An American Original

An American Original
The Life of J. Frank Dobie

By Lon Tinkle

 University of Texas Press, Austin

International Standard Book Number 0-292-70366-x
Library of Congress Catalog Card Number 83-80260
Copyright © 1978 by Lon Tinkle
All rights reserved
Printed in the United States of America

First University of Texas Press Printing, 1983
Reprinted by arrangement with Little, Brown and Company, Inc.

Quotations from letters and journal entries by Bertha McKee Dobie copyright © 1978 by Edgar B. Kincaid, Jr.
Quotations from letters by J. Frank Dobie, R. J. Dobie, and Ella Byler Dobie and excerpts from unpublished material by J. Frank Dobie copyright © 1978 by The Capital National Bank in Austin, Trustees of the J. Frank Dobie Library Trust, and Edgar B. Kincaid, Jr.

For María, and our three sons,
Jon, Alan and Anthony,
and for
Robert S. Sparkman, M.D.,
bibliophile, scholar, surgeon

Contents

1. The Certitudes of Childhood   1
2. All the Love in the World   25
3. The Western Side of a Train   95
4. Mr. Texas   151
5. A Certain Development   179
6. A Joy to Him and a Joy to Hear   237
    A Bibliographical Note   251
    Acknowledgments   257
    Index   261

Illustrations

Between pages 104 and 105
Frank Dobie at Southwestern University, 1910
Bertha McKee
Lieutenant Dobie, 1917
In the Sierra Madre
Dobie the hunter
At Cambridge University, 1944
With his horse
As a guest at the McCombs ranch, 1949
The listener
"One of the most famous grins in history"
Dobie and Lon Tinkle "on location," 1959
"The best copy in Texas"
Bertha McKee Dobie

An American Original

1

The Certitudes of Childhood

> As rural life gives way to urban life and as mobility overcomes stability, human attachment to certain patches of the earth's surface becomes less common. Yet the potentiality of such attachment remains universal. It is very different from attachment to a country, a party, a church, a cause, a person or any group of persons. It is behind much patriotism. With some people it goes deeper than principles and embodies the profundity of life.
> — From "A Plot of Earth"

Frank Dobie was born on September 26, 1888 (the same day as T. S. Eliot), in a small ranch house of whitewashed rock, near Ramirenia Creek in Live Oak County. He grew up there, under the limitless sky — it was almost a bowl from horizon to horizon — of the South Texas "Brush Country," which runs — or slouches or drowses — to the Gulf of Mexico between two rivers with Spanish names, the Nueces and the Rio Grande. It is a country of sun, silence, solitude, and above all, space. In summer, when the cantaloupes yellow in the broiling heat and burst with sugar, the sky is metallic, almost blinding; when the unpredictable wintertime "northers" scourge the land with icy rain, it goes suddenly blue-black. The Brush Country is harsh. Most of the vegetation stings or claws. In times of drought, when the beautiful live oaks were dying as though struck by a sudden pestilence, Frank would often say, "The thirst of those trees for water makes me suffer inside so much that I often want to weep for them." And his mother Ella's most persistent memory of ranch life was the bawling of calves dying of thirst.

In the phrase of one of his friends, it is "a bitterly beautiful land," and in Dobie's mind as he grew up, the ideas of beauty and jeopardy were one. The ragged, dusty, gray-green cactus bursts suddenly into bloom: the spectacular blossoms, purest yellow, purest scarlet, are destined to as brief a life as so many butterflies. "Why son," his mother told him once, "you think more of the ranch than of your own people"; and he was to write of his almost animistic kinship with nature that "certain mesquite trees and certain live oaks along the road were personalities to me and cherished as friends."

For a time in his boyhood the family mail came to Dinero, six miles away, and Frank would ride over once or twice a week to get it. "I knew certain places where I'd seen deer cross the road. I always remembered them," he writes in *Cow People*. "I knew two glades where quail — bobwhites — were plentiful. I knew an opening in the brush where I nooned once in a wagon and let the horses graze. I knew a hollow live oak tree off the road a bit where buzzards annually nested and the little buzzards could not fly away until they had turned from whiteness to blackness. . . . I knew where I was almost sure to see a paisano [a bird also known as the roadrunner] running down the road, though I might see one anywhere. If it had rained, I could expect a certain caliche hill covered with ceniza bushes to be turned by their sudden flowers from ashen gray to almost solid lavender."

Out alone on his good horse Buck, with salt sweat trickling into his mouth or chilling his hair when a breeze came up, he would stop to savor the taste of broomweed or the feathery mesquite leaves, or pause in the shade of a live-oak mott, or gallop toward the horizon, spouting fragments of poems to the endless sky. "His chemistry mixed with mine," he wrote of Buck. "He was good company. I loved to hear him drink water, he was so hearty in swallowing, and then after he was full, to watch him lip the water's surface and drip big drops back into it. . . . A man who has had a good horse in his life — a horse beyond the play world — will remember him as a certitude, like a calm mother, a lovely lake, or a gracious tree, amid all the flickering vanishments." Once Buck had been broken to riding at the age of three by a Mexican vaquero, nobody else ever rode him but Frank. He was willing and smart, with a sure instinct for his rider's wishes, and he was Frank's horse for work on the ranch.

There were plenty of chores, mostly enjoyable; and almost to his dying day, Frank liked to chop firewood, cultivate flowers and vegetables, and prune his fruit trees. He had a green thumb, inherited from his mother, whose famous flower garden was one of the few in the county; and he had a knack for doctoring sick animals. Once when Buck caught a hoof in wire and almost tore it off in his struggle to get free, Frank was able to nurse him back to soundness. Cattle, who have uninspiring personalities, interested him far less than horses, though he once remarked that cows "exercise a wholesome effect on the mind" because they are "a calming influence and they tend to bring orderliness into the person who works with them." For the milk cows on the ranch he had an affection, as he came to know them while teaching them to suckle orphan calves, the little "dogies" whose mothers had died. Sometimes he would squirt the dogie with the cow's milk, so that it would smell like her own to the cow; or while she was suckling her own calf he would encourage the orphan to suck from the other side. Frank's father gave him most of the dogies, though not all. As the eldest son, Frank believed himself entitled to them: "Of course, I was there first to get anything."

Some of these calves were pets from the beginning, and served as "riding calves" for Frank and the other young Dobies. His brother Elrich was the family champion at calf riding: not as easy as it sounds, for horse saddles don't fit a "cow brute" and many of the bull calves defied taming of any sort.

He loved his five brothers and sisters, got on well with them, and all his life had an eldest son's sense of responsibility for them. He led their games with verve and imagination. On one occasion, he took his brothers and his sister Fannie, along with several cousins, on a cave-digging excursion, meant to provide a cave "home" under the creek bluff, about a city block or two from the ranch house. They started back home when the sun was going down. From the top of the bluff Frank saw a dead and whitened tree which he promptly claimed was a giant coming to get them all, "like the giant that Jack the Giant-Killer killed." He pretended to see the giant waving his arms and greedily striding toward the little band. His imagination so fired his audience with fright that he himself "became more thoroughly convinced than any other child in the pack, and with a yell led the race to home and Mama."

The Dobie children loved "play like" games, and their favorite "play-liking" was as ranchers. They fenced in their imaginary acres and pastures with pegs and twine and sticks; their mother's empty thread spools served as horses to be "traded" back and forth in deals that depleted some pastures and crowded others; bits of cattle horn, "sawed off in the branding chute in the ranch corrals," served as cattle, oak galls became herds of sheep, dried snail shells simulated goats. Bits of baling wire were heated red-hot, then carefully used to "brand" what passed for the stock, the single exception being the goats. Since trains were needed to deliver the stock from one ranch to another, flat sardine cans doubled as freight cars; matchboxes — pulled by trapped green lizards harnessed with genuine horsetail hair — served as wagons. Their ingenuity was impressive: "We traded 'cattle' for 'dollars' molded in the bottoms of round wooden bluing boxes out of lead melted from solder on tin cans and from bullets that had been shot for practice into oak trees."

Reading was a great pastime on the Dobie ranch. Ella Byler Dobie ran across a "recommended reading" list for the young, pasted it up on a door of her wardrobe, and procured the books for her family. The list, chosen by educators, included: *Pilgrim's Progress; Robinson Crusoe; Ivanhoe; Tom Brown's School Days; A Child's History of England;* Plutarch's *Lives; David Copperfield; Black Beauty; John Halifax, Gentleman;* and *Heroes and Hero Worship.*

Ivanhoe led Frank and his brother Elrich to organize ring-spearing tournaments on the ranch. They established a course of three posts in a line and about a hundred yards apart, each post bearing a metal hoop on a projecting arm of wood a yard long. The rider, galloping at full speed, tried to spear the easily disengaged rings or hoops with a tournament "pole" held in his right hand. Riding Buck, Frank became expert at the game.

Everything, it seemed, nourished his imagination as a boy, not least the rather narrow and bare way of life on a ranch. But books were primary. Tennyson's *Idylls of the King* reinforced the heroic ideal imbibed from the novels of Sir Walter Scott and from the family favorite, Porter's *Scottish Chiefs.* With elation he welcomed each issue of the *Youth's Companion* on his rides to the post office, and he devoured the children's page in the *Semi-weekly Houston Post.*

He was a perfect example of a once-familiar type of "personality conditioning," in an era when books supplied the most universal artistic experience: his life was dream-oriented, using "dream" in its broadest and most imaginative meaning, and literature fed his dream life. (This pattern manifested itself most powerfully in his life when he was an adolescent in college.) From naming the family's black mongrel Joe, earlier called Rover, after the eponymous dog in *Beautiful Joe,* to fancying himself, when older, as "a knight in the image of Ivanhoe," and on to, when in college, reading

Wordsworth aloud on long walks by the San Gabriel River in deliberate imitation of the poet as he walked along "the sylvan Wye," Frank Dobie steadily sought in life a harmony and a correspondence with passions and responses stirred in him by literature. A prevision of reality through the power of imagination seemed to him one of the virtues of art. And the imagination could also allow one to capture the reality of the past.

The reality of the present, given his gusto and vitality, was mostly a matter of joy to him, but he did not savor all the days of the weeks composing his life: he strongly resented Sundays. In a way of living that demanded much exertion and fierce activity in mastering nature but that failed to demand equal energy in mastering school subjects, Frank Dobie's steadiest encounter with discipline came on Sundays — which his father insisted on observing with puritanical sternness. In later life, the mere thought of the melancholy Sabbath and the family singing of lugubrious hymns caused in him a shudder of revulsion. It was the one day of the week when natural joy and exuberance were disallowed. In fact, unlike his father, he had little gift for music, although he loved the rhythms and power of the readings from the King James Version of the Bible that always brought Sunday evenings to a close (and all other evenings too) before nighttime prayers. On horseback the next day, he would try to match those rhythms, coining phrases himself to ride the wind as Buck's running, galloping, trotting, prancing or walking paces varied.

It was typical of his father that when singing to quiet his restless cattle, he chose, not cowboy songs, but Methodist hymns. R. J. Dobie (self-styled, because he did not like his name, Jonathan Richard) was a pillar of the community who served for years as county commissioner, sat on juries nearly every term of court, and built two schoolhouses and two Methodist churches. He was so rigid about Sabbath observance as seriously to inconvenience himself and, on one occasion, to infuriate his brother-in-law (also a rancher, like most of the men in both families). That year Uncle Frank Byler had sold a number of steers to R. J. Dobie, the two settling on a delivery date without consulting the calendar. A fortnight or so later, on a Sunday afternoon around five o'clock, the Dobie children on their front porch heard the sounds of cattle being crowded into the pens two hundred yards from the house, heard the yelling and "the slapping of quirts on leather leggins." The boys made a break for the pens by the windmill, but their father sat calmly where he was. Presently, Uncle Frank rode up to the porch and exchanged words with his brother-in-law which the boys did not overhear. But they saw his fierce, flashing eyes when he rode back to the pens and tersely commanded his vaqueros, "Vámonos!" They left and Uncle Frank called out to his namesake, "You can tell your pappy to count them when he wants to. They are all there." They were counted next morning — and laboriously branded without the easy help Uncle Frank's vaqueros would have provided on Sunday.

Frank, who grew up to be such a partisan of the unorthodox ("I am glad," he wrote to his sweetheart, "that I can cut an unaccountable figure"), was mortally embarrassed by his father's lapses from conformity. Though modest and diffident, the elder Dobie stuck to his principles; and, though he feared no man, he feared his God. Once, when he was supposed to receive a shipment of cattle on the far side of Ramirenia Creek, it was flooded by a big rain. R. J. Dobie had to cross, but no one was eager to risk it. R. J. advised his vaqueros to remove their shoes and boots, and then, before leading the ride into the swift current, got down on his knees and prayed for a safe crossing. When Frank heard about this, he was "shamed by such humility on the part of my father," as he was shamed by his modesty every summer at the Methodist "encampments" by the sea at Corpus Christi. Refusing to wear what in those days was called a bathing suit, a garment about as revealing as long johns, R. J. took to the water in old pants and an old shirt, making himself "the most conspicuous person in salt water from Sabine Pass to Point Isabel." And on Sundays, when most ranchers dressed to the hilt, R. J. wore a white shirt, all right, and a white starched collar, and was careful to put on his coat — but he often omitted a necktie. Thinking boots and spurs showy, what nowadays we would call status symbols, he did not wear them; and, unlike most ranchers, he did not give his "place," as he called it, a name. The only "romantic" element on the ranch, Frank recalled, was an early Spanish ruin, old Fort Ramírez, reputed to have buried treasures — for which the Dobie clan searched in vain.

Frank was to write, "I often wish that before he died my father

THE CERTITUDES OF CHILDHOOD 9

could have known what a low opinion I came to have of myself for being embarrassed during the prolonged years of puerility at his not acting and dressing as other men acted and dressed." He came to see that although his father was "the least self-assertive of men," he was also firm and fearless in his dealings with others. In later life, when he was writing chapters for an ultimate autobiography, Frank confessed to this writer that he had reached a "block" — he could not write the chapter about his father, for reasons he could not discover. He sought to understand why, without success. This was about 1957. Later, the block disappeared and the chapter in *Some Part of Myself* titled "The Cowman Who Was My Father" is one of the best, although it conspicuously lacks the tone of considered affection and admiration that animates the chapter on his mother. I have found no other clues to explain that temporary "block" and Frank's apparently constant lack of a sense of identity with his father. Perhaps the latter's respect for authority, although it was mostly "divine" authority, was an unconscious rebuke to his son's own talent and propensity for being a law unto himself.

Frank was always close to his remarkable mother; and it seems to have been from her that he took his energy and his joie de vivre. Brought up on Rancho Seco, forty-odd miles away in neighboring Nueces County, Ella Byler Dobie often wrote her absent brood that she truly believed no place on earth could be more satisfyingly lovely than her country in the spring, or in autumn with its wonderful subtropical sunsets and velvet, murmuring nights. She had Frank's delight in nature, and a zest that relished the fresh food grown on the ranch: the mustang grapes, the incomparably sweet watermelons and cantaloupes, the native squashes and beans, the agarita berries which (after laborious preparation) yielded unrivaled jelly, the tender meat of quail and kid and deer, the gamy savor of wild turkey, and all the hot spicy dishes South Texans had learned from the Indians of the Mexican central plateau. Although she was to remind her children, later on when they were grown, that in her ranch days she rarely got to sleep more than four or five hours out of the twenty-four, she was always gay and enterprising, full of ambition for her brood, and equally full of common sense. Like so many women of gusto and spirit, she was astute in financial matters — and in this too her son resembled her, or thought he did. He always had some kind of deal going on the side, even in his teens. Like Frank, she had a shrewd eye (in her case, quite unclouded by romanticism), and few illusions about people, despite her always benevolent manner of life. Once, after Frank had become a teacher at the University of Texas, he told her he enjoyed ranchers' talk more than that of his pedantic colleagues. She could not believe he meant it.

"Law me," she exclaimed, "some of 'em don't have brains enough to fry an egg in."

It was she who taught Frank to read. Though many ranch homes had two-book libraries at best (the Bible, and perhaps a farmers' almanac), the Dobies', thanks mostly to Ella, had between two and three hundred volumes. As small children, Frank and his sister Fannie were taught by a governess until their father, with his brother and a neighbor, built a schoolhouse on the ranch. The teacher usually lived at the Dobies' house; the children came from all over the area, generally on horseback. The school, called Hillview and built in 1896, was succeeded in 1900 by a larger one, called Long Hollow. Droves of wild turkeys used to graze up close to the little building, and curious coyotes lurked in the dense thickets around. The boys set traps for them or entertained themselves by racing the horses they had ridden to school. Once Frank and the other boys rode off one day at noon recess and lunched on roast sweet potatoes stolen from a Mexican tenant on the ranch. They didn't get back until afternoon recess, and Miss Ella Simms, despite the fact that she was boarding with the Dobies, gave them all a mighty whipping. When the term was over, she presented the Dobies with a leather strap, given her after the sweet-potato incident by her sweetheart for future use. The boys named the strap for him, Orsineth Hatfield.

Discipline in the Dobie family seems to have been moral much more than corporal, but it was earnest and high-minded. Frank liked to quote his mother's directive: "Never forget whose son you are." Pride of family was strong, as was family loyalty. Self-reliance and pluck were simple necessities. Achievement was expected. The Dobie children were imbued with the two most formative dogmas of the American frontier: the belief that any man worth his salt will earn his own living by the sweat of his brow, and the belief that any self-respecting person is as good as any other. In later life Frank was often to be rigid and huffy in confrontation with authority, but he was never a respecter of persons.

Nor was he ever lazy, though he loved and dwelt on the implications of the charming verb "to linger." He used to tell of his encounter, in later life, with a venerable "philosopher" in Oaxaca, who spent his mornings and afternoons lolling in his hammock under the shade of a giant peppertree. After some daily observation of the *americano* who greeted him regularly as he passed, the Mexican sage shared his wisdom: "Ah, señor, how good is God! He gives us the nights to sleep in, and the days to rest in!"

Mexicans had been raising cattle and horses in the Brush Country for a long time before Texas won its independence from Mexico in 1836. They supplied the know-how of ranching skill and techniques, and provided the vaqueros for the successive bands of colonists — from Germany, England, France, Ireland, Scotland, and especially the older American states — whom the new Texas government tried desperately, and with some success, to lure to the land-rich and money-bankrupt new republic (it would become a state in 1845).

In Frank Dobie's boyhood, most of the children reared in the Brush Country were bilingual. Most, that is, except for the Mexican young: they were there first, or at least their ancestors were; it was only right that the newcomers should learn their language. Just as naturally, the newcomers assimilated many of the cultural traits of the natives — the almost mystical sense of identity with nature and with animals, the pride in *macho*, or manly, performance, the delight in storytelling and in ballads and folklore, and an easygoing tolerance of human imperfections: too easygoing for most of the "Anglos."

Frank's early conditioning was influenced by the shared wish of his parents that their children be well educated, even through college, which was a rare thing for youth at the turn of the century in Texas. Both parents believed it their duty to bequeath to their children a more ample life than they had known. Achievement was expected to be the ideal of youngsters who had the benefits of education and of solid family background. When young Frank Dobie thought his younger brothers and sisters were losing sight of that ideal, he sternly called them to attention; and when they later followed him to college, he thought it his duty to monitor their performance. He liked to quote to them his mother's reminder: "Never forget whose son you are." The Dobies and the Bylers were prideful Scots — and Texians, the old stock and first-comers from the States. Frank's Virginia-born great-grandfather migrated to Texas in 1834.

It was Frank's mother's decision, primarily, that he and Fannie should go to live in Alice with their grandparents in order to continue their schooling. But even in the Alice High School, she felt they never went beyond what she considered eighth-grade studies. It was really her teaching the children to read early, and guiding their studies thereafter until they entered Southwestern University, that anchored their education. She had been a young schoolteacher in nearby Lagarto before her marriage.

Before they went to Alice, their longest journey had been the wagon trip, made once or twice a year, to Beeville, the nearest big town. It was the marketplace for gathering necessities to be stored against the winter: flour and sugar bought by the barrel, green coffee to be parched and ground at home, frijoles (pinto beans) bought by the tow sack, lard (to supplement that rendered at the ranch) by the five-gallon can. Once a month the family drove into Ramirenia for church, joining the congregation for "dinner on the grounds," each family bringing "its best food and a lot of it," as Fannie Dobie recalled. And once a year the Dobies went to Dinero, for a camp meeting held there on the Nueces River. They generally took a vacation in summer: a camping trip of a week or ten days along the Nueces, or one at Corpus Christi, and once even in the Texas Hill Country, so dear to Ella Dobie. The children loved those days given to swimming, fishing, playing. "Papa would fix the camp very comfortably and conveniently, and we would have a wonderful time."

But in 1904, when he was sixteen, life at the family ranch ended for Frank. "At that time," he wrote, "in our environment, college was as remote as the pyramids of Egypt." But his mother's determination won out, and he took the daylong, forty-mile drive to Grandma Dubose's house in Alice, to get a high school diploma. Of his two years' schooling there, Frank recalled in later life only two things. On being assigned a theme (the only written assignment he had before college), he chose to write on war, beginning with Sherman's famous dictum. The teacher liked his effort and started to read it aloud to the class. But at the word "hell," the class fell into embarrassed dismay, and began to giggle and squeal at hearing such a taboo word publicly pronounced. Their embarrassment was no match for poor Frank's. Then, a few weeks later, he had, as class salutatorian, to deliver an oration at the graduation exercises. His teacher practically wrote his speech for him since Frank had discovered that he really had nothing to say. Being uninvolved in the platitudes he had been coached to deliver, and which he had manfully practiced in the cowshed, he was afflicted with fear once he was on the stage of the Knights of Pythias hall. No amount of whispered prompting from "Professor" Benton could save the day. Midway, the salutatorian simply gave up, stopped abruptly, and sat down in desperation.

He was also struck dumb by falling "tremblingly in love" with a classmate, and was "unable to make out a case for myself," luckily for both of them, as he said later.

School may have posed problems, but Frank enjoyed his grandparents' home. The house was full of reading matter, from Grandpa's file of the magazine indispensable to him, the *Confederate Veteran*, to sets of Bulwer-Lytton, E. P. Roe and Charles Dickens, with random volumes of Mark Twain, Sir Walter Scott, Longfellow and a few others. Once again, as at the ranch, the "formal" instruction in school would matter far less to young Dobie than the people around him and his own voracious appetite for reading. One neighbor recalled often seeing him at Grandma's house, usually curled up with his feet under him, sitting on the porch and engrossed in a book. Like her daughter, Frank's mother, Grandma Dubose respected learning, loved to garden, disciplined herself to dress tidily even while doing household and garden drudgery, and found the center of her life in her church.

Grandpa Dubose, who had driven the stagecoach to Brownsville for a time after moving to Alice and who now made a meager living as justice of the peace, never went to church, to the scandal of the rest of the family. His vast fund of anecdotes included experiences and adventures in the Civil War, in trail driving up from Texas to Kansas and across Texas as a cattle buyer for a Texas coast "packery" in the days when many ranchers thought the chief value of their cattle lay in their hides and tallow. At the "packeries," the flesh was thrown away, food and bones for buzzards and coyotes. Like Frank's father, Grandpa loved to sing, and he stirred Frank's imagination with his rendition of haunting, melancholy trail songs — songs sad in part because they were meant to exploit a slow tempo in quieting and soothing restless herds.

In the shipping season, Grandpa often worked on the loaded trains for trips of a week or so as a sort of watchman over the cattle. When he was away, Frank milked the family cow, turned it out to graze by day, and carried in stovewood. He did not lack for other reminders of ranch life. "Grandpa knew all the ranchmen, horse traders, sheriffs and rangers of the country." The headquarters of the Texas Ranger Captain Rogers was just beyond the yard fence of the Dubose home. Although Frank's widowed grandmother had married a second time, he always called his step-grandfather "Grandpa" and loved him and his sons by his first marriage as if they were blood kin.

As the child and grandchild of ranchers, on both sides of the family, Frank had always owned cattle. In his boyhood years he had acquired, sometimes as gifts, or in trades, or by his earnings working for his father or for fellow ranchers, a few mares and some cows. Now in his teens, in Alice, he wanted to add substantially to his stock; he appealed to his father for a loan or for help in borrowing enough money to buy a hundred yearlings. His father was pleased that Frank wanted to "make something," but had no pasture left to offer him. So he suggested that Frank might sell his steers to Uncle Jim Dobie and then, if pasture could be leased, borrow around six hundred dollars to buy fifty more yearlings. The two elders met and agreed, as Frank's father wrote him, "to get fifteen hundred dollars and invest it in yearlings for you," and to arrange for the pasturing. By the time of his sophomore year in college, Frank owned 144 head of cattle, and he continued for years to make arrangements for them with his idol, Uncle Jim.

Years later, he was to write in *Cow People*, as the caption to a photograph of Uncle Jim, "His name was a synonym for honesty." In the picture, taken in a bank in San Antonio in 1900, Uncle Jim wears a fine worsted suit, complete with watch chain, four-in-hand tie and starched collar. Awkwardly seated, as one who feels himself at bay, Uncle Jim glares at the camera suspiciously. "In a stampede," Frank wrote, "he wanted only one good man with him to stop the cattle and put them into a mill. The idea of shooting six-shooters ahead of cattle to stop their running was absurd to him and other genuine cowmen. He was saving without being tight. His generosity to me is still in my consciousness."

Frank enrolled as a freshman at Southwestern University in 1906, just as he was turning eighteen. It was natural that he should go to a Methodist college; and in any case there wasn't much choice in Texas then. Higher education was largely restricted to the two state schools, the University of Texas at Austin and the Agricultural and Mechanical College of Texas at College Station, both founded a decade or so after the Civil War. Southwestern, a merger of four earlier Methodist colleges grouped by the Methodist Church at Georgetown, was almost as much a vocational training school as the state-owned Texas A & M. The latter graduated mostly engineers and trained farmers in Dobie's time, while Southwestern produced "preachers and teachers."

A preacher son would have suited his mother best of all; Frank's father hoped he would become a lawyer; his hero, Uncle Jim, wanted him to be a rancher. That he became a teacher was probably due to a few remarkable men he encountered at Southwestern. Even enrollment day was auspicious. The president of Southwestern himself, physics professor Robert Stewart Hyer, singled out the shy boy and made him feel welcome. Dr. Hyer, one of the most admired men in the history of education in Texas, asked him if he liked to read: the right question for the right student. Dr. Hyer told Frank that he made it a practice to read at least one book a week new to him, and recommended this wisdom to the young man.

"Right there," Frank writes in *Some Part of Myself*, "I determined to read a book a week myself, and in the more than 2,600 weeks that have passed since Dr. Hyer spoke, I have, without being methodical, been absorbed by that many books, not to speak of many thousands glanced through or searched into for something I could use."

Dr. Hyer also told Frank that he was a lay preacher and always preached the sermon on the first Sunday following the opening of the school year. This year, he said, he would base his sermon on a book, James Parton's *Life of Thomas Jefferson*. Frank attended, and remembered that sermon all his life. "That essay-sermon, which ranged over the great literature of the world and its influence on the mind and spirit of man, elated me with ambition to know." His admiration for Dr. Hyer grew over the years, but that first-day encounter was a happy one for a bookish youth growing up in a state where to be called a bookworm was the supreme and most dreaded insult for any adolescent.

Frank as a freshman was very much a loner, "an unspoiled country boy lost in a new environment," as T. Rucker Stanford, his future brother-in-law, remembers him in that first year. Most Southwestern students, including the Stanfords, came from the rich Brazos Bottoms, where, thanks to King Cotton, a prosperous and sophisticated way of living prevailed. Shy, sensitive, proud, at times paralyzed by feelings of inferiority, Frank never took part in the dormitory rowdyism and preferred long solitary walks in the countryside to athletics. Skirting the playing fields on Saturday afternoons, he would walk alone, reading or reciting aloud from the English Romantic poets, chiefly Wordsworth — the one poet absolutely right for young Dobie at that time.

He had been introduced to Wordsworth by the legendary Professor Albert Shipp Pegues, of whom he later wrote: "His survey course in English poetry transmuted the world for me. In recollection this course has blended with one more advanced in the Romantic poets that I took as a junior. I had read some narrative poetry . . . but only Tennyson had held me in thrall, and he seemed always of the afternoon. The Romantic poets, Burns as well as Wordsworth, Coleridge, Byron, Shelley and Keats, were of the morning, and they were as much a part of Albert Shipp Pegues as love is a part of Juliet. Pegues himself was regarded as being very romantically in love with his comely wife. He drilled us on metrics and illuminated the language and thought of poets; above all, he made us enjoy poetry. The juices of vitality pulsed through his handsome body and features, and he read poetry with burning eyes and absorbed voice. He knew much of it by heart and required us to memorize 'touchstone passages.' No other teacher I came under, least of all in graduate work, so enlarged and enriched life for me, so started up growths inside me. He opened windows; he carried whoever would go with him to the Elysian fields. Many students, perhaps a majority, did not have it within themselves to dance to his piping of divine poetry."

Professor Pegues's "idealism," according to Rucker Stanford, appealed more to Frank than it did to most of the students, although Pegues's classes were notoriously overcrowded and popular. Like his and Frank's friend Lowe Simons, Stanford felt uneasy at Professor Pegues's great influence on the students; both thought that he was, under the Chesterfieldian courtliness, a hypocrite and "as hard as nails." For Stanford, the great and noble man on the campus was President Hyer, who stressed every year in the opening convocation that "scholarship is the purpose of this university." Another favorite theme of President Hyer's was the doctrine, so dear to Dobie's favorite poet, Wordsworth, of "plain living and high thinking." Dr. Hyer's personal hero — and Frank's for a long time — was Robert E. Lee. Grandpa Dubose had conditioned Frank to revere the Confederacy.

Rucker Stanford also recalled that Dobie was much liked, despite his solitary ways, because he was so very "even-tempered," and always characterized by a sharp sense of humor: "I remember how he used to get tickled at something, and couldn't stop laughing. Even in those early days he had that grin that later became such a Dobie trademark." He added that Frank, once he got angry, would fight back rapturously. But in those days he was not quick to anger. He was not, however, the sort of freshman that older students automatically bullied.

Stanford recalled that Frank never had a date in the time that the two were in school together. Of course, dating was not encouraged on the Southwestern campus, co-ed "fraternizing" occurring only at exceedingly supervised and faculty-chaperoned once-a-month gatherings. Until 1909, when the rules were somewhat relaxed, there was a very strict separation in the classroom and campus life of the two sexes. Dobie, said Stanford, was one hundred percent interested in his schoolwork, and was an observer of life then much more than a participant.

Stanford and his younger brother both recall that Frank's major characteristic as an undergraduate was his gentleness. He was often melancholy, and often overwhelmed with nostalgia, as when he wrote home one spring, wishing he were at the ranch to help with the shipping, saying that he could sit in his dormitory room and "hear the spurs jingle as I walk on that rock in front of the barn," see the horses coming down the hill, and "hear the brush crackling." Philosophically he continued, "Beside such a life all other life is dull and tepid, but also there is nothing in it but a passing pleasure, a transient enjoyment that comes and passes away forever."

Gradually, Frank outgrew or overcame his outsider role; by his junior year he was not only working for the student paper, *The Megaphone*, but doing part-time reporting for the Georgetown paper, the Williamson County *Sun*, serving as cheerleader for the baseball team, and writing for the school literary magazine. He was an officer of the Alamo Literary Society, in whose formal debates he eagerly took part, and, as he reported home, he was busy attending recitals, concerts, glee-club programs "and other things." As a new "achiever," his big triumph was being elected editor of next year's college annual.

Moreover, he had found a cause, one that aroused his innate democratic sympathy, his dislike of hierarchy and elitism, and his propensity for taking the side of the underdog. Of the 633 students at Southwestern in the autumn of 1908, 119 belonged to fraternities or sororities, and the vast majority, 514 nonfraternity students like Frank, were "Barbs" (barbarians), as the "Greeks" called them.

The Barbs were so hypercritical of the Greeks that they wanted the administration to kick the fraternity system off the campus, something vigorously opposed by the powerful alumni and the board of trustees. A Barb committee of a dozen dormitory residents, including Frank Dobie and Rucker Stanford, wrote a letter to "friends and patrons" of the university, inviting an investigation of the evils of the fraternity system at Southwestern University — and called a mass meeting of nonfraternity men to endorse it.

Their hope, as they said in their letter, was for "a United, Loyal Student Body and a Greater Southwestern." There were only three fraternities on the campus, only four sororities. Dr. Hyer and the rest of the administration thought the matter of minor importance and kept the hostility within manageable bounds. But the friction escalated the following year, when two of the signers of the letter were elected to run *The Megaphone*. These two were J. Fisher Simpson, editor, and J. Frank Dobie, business manager. (Frank's letters home were now written on *Megaphone* stationery, with the two officers listed on the letterhead.) The student paper created so much stir about the problem of "snobbery" on the campus that Dr. Hyer felt obliged to remonstrate with his young admirer Dobie and to warn him to spend more time on his studies, as he well might: Frank's grades for the spring term of his junior year were his poorest ever, and he failed mathematics. For a time in 1909, in the autumn, Dr. Hyer had to suspend the paper's publication in order to keep peace and restore perspective on the campus. His solution, on authorizing publication again, was to let the Barbs have the editorial post, the Greeks the business manager's post. Frank Dobie was sufficiently chastened by the experience to warn his mother to expect a bad grade report and, above all, since she would be seeing Dr. Hyer at the annual Methodist Summer Encampment at Corpus Christi, to warn her against expecting any praise of her son. "Dr. Hyer thinks I have spent entirely too much of my energy in fighting fraternities and by so doing helping to keep things in a broil at Southwestern." He wrote later in *Some Part of Myself:* "I cannot remember when I was not on the side of rebels."

To young Frank — in the recollection of a contemporary he was becoming known on the campus as a rebel and something of a show-off — keeping the wide world of Southwestern "on the broil" must have been gratifying, particularly since it was, after all, in a high-minded cause. Frank was still shocked when fellow students swore, still dreaded alcohol, and on learning that his younger brother Elrich was being allowed to "go out with girls during week nights," he was quick to admonish his mother. *He* had never enjoyed such a privilege at Elrich's age; aside from the unfairness, it was wrong. "If he was at home reading *Peck's Bad Boy* I think he would improve his time better than by continually running after some little hair-brained [sic] specimen of the female tribe. It looks like Elrich is old enough to have one serious thought: to have at least enough judgment to know he ought to improve his time."

The moral strenuousness of his upbringing, combined with his naiveté, his sensitivity, and his profound concern for the figure he cut, was bound to make him rigorous and righteous in deliberately confounding standards of ethics, equity, propriety and taste. "When I Was a Prig" he titled a handwritten autobiographical fragment years later. "Puberty," he notes, "brought priggishness with it. I heard a lot and read a lot about purity. My father was no prig at all, but his saying that he would rather see my sister Fannie in a coffin than dancing in the arms of a man had a strong effect on me. I came to believe that the delights of the flesh were sinful and to feel shameful towards all implications of sex."

Two instances: When a young cousin, the son of a doctor, asked Frank if Aunt Fannie had died in childbirth, Frank did not know, never having heard the cause of her death. Moreover, he had not been interested in the cause of her death because he saw "no termination to life." But he felt compelled, when questioned, to deny emphatically that "Aunt Fannie had died of childbirth." In the other example, his mother, two or three years before they left the ranch, had a severe attack of what was then called sciatica. "I rode to Mathis in the night to summon a doctor." On the ride home the next day he stopped in Lagarto to pick up the mail. He was aware that the postmistress and several others there knew the doctor had passed through on his way to the ranch. The townsfolk were curious and perhaps solicitous, but young Dobie was in agony at the idea "they must be thinking that Mama was having another Baby. I proclaimed sciatica as her trouble and I located it in her hip."

He developed, he says, the idea that "to all females of the human species the male function was repugnant, though the joy of a black and white cow with a shorthorn bull, or a bay filly with our Dandy stallion, of pullets under roosters and sows under boars all bespoke the contrary. However, I did not rationalize on the subject. (Thinking has never been natural to me.)"

This passage is followed by a comment on his father's tielessness at church: "I was humiliated beyond expression at my own father's boorish crudity," and says of himself: "I could make a long chapter out of the confessions of a fool." He then relates an episode of outraged indignation that happened while he was a graduate student at Columbia. He went with another doctoral candidate to visit the Edgar Allan Poe shrine at Fordham, Poe being a particular enthusiasm — at the time — of Dobie's. "We found a marble bust of Poe missing from its proper niche and on the floor of the public toilet." The classmate thought it funny; Dobie found it a desecration of his hero. He writes, "I felt a moral compulsion to be indignant." And: "My companion's placidity offended me as much as the desecration. Looking back now, I cannot say what percentage of prig and what percentage of fool made up the Me. If the mechanics of Poe had not come to squeak so loudly in my ears, perhaps I should feel more tolerant of the fool."

It was not until his old age that Dobie wrote anything smacking at all of ribaldry — a last proof, perhaps, of his lifelong rebellion, or better, of the slow process of liberation, on all fronts, that marked his adulthood. Perhaps the first step was his enrollment at Southwestern, and the next, a trip undertaken between his junior and senior years, to take summer courses, with several classmates, at the University of Chicago.

This trip, when he was twenty, was his first venture out of Texas and his first visit to a real metropolis, just as his enrolling at Southwestern had been his first trip out of "ranch country." He thoroughly enjoyed his stay in Chicago, after overcoming a first dismal attack of homesickness. He still wrote his mother on Sundays, still went to church religiously every Sabbath.

He went, inevitably, to the Newberry Library (where he read Texas newspapers), the Field Museum of Natural History, the Art Institute, Hull House, the stockyards, and had a thrilling day at Buffalo Bill's Wild West Show, shouting Spanish phrases of praise to Mexican vaqueros in the troupe. The Art Institute was his favorite; he went there several times, and described it as "great." He enjoyed the Texas Club picnic in Jackson Park.

A ten-hour boat trip up to Milwaukee was a revelation to him, for natural beauty, for the elegance of many homes, for the incredible sunset on the return. Another "incredible" matter for him was the consumption in Chicago of beer and whiskey at bars and "buffets." He marveled at it but was not converted. (Two years later, in Alpine, he participated in a "prohibition" rally and made a speech which he pridefully reported in his family letter.) One sidelight of his visit to the stockyards: "Away off in one corner, in pens marked 'quarantine,' I found the Texas cattle. I felt at home out there listening to the bellowing, and breathing dust."

He was overwhelmed with nostalgia. By mid-August: "I am getting tired of noise and sights and crowds. I would give a great deal to be either at home or with that unsurpassably good and extraordinary bunch of boys who roomed in Sec. 8 of Mood Hall and who

— don't mention it — ran and will continue to run Southwestern University's political and financial enterprises." He closed his letter "to prepare for church."

His mind broadened, perhaps, by this excursion, he made his peace with Dr. Hyer on returning to Southwestern, and promptly rejoined his Sunday school class, as he proudly told his mother. And at its first meeting Dr. Hyer, whom he had never ceased to revere, gave a "great sermon," admonishing Greeks and Barbs alike "not to join either side so closely as to exclude himself from intimate relations with the other side." Frank's comment: "Good advice, but such is impossible with many." It was a community generally hostile to pluralism or to any sign of nonconformity.

Frank was elected secretary-treasurer of the Sunday school class, got a job as student grader for a history professor he liked, S. H. Moore, and later in the year was elected president of the Alamo Literary Society. Moreover, as he wrote his mother, he discovered a great liking for "parties."

"Frank liked the girls, and they very much liked him," said his contemporary Mary Thomas Simons almost seventy years later. Despite his pigeon toes, and the bowlegs early formed to the saddle, he was a handsome boy. Middle-sized, at five feet eight inches and one hundred and sixty pounds, he had a ruddy complexion, copious hair, twinkling clear blue eyes, and an extraordinary, infectious smile. Mrs. Simons, who was to marry his former roommate and best friend, was herself thought to be in love with Frank when they were both in graduate school at Columbia. The friends who had this idea were mistaken, but she and Frank found one another both entertaining and sympathetic, then and for the rest of their lives. Another girl, Alice Beretta, who was vividly remembered from her school days by the painter Georgia O'Keeffe as well, was said by Mrs. Simons to have been profoundly in love with Frank. He did not reciprocate, but was a loyal friend then and always thereafter, and an advisor whenever Alice got into trouble ("which was often"). She had brought to the Southwestern campus a radiant vitality and a sophistication not known there before, as well as a piquant aura of scandal. Her mother's runaway love affair had shaken the state; and Alice, too, was to become notorious. Still another young woman, soon to suffer an unrequited love for Frank, was Una Jackson, whom Frank, in Mary and Lowe Simons's opinion, treated rather callously. In their view, Frank in his later writings somewhat romanticized his early infatuation for Bertha McKee, whom he had met in his junior year and got to know when both were working together on the college yearbook as seniors.

"With her," said Mrs. Simons, reflecting on a lifelong friendship with them both, "Frank was always so generous, so kind, so protective." She paused. "Bertha had a good deal that Frank lacked in college — everybody acknowledged *her* gifts, and she was poised and composed as well as beautiful." Aloof, gifted, the commencement valedictorian, Bertha "was very strictly brought up and she was the essence of gentility. She was small, brown-haired and brown-eyed and very beautiful," though not considered at Southwestern to be the equal of her younger sister Lucile. Bertha, Lucile, and Emily McKee, the middle sister, were thought to be "well off" because their father was a teacher and all three girls were in college at the same time. Of the three, only Bertha was in fragile health. Having barely survived a serious illness in childhood, she suffered gravely from a wide assortment of ailments for the rest of her life — which lasted eighty-four years.

In the first term of 1909–1910, his senior year, Frank was very much attracted to his roommate's young sister, whom he described to his mother as "the prettiest girl on the campus," and he mentions her several times in his letters that autumn. But just then, or just before then, he had had that vision of Bertha, that *coup de foudre*, which he was always to claim as decisive: a glimpse of her sitting at a table in the library, dressed all in white.

The girls at Southwestern boarded in a building known as Women's Annex; and that year, for the first time in its history, Southwestern began to allow them to receive company once a week in the parlor. On the first day of the new rule, Frank went up, as he wrote his mother, "to celebrate the occasion." And at graduation time, he planned to escort Miss McKee, the outstanding girl of the class, a beauty, a poet, a brain; but unfortunately he and a dozen of his Mood Hall classmates fell sick of the mumps and were quarantined. He sent her a bouquet, but was forced to miss Bertha's star performance at the graduation exercises, her valedictory address, in which she exhorted the audience to remember the power of "magic" in life and to "follow the Gleam."

Frank's college life had been very happy, and he hated to see it come to an end. It was at Southwestern, in his freshman year, that the notion of becoming a writer had begun to crystallize in him when Professor Pegues had read to the class one of his compositions, a narrative of his schoolboy days at the Dobie ranch. And it was at Southwestern that he bought his first book (other than textbooks), the *Rubáiyát of Omar Khayyám;* there that he began making lists of words and definitions, meditating upon their "prolonged shadows" and "cultivating the art of connotation" that "has helped me in an unending strife to be precise, specific, concrete, definite." His maturation as a writer was very slow (he did not publish his first book until he was nearly forty), which seems curious, considering how early he identified his natural bent and how stubbornly he followed it. Something in him rebelled against structured thinking: "I admire intelligences that make systems of thought, but I cannot follow them, except by an effort that I am unwilling to exert," yet he was drawn to Bertha's speculative, incisive intelligence, drawn to the academic life and especially to teaching, though pedantry and scholarly snobbery drew his constant fire and he would never take his Ph.D. Never introspective, so unsure of himself that, even after four years in the college debating society, his knees trembled whenever he rose to speak, he seems to have come to self-definition by a long process of trial and error.

Perhaps nothing in his life was so formative as his courtship of Bertha McKee.

2

All the Love in the World

> I wasted my golden youth on causes. The only salvation for the human race is to arrive at a just sense of values. And a just sense of values is not implanted by a political victory in an election. The mob might be right once in a while. But if the majority always had a just sense of values, we'd always elect a good man, a strong man, and turn things over to him. If you work for causes, you've got to be leading society around every two or four years. Enlightenment is the only answer.
> — From an interview with Joe Goulden, Dallas *Morning News*

WHEN, AT COMMENCEMENT, "B. McKee" thanked "Mr. Dobie" nicely for his bouquet of carnations, she was initiating a correspondence that would continue for the rest of their lives, and he, a courtship that took six years. It was inhibited by their caution, their poverty, and their geographic separation — for which we may be thankful, since they kept in touch by letters, most of which have survived. Through these letters we can look on as the two naive, romantic, earnest young people are mirrored in one another's eyes, trying on attitudes, posturing a bit, taking themselves with the utmost seriousness, trying to find out by reflection and refraction who they really are.

They began, of course, very decorously; and it is clear that Frank had warm friendships with other girls, at least until the year of their engagement. Bertha, who understood him much better than he understood himself, probably sensed to what degree his ardor was fed by fancy, and was too cautious to rely entirely on a heart made fonder by absence.

In the summer after graduation, Frank got a temporary job as a reporter on the San Antonio *Express*, pending the opening of school in Alpine, high in the Big Bend Country of Southwest Texas, where he had accepted a post as a teacher of English at a salary of one hundred dollars a month. Bertha was to teach Latin at Dalhart, in the Panhandle. "Teaching is a heavenly profession," she wrote him that winter, and she planned to take education courses the following summer, with the hope of working on a master's degree thereafter at the University of Chicago. Frank's early letters to her were lost in a fire, but we learn from her replies that he was thinking of founding a magazine with a regional emphasis. The dream did not come true, but was prophetic of his future activities on the *Southwest Review*. "Texas events as a basis of fiction," Bertha wrote in December 1910, "the thoughts and feelings of the early settlers, especially appeal to me." And: "You know Texas has a history richer in stirring events, picturesque scenes, and dramatic intensity than almost any other state in the Union, and yet so little of all that material has been used. . . . I would like to see Texas come into her own in a literary way, as she has begun to do educationally. O, to help realize that desire!"

Next summer, back at Southwestern for her education courses, she risks a more personal note: "You say you wonder whether I really care anything about writing to you. Do you think I often do things I don't want to do? Believe me when I say I enjoy your letters and appreciate your friendship." In the autumn, Frank happily returned to Southwestern as "secretary to the president," but his duties were primarily to set up the organization of Southwestern alumni in preparation for a fund-raising campaign. He was also to teach in the "prep" school. Bertha was off to teach at the Alexander Collegiate Institute (now Lon Morris College) in Jacksonville, in the Piney Woods of East Texas. They met in the following spring at the homecoming celebration of Southwestern, held in April; then Bertha went to the University of Chicago summer session, while Frank remained in Georgetown. Then she returned to Jacksonville, where she was to teach for two more years. In January of 1913, Frank went to New York City to work for his master's degree at Columbia.

Except for his courses with the legendary Brander Matthews, Frank felt afterward that Columbia had taught him less than he learned simply by living in New York. He went to the theater two or three times a week, seeing Julia Marlowe, Forbes-Robertson, the Abbey Theatre company, and Anna Pavlova; and he went to hear Emma Goldman, from whom, he said, he got no ideas, "only glimpses of another world and a feeling of vitality." He made friends with the budding playwright Hatcher Hughes, and with a group of young men who ate at the same cheap restaurant and together bought their favorite waitress a wedding present. In the fall of 1913, he spent two weeks hiking and camping in the Lake George region. Its fresh greenness and hazy blue hills were as sharp a contrast to the little cowtown of Alpine in the Big Bend as were the towers and traffic of Manhattan.

But when he left New York in the first week of June 1914, happy prospects beckoned him back home and into the future. After his three semesters at Columbia ("I finally passed enough courses to get an M.A.," he wrote a friend), he felt fully qualified to practice his profession. Like a doctor or a lawyer or an architect, he had his license. If he had cared for security, which he never did, he had his future reasonably roadmarked. Anxiety on that score need not afflict him. He was prepared and certified for the vocation of teaching. He had already given proof of having classroom charisma.

More alluring and more immediate signals of felicity elated him. He knew now that he could not be happy without Bertha McKee. They were to meet at a Southwestern University commencement reunion in Georgetown on the way home, Frank proceeding from New York to Beeville and the ranch, and Bertha traveling from the Alexander Collegiate Institute in Jacksonville to her home in Velasco. The encounter was crucial for Frank, necessary for Bertha. She now knew she "cared for" Frank, she knew how he felt about her, but she was not at all certain that she cared enough to select him as the most important man of her life. In his newly won confidence with his M.A., in the happiness of his return home and above all to the ranch, he nearly persuaded her at the Georgetown encounter. He wrote her soon after, "I believe I can win you now."

At twenty-five he was a purposeful young man that summer, invigorated by his successful testing at Columbia and in the "big city," reassured that the Southwest was where he most wanted to live and work, where awaited him a place at the University of Texas and a girl he loved who nearly loved him back. Bertha would also be at Austin in the coming year, having won a fellowship at the University of Texas graduate school.

After the tryst with Bertha at Georgetown came the reunion with family and the experience of the ranch. On June 24 he sent Bertha a triumphant description of his happiness, assuring her that he was having "a great time and leading a life just as intellectual as I led at Columbia University." True, the ranch had changed: a railroad had been built within six miles of "this place," and the "place" (as he and his father insisted on calling a "meager" ranch of seven thousand acres) had been cut in two; the country was settling up, so there were no longer big herds or long, hard drives — "but still, for which I reverently thank God, the coyotes howl — I can hear them now."

There are, despite the changes, other old pleasures of recognition: the old trails wind in the same old way, "and a man can keep out of sight of other human beings and in sight of fat cattle." He had not thrown a rope in three years, but his first throw was just right (he was helping doctor some steers — "worms try to eat them up alive"). He tells Bertha of "the great feeling of the jerk of a steer on the horn of the saddle." He had to do the work alone that morning. His Mexican vaquero, Genardo, got his fingernails "pulled off by getting his hand caught between the saddle and the rope." There was another accident that day. A poor cow got caught in quicksand and nothing Frank and Genardo tried could get her out.

He describes the ranch to Bertha in a letter whose directness and verve are prophetic of his mature style:

> The ranch is thirty miles due west of Beeville. It is traversed by the Ramirenia Creek, which is so crooked that one is always in doubt whether he is on "this side" or the "other side." Also the Arroyo Largo runs by the old house and it is the dry branch that Elrich and I used to like to swim on horseback when it got up after a big rain. The ranch is transfixed by ten thousand prickly pear and other kinds of thorns. The sun *stands* immediately over it at noon from ten o'clock until five o'clock every day from May until September; but the moon shines there better than anywhere else on dry land between the Fort Davis Mountains and the Jacksonville pines. There are more stars visible through one rift in the branches of the old oak back of the barn than from all the roof-gardens in New York City. It is generally so dry that the crickets get hoarse from thirst. These are all the geographical facts I can think of about the place, which I have so often blessed in absence and damned in presence.

But ranching was not enough for a man of his complexity and essentially multiple, not merely dual, nature. He knew it. Part of his exultation that summer came from his certitude after the meeting with Bertha, part from the ease with which right after that meeting he stopped over in Austin to set up arrangements for his first year of college teaching. He was in debt from his schooling and he was in no way financially able to offer immediate marriage. His salary at the University of Texas was scant, one hundred dollars a month, and he planned to augment it by writing and by speculating on cattle. He had to have money, "to make money," as he wrote Bertha — along with his repeated assertion, "I love you and I am going to win you, if I can."

To make money that summer, soon after allowing himself a "holiday" working at the ranch, he wrote friends on Texas newspapers about a reporting job, and landed one in Galveston on the afternoon paper, the Galveston *Tribune*. But he had two friends from Southwestern on the staff of the Galveston *News*, and he wrote Bertha that he "ran" with them. They enjoyed eating together at a little café run by a Roumanian who called his place the American Restaurant. The work was fairly routine, but he loved the fact of writing and he loved the ocean, which set him to dreaming again of adventures still to experience, and he loved swimming in the surf. Here, as at the ranch, he delighted in concrete details, the palms and oleanders and the bougainvillea lining Galveston's "beautiful" street (ironically named Broadway), the sound of the surf, the sea, the sand, the sky, the sun.

An unexpected letter compelled him, in his summer euphoria, to take thought of the immediate future. Professor Pegues, the hardest man in the world for Frank to turn down at the time, wrote to offer him a teaching post at Southwestern, and Frank had the audacity to ask Professor Pegues to hold the position open for a year. He admits he made this suggestion because he could not bear to be away from Bertha the coming autumn. And he wanted to test at Austin whether he should stay in teaching or choose journalism as his ultimate career, a choice that plagued him for years.

The starting salary at Southwestern was two hundred dollars more a year than he would be getting at Austin, and in the second year would go up by three hundred dollars more. It was so tempting that Frank telegraphed Dr. Morgan Callaway at the University of Texas to ask if he might resign (he wrote Bertha that he hoped Dr. Callaway would say no). Frank wanted to avoid giving Professor Pegues any hurt, but he told Bertha, "It seems to me that it would be easier to progress out of Austin than out of Georgetown."

Dr. Callaway ultimately decreed it would not be "just" to the university at Austin for Frank to resign his instructorship. With relief, Frank forwarded Dr. Callaway's letter to Southwestern.

In Galveston, on the *Tribune*, he was given the title of dramatic editor, which meant only that he rewrote publicity material on current movies that others had seen and reviewed, except for the ones he wanted to see and review himself. This was not often. He was far more excited about the prospect of interviewing celebrities who came into Galveston as steamship passengers because of the war; many were Germans, Austrians and other Europeans who were on their way home from Central and South America and elsewhere. His working day started at seven-thirty; he was usually free around four-thirty, when he would go out to the beach to swim. Often he stopped by the Rosenberg Library, only a block from his rooming house, before walking the dozen or so blocks to the oceanfront. Later he would go into town for dinner at the American Restaurant with his young colleagues Lowe Simons, Harry Benge Crozier and John Reagan. Sometimes he met old trail drivers there, whose talk reminded him that at one time "I used to almost weep because I was born too late to go up the trails but I am not a bit sorry now — for I would not have known you then, unless you had been born that early too, and I am sure you had been repulsed at the mustaches and six-shooters and other impedimenta with which I had adorned myself."

His most stirring, and most successful, moment as a reporter that summer came when his managing editor sent him to write a feature story on a young girl who had been found drowned on the beach, and whose identity was unknown. Hundreds of people streamed by to view the beautiful, tragic creature; nobody claimed the body; nobody could identify her. Frank's article focused on the reactions of the curiosity hounds who thronged the mortuary. The managing editor put it on the front page, and that night at dinner Frank heard neighboring diners at his restaurant buzzing with discussion of the story, which was, in the style of the day, unsigned. The praise was paradisal to his ears.

His account, "Scenes at the Morgue," in its description of the stream of visitors to view the young corpse, concludes thus: "Coarse men leer, and passing out put a cigar in mouth and hat on head before reaching the door. Two little girls titter, and others of their age are afraid, and others feign agitation. A young man with the face of a poet looks at the forever lifeless features and then at the spectators, whom he no more resembles than does the dead woman there, and passes without a sound into the street."

He was so happy in his work that he wrote Bertha he hated to have to leave Galveston to take up his teaching duties in Austin. For the first time he was really "enjoying" working for a living. He formed the idea of becoming an authority on Mexico, so that when "intervention comes, I could do something fine." He would return to teaching, resolved to give it only one more year of his life. He would like to write the life of "that *charming* man, Pancho Villa," and he felt in his bones that within ten years he would know Mexico as few experts did. He was somewhat influenced by the flamboyant career of the then much-glorified "international correspondent" Richard Harding Davis.

It might make her afraid of him, he wrote her — undoubtedly meaning it — but he felt it was his duty to tell Bertha about a family scandal; and he sent her a clipping from a Galveston paper on an outrageous encounter that was publicized all over the state. Two of his uncles, both of whom had served as Texas Rangers, got into a shoot-out with a raging husband whom one of them had wronged. Two men died: the husband and the brother who was innocent.

Uncle Ed Dubose and Uncle Judge (as he was called) Dubose were both at the time of the shoot-out serving in the Immigration Service at the Brownsville-Matamoros border. J. G. Schoenbohm, the wronged husband, was living with his unfaithful wife in Alice (where Frank, and later Fannie, had been sent in 1904 to stay with the Dubose family while going to high school). He lured the brothers Dubose into an ambush of sorts after following Uncle Ed to Brownsville, nearly two hundred miles south of Alice on the Rio Grande. Using a false name, Schoenbohm wrote Ed please to meet him one late afternoon in the lobby of a Brownsville hotel. Ed, he said in his note, had years ago done him a great service and he was able at last to show his gratitude. Ed showed the note to his brother; neither could remember playing the Good Samaritan unrewarded or unthanked. But Ed's curiosity won out; and Judge, conquering his better judgment, went along primarily to protect his exuberant and wild brother. In the lobby they were directed to a room up the stairs. The assassin, who had stained his face and hands to defy identification, opened fire from his hiding place on the ground floor. Nineteen shots were exchanged. The paper reported that "Dubose, with his automatic, almost drew a circle of holes around the man's chest."

The Dobie family had known that trouble was brewing and that Uncle Ed was far from innocent. Frank Dobie's youthful passion for the upright, instilled in him by his stern father and his strong-minded mother, was profoundly shocked.

Not long after the shoot-out, in September 1914, Frank paid a visit to Bertha at her home in Velasco, just north of the mouth of the Brazos River. He was in the euphoric mood of a young man who has found both his true love and his proper vocation — as he thought: "the news-paper game." "Everything in life nearly tastes good now," he wrote her. "I shall like teaching in Austin, but not so much as this." He was full of high seriousness, due undoubtedly to the family scandal and also to his father's illness and rapid aging: in a very real sense, Frank was coming to think of himself as head of the Dobie family, and he became both paternal and judgmental with his younger brothers. Always longing for adventure and bold testings, perhaps disappointed with himself for not immediately pursuing the dashing career of a reporter like the spectacular Davis, he was reconciled to his decision. He would be content, he said, to bring to the world whatever little bit of *beauty* he might be able to contribute by teaching English literature. "If I were just willing to do what I *can* do my life might be worth more."

It was his third visit to Bertha that summer. Although Frank was so much in debt that he had little prospect of marrying within a year, they became engaged on September 6. Two days later she wrote him: "I have been lonesome for you today, and I have spent a good deal of time *realizing* yesterday and this morning. While they were, I was too happy in living them for thinking. And all this day, too, I have had a curious sort of feeling that I'm walking with a stranger; for I don't know very well yet this new me who loves you and is happy."

Back in Beeville, Frank rode out to the ranch before going up to Austin (the family had moved "into town" in 1906).

He was "obeying an impulse," he wrote Bertha, an impulse that came over him when he went out one morning, at home, to feed his horse and to shell corn for the chickens. Not to follow the impulse, he said, would leave him with "lingering pains of regret for a month." On the trip he nearly lost his horse in quicksand when the mount sank up to his saddle skirts. Frank barely got him out with his rope, and he told Bertha of the animal's magnificent struggle. He slept one night alone on the creek, gun at the ready, in a token of farewell.

And so, characteristically, they began their new lives: Bertha *"realizing,"* and Frank with a symbolic gesture. Each wrote to the other about rereading their old letters. Frank was often, in later years, to remind Bertha that her first to him at Columbia had enclosed a peach blossom. The first thing Frank did on his arrival in Austin was to look over the private home where Bertha would be living. He found it charming, but a long way from his room.

If the most lasting and rewarding loves are founded on deep similarities in temperament and in subconscious values, in being more like than unlike, then Bertha McKee and J. Frank Dobie had a superb conjugal endowment from the start.

What was to separate them so often was a physical difference: Frank Dobie was a robustly healthy man, as he often told her in his letters — he was much concerned with health — and Bertha McKee had been marked by illness from childhood on. He was to become more preoccupied with her health than with his own.

But they were united in their love of poetry and literature, in their instinctive impulsion toward teaching others and taking that vocation seriously. They were alike — although some who knew Frank only in later life will be surprised to hear it — in that both shared a trembling and profound sensitivity, a depth of artistic and emotional response that was rare — and for most people, inadmissible anyway — in the Texas of their youth. In 1915 Frank would be distressed beyond measure, and shocked into searching his soul, when a friend remarked of him that teaching English was making him a "sissy." Aggrieved, he asked Bertha whether she thought so, because (Lyndsay) "Hawkins is really alarmed about me." Bertha earnestly reassured him that she thought him "the most manly man" she had ever seen, although "the most sensitive." Hawkins, a Southwestern classmate, may have felt that his old friend had picked up urban manners in New York, or he may have been pulling Frank's leg. (One of Frank's earliest students at Austin recalled that in those days he "had an English accent.") Frank, much troubled, said he had observed that teaching tended to render men effeminate, the result of "slow, patient, painstaking study."

Just a week after they became engaged, he wrote Bertha that for him the two chief virtues were Truth and Purity. What he meant at the time by Purity we may guess from one brief sentence in *Some Part of Myself*, where he wrote that his ignorance of sex as a young man was "ludicrous." As for Bertha, she was to astonish her rather earthier friend Mary Thomas, a year or so later, by a sobbing admission of her fear of pregnancy: she and Frank had been "kissing."

They were wholehearted in their belief that a great love was life's highest good. All Frank's letters either say to Bertha literally or exhale through the lines like a fragrance from the flowers he so often enclosed: "I am a happy man because I am in love with you."

Frank attended the University Club "smoker" to inaugurate the new school year, and to meet his new colleagues. He was charmed by the occasion; he wrote home that "all the men in my department have been as gracious to me as they could be." He was rooming at 808 West Twenty-second Street, the home of Mrs. Dimmitt, who had one other roomer. In 1914, Mrs. Dimmitt's house was "the last one out but one — then come the valley and the hills." It was only four blocks west of the campus.

The day before the faculty smoker was Frank's birthday. Bertha had gone on a long walk with him to celebrate his anniversary. He wrote his mother that they had walked along the river "and life was sweeter than I dreamed it could be. I thanked God that I had been born."

The University of Texas in 1914 seemed to have the "simplicity" that had characterized Southwestern — or so Frank Dobie thought at first. One of the elements of "chance" — on which he placed such store — happened to him at the outset of his Austin tenure, the accident of association with the man who became one of the greatest names in American folklore, Stith Thompson. Both were starting their first year at the University of Texas, although Thompson's Ph.D. from Harvard was earning him two hundred dollars a year more than Dobie was getting. With two other instructors in the department, they were officemates in a big room.

All four, as Frank Dobie wrote later, were extremely conscientious "toward freshmen and maintained constant receiving lines for conferences on their themes." But, as Frank later wrote to Mody Boatright: "Stith knew where he was going, and I didn't have any idea where I was going beyond being in love. I wanted to teach the survey course in English poetry to sophomores so as to help them fall in love more deliciously, but poetry teaching was not permitted, at that time, to a 'poor M.A.' " One day officemate Thompson asked his colleague Dobie to join the Texas Folklore Society and to pay a dollar in dues to help defray the cost of printing Publication Number 1, which Thompson was editing. Dobie agreed, although he had never heard of the society, or indeed of "folklore." He told Boatright that so far as he knew it was the first time the word had been "used in front of me," and he certainly didn't know what it was. "If Stith Thompson hadn't said *folklore* to me . . . I don't know where in the devil I'd be today," he recalled in 1956, "or where the Folklore Society [of Texas] would either." This was only one of many "chance" connections that Dobie held to be totemic or symbolic in his life.

One of Dobie's most characteristic, and appealing, traits was his indomitable optimism ("perhaps his only real flaw," once observed the man who was his closest friend in later life, Roy Bedichek). Never did his faith in the ultimate goodness of destiny, his almost Tolstoyan respect for the wholeness of meaning in nature and life, stand him in better stead than in the poverty-plagued two years between the sixth day of September 1914, when he and Bertha McKee pledged themselves to each other, and the twentieth day of September 1916, when they at last had enough money ahead, or maybe enough debts settled, to marry and set up their household in Austin.

Bertha's case was particularly trying, since it involved injustice. When she won the fellowship, which yielded only a meager one hundred dollars a trimester, she accepted it with the belief that she could "manage" with what she had saved out of her teaching salary at Alexander Collegiate Institute. But ACI was strapped for money, too, and could not meet the last three months of its payroll. Despite appeals to Bishop Mouzon and other Texas Methodist leaders whom she and Frank both had known at Georgetown, Bertha was never able to retrieve the salary due her.

As a result, by the end of the fall trimester at the University of Texas, she found she could not live on the money she had. Frank's several attempts at speculation in cattle had, because of an exceptionally severe drought, only plunged him further into debt. Marriage at the moment was neither sensible nor possible.

Nonetheless, Bertha's Christmas letter of 1914 to Frank, written at Velasco on the twenty-fourth and sent to him at Beeville, summarizes her delight with their trimester at Austin. "O, my Dear, I have thought of you almost every minute since I left Austin. Whatever my tongue might be saying, my heart was beating your name. I have had a good deal of time to think; I have thought a great deal of the past and hugged sweet memories close, and I have thought about the future too. How the memories come thronging: the morning we sat under the tree in the valley; the day we played 'hand-gull'; the last time — I think, O, no the last time but one — that we went to the river alone together and then came back to town for supper; one late walk with the mist on our faces; one night on the sideporch; the Sunday we read *Aucassin and Nicolette;* a certain afternoon of jumbles; Thanksgiving day, which wasn't like any Thanksgiving day I had ever known; and oh, a dozen others, sweet sweet memories. Guess which two I like best? I know!"

Their decision, arrived at mutually and with Frank taking on a good deal of responsibility for the solution, was for Bertha to go back into teaching after the New Year. Frank had good and useful friends in Galveston. He got Bertha a position that had become vacant there at the Ball High School, teaching both English and algebra to first-year high school classes. The pay would be eighty dollars a month, enough to tide Bertha over until Frank could become at least modestly solvent.

Although she accepted the post, she did not like it. She felt humiliated by having to teach high school freshmen — a comedown after teaching college students — and she detested teaching algebra. But as long as she possibly could, she concealed her feelings from Frank. She consoled herself, as she told him later, with the thought that at her age (she was twenty-four) it was no great matter to take a year out of her life to serve their future.

From Galveston she wrote Frank practically every day, a long two- or three-page handwritten letter; Frank responded in kind, except that his letters were usually twice as long and sometimes he wrote twice a day.

Here are passages from two letters that crossed, each written on January 12, 1915. Frank's was longer, but no more loving. Bertha told him, "I have never got over the strange ecstasy of loving so much. Don't you think it quite wonderful that I should have learned so much about love in just four months? But then I had *you* to teach me." On the same day, Frank wrote: "I never was so terribly lonesome for you as I am tonight. I have been reading — but I would rather hear one beautiful word from your lips than to contain in my memory all the works of the immortals; I would rather touch your hand than possess all the libraries in the world. This is no figure of speech and some day I am going to come and carry you off with me. I will come in a great black coat and I will lift you up and wrap you in it, and then we will go where the world won't bother us — where there are no labors to grind, no miles to separate, no debts to pay.

"This evening I walked to our rock, whence I could see the place where we *studied* one morning, the place where we read *Aucassin and Nicolette*, my arms about you and both as happy as angels. How the memories trooped to me there! Then I went to look upon our little house in the shadowy valley.

"Even though I want you desperately, powerfully, terribly — for I do want you so — don't worry, sweetheart, about how I'm getting along. I am glad, glad to be a-living. There is no law of God or man that could keep me from you, but there is not a hair of your head that I could hurt when I come to you; to get to you I could become a thing of iron and fire; to hold you I should become as gentle as an infant. Sometimes my heart is all in tears with the tenderness of love for you. Goodnight. Frank."

In their letters, he calls her "Burbie," her family's pet name for her, and she calls him "Cher." Frank made a distinction between "Burbie," her playful and spontaneous self, and "Bertha," her intellectual and conscious self.

Her new life began more pleasantly than she had anticipated. Frank's close college friend, Lowe Simons, lived in Galveston; and he met Bertha at the station when she arrived from Velasco. She taught a Sunday school class because the Sunday school superintendent was an old friend; two of her colleagues at Ball High

School were sisters whom she had known at the University of Texas. Still others Bertha knew, and she soon was going with friends on walks along the beach, or on car rides, or to the "picture show." She had enough free time to begin to embroider things for her "hope box." In good weather, she played tennis.

But in his letters Frank's most frequent adjectives for her were "delicate" and "exquisite." She felt obliged to give him good reports of her health, a constant preoccupation with him. She wrote in the first month, "I have never had so much energy in all my life and scarcely ever — at least as it seems now — felt so gloriously well." She kept a bucket of water on top of the oil stove that warmed her room "to keep the room fresh." She walked a great deal. Before the terrible flood of 1900, when six thousand persons lost their lives, Galveston had been the most important city in Texas, with many beautiful houses. Bertha loved "lovely homes."

Now, all this sunshine at the outset came partly from a determined cheerfulness. The move from university campus as a subsidized fellow in the graduate school to "schoolteaching" in the first year of high school was painful for Bertha McKee. Only gradually did the extent of her sacrifice surface in her conscious mind; and when it did surface, she cast it back.

Frank was in one of his spells of rebellion against teaching as a livelihood. Bertha thought he would probably choose journalism as a path to writing books. She told him she had mentioned the matter to their close friend Lowe, who disapproved of Frank's plan to stop teaching. But as for herself, she states forthrightly and with the sanity typical of her letters, "You know what I think of the matter: that you should do whichever you have most ability and desire for; that all the love in the world cannot make a man very happy for long if he does not like his work; and that difficulty and distance of success are minor considerations, provided success does sometime come." She was a brilliant woman, as well as a beautiful one, of clear-sighted logic and impressive literary sensibility, who had always felt that she could lead a life of some distinction on a college campus, as indeed she could have and later did. What had cost her real pangs to leave, Frank was steadily excoriating. She occasionally objected that he was really being intolerant of others' points of view.

A few letters later, she says that "I could mass evidence enough from your recent letters to indicate that you had given up the hope of accomplishing anything in particular and that you were part resigning yourself to a state of obscurity." She also apologizes for conveying a false impression of her health. The exercises Frank insisted she practice had helped her mightily: "Why, it is ridiculous to speak of ill health. Organically I am entirely well."

Frank could enjoy teaching, sometimes even exult in it, and was a great success with the students — but he did not want to earn the Ph.D. simply as indispensable certification. Unorthodox and independent to the ultimate limits of his temperament, he did not want to take several years out of his life for a "discipline" he felt he personally did not need. He wanted to write, and to test himself as a writer who could make money out of what he wrote.

Bertha was immensely sympathetic. She had within herself the same conflicting impulses. She was creative as well as critical in mind; she too was trying her hand at writing short stories. But she, like Frank, had such a natural gift for teaching that she could not lightly ignore its personal rewards, or the satisfaction of performing a socially valuable service. The latter argument appealed but little to Frank, though like all teachers he was elated when his teaching enlarged and encouraged a spirited mind. His choice was a tough one. The ideal, perhaps, was to combine the two, counting writing as the "journalism" fulfillment. But what Frank saw exactly was that the kind of writing he was destined to do — original and innovative, rather than derivative — might well be crippled by the Teutonic modes of inventory scholarship then prevailing. He wrote Bertha that, with her as his wife, he could be happy as an English instructor, but the hard fact remained that he had no wish to be what was then called a scholar, and "one does not become a professor without first becoming a scholar." If he cared enough, he told Bertha, he might fight the system (which at that time in the English Department at the University of Texas was exceptionally inflexible) and "be a successful teacher of the high and the beautiful. I am not provided with the weapons of the academicians. I am provided by nature with those of the journalists: a man can fight better with his own than with another's arms."

A month after this letter he made a trip to Georgetown (hardly more than thirty miles northeast of Austin) to visit his younger brother Lee, who — unlike Frank — had become a "fraternity man" at Southwestern. Frank was flooded again with delightful reminders of his happiness there, and of course saw the teacher whom he and Bertha both idolized, Professor Pegues (who was not a "scholar," no matter how great a "teacher"). Mrs. Pegues pleased him immensely by saying that as he came up the steps he still looked like a "boy." He was seized with yearning for the old life. "I wanted you there today. All the charm and tenderness of that place, which — as a place — is the only dear place to me on earth, came back to me across the years. I saw you in many places and I remembered many a boyhood glimpse that I had thought to have forgotten."

Deep down both knew, however, that the privileged moments of their idyllic college life in a sylvan setting were preparation and not fulfillment. For neither one did this special interlude in life remain the most vivid and happiest time lived through — as it did remain for many college students in "the good old days." Deeper down, what both realized was that Texas was changing very rapidly, growing, maturing, and becoming more like than unlike the rest of the nation. This fact was to form one of the central issues of his, and therefore Bertha's, life. Only two years after that report in early 1915, he was to tell Bertha that he could never "go back" to Georgetown — meaning symbolically that he could never again find there, as at the one right moment he once had, his essential self.

Bertha began to suffer from headaches and fatigue. Frank was so troubled he called her long distance one night in February because he "wanted to make her well." (She reported in her next letter that he did.) In mid-February, her teaching chores were augmented when seventy-five new pupils came to Ball High School from the ward schools, and classes that once had had twenty-five now had around forty. Bertha said her teaching would be a "battle from this day forth." She had "one roomful of young hyenas for two eternal periods."

But there was the prospect of a visit in March. Frank went over to Georgetown on a visit in late February and remembered to send her violets from there. Bertha was touched, and wrote him, "I think you have the finest sensibilities of anyone I ever knew."

A few days later she admits she also thinks he is "vain, . . . but with a vanity that delights me." He characterizes himself as a man like Rossetti, according to Pater's phrase: "Rossetti is like one of those who, in the words of Mérimée, 'se passionnent pour la passion,' one of love's lovers." In their letters they frequently cited French passages to each other.

Frank's weekend-long visit was their first meeting since the separation at Christmas. The visit was memorable for both of them. Bertha wrote him two or three days later: "Do not think that in marrying you I shall feel any sense of loss of things dear to me. Once I should have thought so, but not now. It is not now as once it was that you are merely first; you are all. Should I tell you this, should I thus let you see my heart absolutely without reservation? I do not know. I think so, for you, too, love greatly. Whether I teach or not is a trivial question; whether I do my part in making our life happy and beautiful and full is all absorbing. Whether it is well that one's life plan be so changed I do not know; I merely know that it is so." And she assured him that "a few lean years" did not worry her. "You will win ultimately, that I know. Nor is this confidence merely the undirected confidence of the woman who loves. As I told you, my reason and my love are singularly detached and I can judge. I have judged." She concludes: "I woke once last night at two to think of you on your journey."

They had chosen March for their spring visit because it was the sixth month after their engagement pledges of the preceding September. The number six came to have for Frank a special meaning, as he told Bertha that autumn: "Bertha, I think we surely had better be married on some day that has in its month number the number six. I am in earnest. Look you: I was born on the twenty-*sixth* of the *ninth* month, which latter number *nine* is common by the kinship of three to *sixth*. In the *sixth* month of the year I besought your love (June). On the *sixth* day of the *ninth* month (again the number nine), near my own twenty-*sixth* birthday, we became engaged. *Six* months later, on the *sixth* day of that month (March) I saw you in an entirely unforeseen manner at Galveston. By a strange turn of fortune, we are to be blessed with a love meeting on the next *sixth*. We plan to marry in the year approaching your own twenty-*sixth* birthday. You were sixteen your first year at Georgetown — the fatal place. Also I am one of *six* children, and you are one of *three* children. Verily, verily, according to the philosophy of numbers our binding tie is *six*. Furthermore you are about six hundred times nicer and more lovely and finer and everything than anybody I know, and I love you about six thousand times as much as I would love you if I just loved you ordinarily. Oh, Burbie, Burbie, I do love you gladly and madly." It was another sign of his attachment to the concrete and particular rather than to the abstract and general. An example: Just before the March meeting, Frank enclosed with his daily letter not the usual flower but bird feathers. "I found a dead redbird and I plucked a few of its feathers that you might note the delicate and exquisite tippings. Observe how much brighter the red color is on the outer side than on the inner side." Perhaps another sign of this attachment to detail occurs in his postscript to the letter, a fairly long one: "I want you to tell me when you did first kiss my picture. Tell me please. I kissed yours first once in New York. Oh I want to kiss you goodnight now — no, not 'goodnight,' for I want to hold you close and kiss you a thousand rapturous kisses."

Meantime, he was attending all the special lectures given during Home Economics Week at the university. He wrote Bertha about "counting calories" even then, giving her an inventory of his habits. He worshipped exercise; he had decided to quit coffee. This made him feel much better, but it would have been absolute paradise to have a glass of wine instead. He confessed that he started far more books than he finished. "I love beginning them," he said. He was disgusted by chauvinists who overpraised American writing. He himself found it "senile, puerile, devoid of color, of the beautiful, of the waveringly beckoning; I have found it the product of hot-house pundits and of butcher-shop artisans." It lacked "the enduring quality of youth — the quality of Shakespeare, of Stevenson, of Victor Hugo, of Shelley." He ferociously rejected an essay in the *Century Illustrated Magazine* that found the literature of America "youthful but not boyish." Finally, he vaunted his own cheerfulness and wondered why Bertha so often saw life "in black." He deplored again her fondness for melancholy and pessimistic authors.

On that same day, in a second letter: "Someday you shall be proud of me. As a matter of fact, you need not be ashamed of me now, for I am the youngest by two years of all the instructors and I am the best instructor among them — the most interesting. I know it, lady, and furthermore I do as I please, skipping what I want to, and adding what I want to. Furthermore, I expect to do as I please all the rest of my life and never conform to anything wrong, myself the judge, and thus be a site more successful than some of the immortals." He interrupts the flush of his anger to note, no doubt to the considerable amusement of Bertha McKee, that "a woman who has not been married very long, wearing a pretty coat suit with a sash behind it exactly like the one on your brown dress, went by with her husband just then."

The vivid reminder of Bertha did not long deter the course of his righteous anger. He continues: "My idea of success tonight is: 1) You very happy and well; 2) a secluded back garden to smell like the side street through which I am going to walk back [an allusion to a fragrant alleyway passed earlier on the way to the Driskill Hotel]; 3) freedom from service in the cause of the great American public; 4) the absence of any corking and carping ambition. Of course my idea of success is apt to change by midnight. Whatever it is or may be, you must know that I would not let you love me in that self-pitying, man-pitying, unconsciously patronizing manner in which women love those men of whom they are ashamed. I have too much pride and self-respect for that." Just before his assertion of his manly ability to do what he pleases, he had confided to Bertha that he had "invented a rose leaf jar," that is, a tobacco jar in which he placed the "red petals of falling roses." He told her: "It is nearly full now, and you cannot imagine what an exotic beauty is obtained. And the fragrance."

Bertha, who was far more addicted to analysis than Frank, urged him that spring to consider carefully the wisdom of marrying *her*. She could not be the conventional housewife, she reminded him, and confessed that the kitchen was less fulfilling for her than the library. He replied vigorously: "Bertha, believe me when I tell you that I am glad you love a poem better than you love a dress and that you can criticize a novel better than you can cook a cobbler. You may think it foolish — but I am glad that you are not *very* practical. I like you just as you are. And I have been wanting to tell you that I am very much ashamed of the tirade I made against your reading Hardy; at the time I imagined that Hardy was killing something in you that I love; now I know that one reason I love you is because you have an ambition to do something fine in our field — literature." He enclosed Easter violets with his Easter wishes.

Not discouraged by a failure to land a post on the Dallas *News*, he discussed with his superior, Professor Royster, the prospect of taking a year's leave of absence to give journalism a final testing, and then returning, in all likelihood, to teaching. Royster was blunt. Frank would have little chance of returning because there was "more hidebound clinging to Ph.D. principles here than in any university in the country." Royster was quite certain that a year in professional newspaper work would diminish rather than increase Frank's prestige. But Frank's urge to write was as powerful as ever. He had developed a number of plots he was gradually turning into stories. As though to prove his talent to Bertha, he wrote her an elaborate description of a dead butterfly he had found and put on a green leaf to admire the delicacy of its beautiful structure. After a rainy night in April, Frank wrote her: "Oh, Burbie, you will never know what rain means until you live in the west — a rancher's bride! It is not Italy nor Paris I want this morning. It is the old, old hills of Live Oak County. I want *you* there; dear heart, you should have to learn to ride with me — if not on a horse by yourself then like Lochinvar's bride. We should swim the roaring Arroyo Largo; we should hear Elrich shout; and then we should ride across shimmering seas of blue bonnets. Oh there is not any healthy joy in the world so good as *that*, and you would not remember that ever you were sick when you were a child, and the idea of staying indoors and reading such books as *The Egoist* would seem to you the most absurd and punitive in the world."

After one of her letters about the novels of George Meredith, Frank's envelope comment, "An intellectual letter," conveys a stern discontent. Often, he rebuked her for writing of anything but her feelings, or more exactly, of subordinating expression of her feelings to nonpersonal observations. Just as often, she reassured him:

"Believe me, Frank, I am happy. I wish for your sake that I were more often joyous. That I am not is due partly to disposition; partly to environment; partly to some events of my life, the first and perhaps the chief being a sickly childhood. But if I am rarely joyous — I mean radiantly, ecstatically joyous — I am seldom gloomy. You are mistaken. I do not see black, but gray suffused with rose. And often you have made me magically, always deeply, happy. It is a subject over which we once made ourselves very miserable in Austin. Do you not expect in me the spontaneity and abounding glory in the mere sense of life that a girl of seventeen feels? You forget that I am a woman." (She was twenty-four, two years younger than he.)

This searching letter, exploring their differences in temperament, continues frankly to the point where Bertha makes a confession. "In one particular you are right. I do not like my work — it seems a sort of treason to say that — but I had not wished you to know. . . . I appreciate your generosity in suggesting that I study next year. But you are mistaken. I have no longer any desire for that. And I want, more than I want anything else in the world, you whom I love with my whole heart." She tells him that at the time of his visit she felt she was "far happier" than he. She adds: "I fear that you will reproach yourself for your share in my being here. I still think that you took a grave responsibility, but I understand now as I did not understand then. And I know now that you were wise. I am very glad for several reasons that I did not remain at the university."

Two letters later, Frank delightedly writes on the outside of the envelope that her letter "came on a Sunday of April odors." Bertha describes the springtime life of a tree just beginning its first "feathering" outside her window, her pleasure in the copious stream of fresh flowers her students bring her, her deep love of the things of nature, and her satisfaction that the superintendent is full of praise for her work. In fact, he has promised her all English classes, no algebra, if she will stay on next year. She will stay on, she says, if the school will pay her $100, or $120 with a combination of high school and night school classes.

And a week later she praises another virtue of the Galveston experience; it has made her "more respectful of the material." She explains: "I think I used to believe that the material and the spiritual were incompatible but now — What is that line from Browning? I'll look it up.

*'All good things
Are ours, nor soul helps flesh more now, than flesh helps soul.'*

Frank responded with approval to the quotation from Browning, and was moved to a confession himself: "For myself, I take much joy in sheer animal life — in swimming, in feeling the waters swish up to the saddle skirts, in *eating rain*, in doing a thousand things." He guessed correctly, in being allowed three guesses, where Bertha had put the lock of his hair — one, in the lavaliere he had given her; two, with his picture; or three, "in the love tale of *Aucassin and Nicolette.*" Frank kept Bertha's lock of hair in his copy of *Sonnets from the Portuguese.*

Exasperation over misinterpreted nuances usually ended in renewed reassurances of total understanding. But in these two hypersensitive lovers, hurts were unconsciously inflicted. Bertha protested Frank's assertion this same spring that "he knows her little": "Why, Frank, I have never flung my doors so wide to [any] other being as I have flung them to you. And I am puzzled to know the characteristic that you say puzzles you. I hope that you will neither forget nor hesitate to tell me of it when we meet." Yet, on the envelope of her next letter, Frank notes, "A true love letter, as all are; the three before this especially too."

To her astonishment at his asserting he "knew her little," he replied contritely: "I know you very, very much — not a 'little' even if I did say it — and don't think that at any time I think you too reserved with me. No matter how wide you open the doors, always some of you will puzzle me — because there is so much to you, you see. But now don't forget to ask me what it is that puzzles me especially."

Each deplored on occasion the necessity of writing instead of speaking what was to be said, as when Frank complains that it is harder to write letters to make her happy than to speak the words to her. When neither feels like writing, Frank is sure the effort of doing so is evident to the other, whereas a passing mood in daily association is quickly absorbed into a proper perspective. Worst of all is the disparity when a letter written in high spirits is answered by one written in melancholy. Both indeed enjoyed the intensity of writing and deplored the absence of each other's comforting daily presence. As Frank put it, he felt he was "much more answerable to your mood than you are to mine," in letters. Was this a weakness or a strength? he wondered.

He went on, that spring, to observe that "this love has caused a revolution in all my tastes and ideas. That which I love to read best is now of love, of the theme that fills my soul. You, on the other hand, who used to write me much of Browning, now write me of German war articles! The psychology of it interests me. Is there not, unconsciously perhaps, something like this? I do not like you when you discuss the German war — the subject is not compatible to you — and therefore write to you of the love things, the exquisite things that I wish always to epitomize you — as they do. You fear that I grow emasculate, that I do not struggle with enough Titanic vigor; therefore you turn to the *strong* material? This is somewhat 'wild,' I admit, now that I see it written down. It is my nature to like Mexico better than I like Germany, and it is your nature to like *Diana of the Crossways* better than you like Browning's Love Letters!" Wild, indeed, but did any man in love ever fail to demand that his beloved resemble him exactly?

She did so, in suffering "starvation" for a letter from him when a day was skipped. On such a day, she admitted, she listened with haunted attention for a telephone call, since he had in the past called her long distance. Each rebukes the other for loving less, each claims to love the more, in these infrequent periods of storm. The first two weeks in May of 1915 were, for them, hurricane season. On the letter he received on May 15, Frank noted: "Which made me very happy. It came on a Saturday after many unhappy letters." It is, by the way, in his count, letter number 100.

So, number 101 is a part of the cleanup operation. Bertha writes: "Now that I have returned to a state of mental equilibrium, I know that what you wrote was written with entire unselfishness; that you were concerned about my happiness for my own sake; that you were not upbraiding me for giving you a less joyous love than you desired. But it is a joyous love, Frank. I feel this morning as blithe as the birds that sing outside my window their madrigals of love. O, my dearest, I know that you love me very greatly, very wonderfully, very beautifully. I thank God for that love and hold it to my heart with the prayer that I may be all my life worthy of it. You know that I love you."

And in her next she speaks of "the reserved Bertha McKee of five years ago, who would have been aghast had she known that some day she would give her love so unwithholdingly."

Mundane matters now compelled attention. Frank wrote that he had won high praise from Dr. Callaway. Bertha was pleased with this sign that Frank was again liking his work at the university, "though," she tells him, "I expect you to contend still that your happiness and your work are absolutely unrelated." Frank was contented enough with himself and his life to ask her detailed questions about what sort of house she looked forward to having, and whether she preferred to buy or rent. She was certain only about the plants she wanted to grow. He also needed information on how much money she would need to "dress well." She gave him a very modest figure and said she no longer wanted to teach "because more than I desire my work, I desire that we be happy together in a real home. And divided interests are weak interests." In the same practical letter she informs him that she has put the lock of his hair he sent in her copy of *Aucassin and Nicolette*, "at the happy part."

Frank sent her Conrad's *Youth*, one of his sovereign admirations. She shared his response, and concluded her reply: "And with you — oh, Frank, let us live to the uttermost and fight the gray thing together. I am ready to seek with you adventures of body or of spirit, wherever or however you will. I was not always so."

Frank notes on her next letter, "A glorious letter. So the one before." She asks, "Frank, would you like to go into Mexico? If you would, I am most absolutely willing to go. The unusualness, the wildness, the romance — although I realize there would be much not-romance — has taken hold of my imagination until honestly I had just as soon go, rather if you wish it. There would be adventure, and what a different life from the life of my planning!"

At any rate, if not Mexico, Frank had at least to decide whether he would teach in Austin the next year or take an available job on the San Antonio *Express* — at a good deal less pay. His decision would inevitably affect Bertha's. From her "eighth year," she wrote Frank, she had wanted to be a writer. She was working at short stories. But only teaching offered any security.

Meanwhile, he had heard of a teaching post in San Marcos, only forty miles from Austin, which he hoped to get for Bertha. "San Marcos is the most beautiful little city in Texas: it is on hills and rivers."

He was able to get to Galveston again in early May, and planned to return in another month or five weeks. The formidable, grand old gentleman of the English Department, Dr. Morgan Callaway, had assured Frank that he should stay in teaching, and had recommended a raise in pay for him next year. But he felt certain that a year in journalism would not make Frank a better teacher. Much pleased, Frank shamefacedly wrote Bertha that he was coming to like his work at the university, but "I should not like for the idea to get abroad!" He accepted an invitation to make the commencement address at the Sabinal High School on May 22, 1915, choosing as the title for his speech, "The Practicability of the Beautiful." He took as his text "Mahomet's beautiful dictum: 'If I had only two loaves of bread, I should exchange one for a lily.' . . . I wish to elevate my hearers to a thirst for the beautiful; I wish to make the beautiful come to them as something needed every day."

II

With the summer of 1915 free after his first year of teaching at the university, Frank tried for reporting jobs, not only with the Dallas *News*, the Fort Worth *Record*, the Galveston *Tribune* and the San Antonio *Express*, but also with the Austin *American*. He wanted most to go to Galveston — the exhilaration of his work there the preceding summer was still with him. He was led to wonder what his life might have been like had he "never forsaken journalism." He tells Bertha, "I cannot think now that all my life is destined to be spent in academic puling." If he doesn't get a newspaper job that summer, he will either go to New Orleans, or to Uncle Jim's ranch in Mexico, or speculate in cattle around Beeville, although that would require taking a loan, to operate on, in San Antonio.

After a visit there, he wrote her of his pleasure in the cowmen he had seen, the pleasure he took in their "manliness" and their "manly" talk. Obviously, he felt a real conflict between the life he led on the campus and the one he led on the range. He knew well that his was a divided nature. Analyzing himself for Bertha's knowledge, he wrote her: "One half of the time I act on impulse, all too decisive, defying a devil or blaspheming an angel; the other half I hesitate between two or more courses, all seemingly reasonable. In one case I have too much will – will turned to obstinancy [sic]; in the other a lack of judgment as to which way to exert it. If you wish to know the great obstacle to my success it is that I hear too many voices, that I love excessively the new, the varied. Still I say I respect myself." He tells Bertha that "analysis of persons is my *forte.*"

They were both interested in folklore, although Bertha's attention to it crystallized first. By 1915 Frank was already writing her of "the world of Mexican lore I could gather, and shall gather. I have been reading a journal of Mexican lore." In the same letter, he remarked that Ruskin had said at the end of his life, "I wish I knew less and had *painted* more." Frank comments, "What a commentary on life, on pedantry – though Ruskin was never a pedant." He adds that he has discovered exactly why he likes Ruskin – "because he is extremely sensitive." He has begun to plan a course in biography, a form that interested him greatly. He did not suppose he would be allowed to offer it, but he found it stimulating to think about the possibility. He decided that his favorite "life of one writer by another writer" was William Dean Howells's life of Mark Twain.

In June, he wrote Bertha about his raise – another hundred a year – for his second year at the university. He planned to be in Velasco the next weekend, sure he would profit by $150 or so on a cattle trade made possible by a loan from Uncle Jim. But, at least at that moment, he told her, "I had a lot rather teach than run devilish steers through brush and thorns into my legs." This was not steadily so.

Galveston offered Bertha the increase she wanted and expected. She was pleased and Frank noted on her letter: "Elle semblait enchantée de la vie."

But *he* was not exactly enchanted with his own life. He was having problems with his cattle at the ranch. "Sensible to the end," as she said of herself, she told Frank she did not wish him to speculate in cattle for her sake, wanted him to run no risks because of her. She has disciplined herself to do the family cooking at Velasco that summer; she tells him that she found the "fourth day far more bearable than the first."

Frank was so elated by a visit late in June and by the letters that followed that he noted, "And the world is all at our feet." He sent her a volume of Victor Hugo's verse; she wrote him that for her the two greatest "tonics of prose literature" were Carlyle's *Sartor Resartus* and Stevenson's "Aes Triplex." She very much liked Lewes's *Life of Goethe*, and made out for Frank a list of the books and writers that had most influenced her. Shakespeare, Browning and Wordsworth head the list; then she enumerates these titles: *Sesame and Lilies; Sartor Resartus;* the Gospel of John and the Epistle to the Romans; Emerson's *Essays; The Arabian Nights;* and *Vanity Fair,* "if fiction be included."

In July, Frank was back in Velasco for a two-day stay. They went swimming in the Gulf of Mexico at Surfside, four miles below Velasco, and went rowboating on the Brazos River, both summertime pleasures that Bertha loved. He gave her a pearl ring, and she wrote to him after his departure: "I am immeasurably happiest when your ring is on my finger. It is as if a shadow of your presence were beside me. I had not dreamed that a ring — a mere thing — could mean so much." And in a letter he got at the ranch on July 27, he made a typical note: "This letter I opened at dawn and read sitting on my horse [he had sent some of the ranch help into Lagarto to bring back his mail]. Oh how it gave my heart a cheer and eyes for the glorious." One thing the letter told him: "Ah, Frank, there is now no happiness, even fleeting, for me but in you. . . . I liked your calling me your morning glory. If I am your morning glory, then you are my day's dawn, which the morning glory blossoms to greet."

Frank's cattle deals were not in as full sail as his love. The scorching summer winds and the long, unrelieved drought had brought misery to the land and the cattle and the people who lived on it. He needed a new suit, but spent the money set aside for it on a necklace for Bertha. She knew this and rebuked him. They had never yet seen each other in the month of August, nor would they this year.

When Frank had gone with Uncle Jim in July to help receive a big string of steers from Bassett Blakely at Liverpool in Brazoria County, Uncle Jim took Frank on to Houston. He wanted Frank to buy a few cattle and said he would sign Frank's note. Frank bought "a hundred and thirty or forty cows" from an acquaintance of Uncle Jim's, and arranged to ship them to Dinero. He accompanied them, riding in the caboose, and sent word ahead for several helpers on horseback to bring a horse for him and meet him at the pens. He leased the Miller pasture of about two thousand acres (it adjoined the Dobie ranch) and put the cows in it. His note for the payment was made out to the National Bank of Commerce in San Antonio. Thus began the major "speculation in cattle" that bedogged his marriage, and later his bank account, until the aftermath of the war in 1919.

He offered Bertha "my history" in an August letter: "Thursday, starting at three o'clock in the morning and stopping at eleven that night, I rode two horses down, sold 20 cows at $3 per head profit, and bought eighty steers. Friday early I started back to Casa Blanca for the cattle. It was the hottest day I ever drove cattle. We were three hours going a mile and a half. By moonlight I finished branding, and after that my Mexican boys arrived with the much expected letter." He adds: "All day yesterday we drove — slow, slow, but with a lot of running. It is six o'clock now. I have just gotten in for *dinner*, from taking the cattle to my pasture. We started with the first light. But I have had good luck; Uncle Frank (who is, papa excepted, the best cattle judge in the country), says I got them cheap. And I drove through a country of 'muchos amigos' — many friends — where the broad hospitality of one cow man to another (who has a herd) showed itself. Oh luck is turning our way, Burbie, and it is going to rain. My spirits are high. Presently I am going to mount a fresh horse and ride down on a prairie to rope a wild cow that can't be caught otherwise. She comes out only with the lateness."

He and the Mexican vaquero Genardo del Bosque set out in the morning to drive home the wild, "fighting cow" they had roped and tied the evening before. Frank wrote Bertha what happened: "I was riding a fractious horse that had tried to pitch me the day before. Well the cow, while I was near, made a run at my horse, tipping him with her horn, while I, at the same time, spurred him hard to make him jump off. He is hard-mouthed; he started off pitching fiercely; I am no expert rider. I was thrown and somehow wrenched my back. Fortunately we were close to the house, and it did not take long to get the mules and wagon to haul me in. Yesterday and last night I could not sit up, or even turn over. But today the pains are quiet, and I can sit up. . . . Of course the people at home know nothing of this, and by the time you get this I shall be walking. So think no more of the matter."

Bertha let him have a diary she kept as a young girl. He tells her on August 25 that he read it "with tender love," and that she "was then — and is yet sometimes — a grown-up like Quaker girl — the most adorable little Quaker girl in the world."* He assures her she is "an angel." The day he read the diary was a good day for him. "All day people have been good to me. The man who bought the cows from me sent some fresh butter ten miles." Another rancher, "a kind of cowboy osteopath," came over and rubbed Frank's back, and returned later to rub in oil: "Oh there are lots of kind hearts in this world." A postscript to this cheerful letter adds, "I am glad for a thousand things: I am glad that my beard is long and my hat big so that when I enter the parlor-car people will look funny. I am glad that I have some *tortillas* and deer meat to eat on the train; I am glad that I can cut an unaccountable figure; I am glad, glad that I love you and you love me. I am Your Frank."

His father completed a sale of one-half of the ranch in November 1915, but he planned to stay until the following summer. He delivered over the stock, "every hoof, horses and cattle," except one. He kept Frank's favorite horse, old Buck. Frank appreciated this thoughtfulness; "I would have felt mean and like a traitor at selling him," he wrote Bertha. He also told his parents: "I would not think about business matters so concernedly or care so profoundly if I were not dying to get a little money to marry on." And he also wanted to pay back his father a debt of $175. He was teaching four classes that fall, all in freshman English. His back continued to pain him after the summer's accident. For treatment, he went to an osteopath, and reported home that the visits had helped him a lot.

Frank suggested to Bertha she might quit teaching after the first term and return to Austin. But her need for money seems to have been as desperate as his, although she did not have the responsibility of paying back a $6,400 loan. She did decide to drop a life insurance policy (Frank told her to be sure to check on any possible "cash

---

* Bertha McKee's parents moved to Texas from Pennsylvania before she was born, but her mother returned to the family farm in Susquehanna County for the birth.

rebate"). He himself was occasionally morose at the extent of his gamble in cattle: "Sometimes when I get to thinking how I may lose money and thus be neither able to marry or to afford you soon anything like a home, the sweat breaks out cold all over me." Bertha sought to heal him of the "anxiety of debt that you have assumed."

He was working very hard, much gratified that he would be given the course in poetry to teach as part of his spring "load." He paid the conventional Sunday afternoon visits to his superiors; he went to church every Sunday morning.

In December he went to Beeville to spend part of the holidays with his family; the news he got was not good. About twenty head of his herd of 168 cattle in the Miller pasture had died of a fever caused by ticks. Those left alive were doing better, but the winter had hardly begun. In the crisis, his father and Elrich and Genardo had worked themselves to the limit of their strength. But the cattle were "too thin" to offer to market. A blessed rain would heal a lot, and he might not lose more than $500. But he wrote Bertha that "if a droughty winter and spring come, I might lose two or three times that much. I would sell out today at $500.00 loss."

For Frank, desperate to have enough money to provide Bertha with a home and a solvent marriage, no vocation he had tried seemed foolproof. With the scruple characteristic of him, he goes to the heart of the matter in this same Christmastime letter: "And now, Bertha, that marrying this year seems out of the question, I once more without arguing, without attempting to convince, must tell you how I view your side of the situation. When you wrote me last week that you would "never, *never* go to Texas [the university], you were talking at a height of revolt against all mankind. . . . Two weeks after you returned to Texas you would be enthusiastic and glad, and if you did not get your thesis done, you could finish it after commencement. . . . If we married now or even a year hence, what of the home beautiful would there be to engage your intelligence and interests?" He doesn't want her to suffer an unpleasant year in Galveston. Their "economic condition" precludes Bertha's finding fulfilling activity in making a home, and most certainly precludes "any such contingency" as adopting the world's view that "a woman found life abundant in the bearing and caring for a baby." She cannot be happy without intellectual fulfillment, and that's why he argues for her returning to graduate school. He accuses himself of failure: "I have bungled the whole business. I ran a risk twice; I lost twice. . . . I am trying to sell my Bee County cattle: if I sell them, I can't see you." He adds that he will telegraph, but in the prospect of not coming at Christmastime and of not being able to talk these matters over with her, he ends on a desperate note that as for Bertha's going on teaching in Galveston — "sacrificing yourself, changing yourself, not feeling yourself to *advance* — this is the bitterest pill I have ever swallowed."

Frank liked to carry Bertha's most recent letters in his coat pocket and to read and reread them on the long walks he took into the woods and along the river. He wanted to read them in some "quiet, beautiful place alone." When he felt the spur to write one evening after coming back from a walk into town to eat dinner, he made do with unused portions of paper in her letters, chiding her of course for not filling the pages. He usually walked alone, as he had done at Southwestern, telling Bertha he was not good at "sports," cared nothing for the "national pastime" (baseball, then) because he "couldn't throw." Of odd facts he related to Bertha in his letters, many are attempts to let her know him better, but many others are simply included as "curious"; for example, his brother Lee thought that Bertha, in a picture Frank kept out, looked like "a Japanese." Another example: he confessed he thought it was "foolish" for a man to wear his clothes the way he, Frank, did and always to wear a flower in his buttonhole. But, without this habit, he would not have sent her the "first red rose of the year" (after wearing it himself for a day). As a matter of fact, he sent only a petal of the rose, but this was a symbol of the beauty that both the flower and Bertha represented. However, if Bertha had been in Austin, he would have put the rose in her beautiful hair, and would have kissed the hair, the rose "and you." Another detail: he wakes to watch the sunrise every morning. "I keep my word: 'Daily I see the sunrise out of my bed, which I still value as a tonic, a perpetual tuning-fork, a look of God's face once in a day.'" Sometimes a poetic note: "In the room of the blue vase at moonset"; or, "The first Sunday of the Fifth Month." Sometimes domestic, as when he offers a budget plan, gleaned from the Home Economics Week of lectures: rent, 20 percent; food, 30 percent; clothes, 20 percent; "running expenses," 15 percent; *"higher life,"* 15 percent. Sometimes horticultural: he dug up the garden beds for his landlady, Mrs. Dimmitt, "and reset all the violets." Or family details: "I am overlord of three younger brothers." Or personal: he can't become a "scholar" because he can't bear to spend that much time indoors. Or congratulatory: Cheers! Bertha has gained seven pounds! And another personal detail: he tended to dislike blond people — "they'd be in character as in color — colorless." His own hair, once light, had darkened because he "wished so hard" that it would.

Frank was deeply attached to the sylvan and (for Texas) unique landscape of Austin. He was especially fond of a colleague's new house because of its flat roof (rare in those days) from which "all the beautiful world around Austin is visible."

His taste in literature was still puritanical, at least in regard to contemporary writing. He relished Shakespeare's Falstaff, he relished Rabelais, but he found much modern drama morbidly unwholesome. Of one play touring Austin, *A Pair of Sixes*, he wrote Bertha he was glad she was not with him. The play had "one good scene; a dozen indecent ones; three dozen silly and boresome ones. . . . It has made me feel low and grimy."

Of his literary preferences, he wrote Bertha that he remembered Boswell "better than anything I ever read; it has taught me more than twenty histories of literature could teach me; its last pages are the most moving that I know of. . . . Many times the tenderness of one scene between those grand old men — Dr. Johnson and Sir Joshua Reynolds — has come back to soften me."

In a letter of March 6, just before a visit from Frank, Bertha sent twenty-one pages, small in size, in answer to Frank's praise of George Herbert Palmer and his wife, Alice Freeman Palmer. Bertha says she has read to many a class from George Herbert Palmer's *Self-Cultivation in English*, the reading of which has meant more to her than any other book in many years. The perfection of the Palmer marriage she found exemplary.

Bertha explained to Frank after his departure that she caused him "unhappiness" last Sunday because she had "grown hard" for these reasons: [because] "I have not received $200 from A.C.I., because circumstances prevented my continuing the studies that had been my passionate interest, and because I am now doing work that is uncongenial and for which I am not suited." However, she will continue her studies, if Frank is willing, "under the happiest of circumstances" (that is, marriage to him). If she teaches next year, she wants to teach in a normal school or junior college. She need not have explained. Frank understood.

She repeats her faith in Frank's gifts for writing, and tells him forthrightly that his talents do lie in literature, not scholarship. "I do think that you can write, if only you have sufficient staying power." She tries to reconcile him with the academic point of view, which must deny him recognition until he creates something. "Once you create something worthy, you will see how cordially they will recognize your creation as more than their learning. I think this bitterness does you no good. It wastes your energies." About the cattle, she hopes Frank can break even. "Then we'll never speculate again, will we, Frank, but be poor and happy all our lives, unless, indeed, you should write books. Then we should be rich and happy. What a towering, impassable mountain, separating you and me, seems that $6,400!"

He continued to work at short-story writing; tried his hand at essays; and "contemplated" articles for the *English Journal*, "iconoclastic" articles. He wrote Bertha a number of times, "I want to be independent and original." And on March 13, 1916, Frank sent Bertha this comment about his life on the campus: "Nobody here knows my best side; nobody here knows me at all. I wonder if all the world walks as little understood and as sensitive as I walk. Are you glad, Bertha, that I not only want you, but also need you? I am." In the same letter, he continues his analysis of their "likeness" in observing "for people like us, Burbie — for you and I are remarkably alike in the uncontrollable flexibility of our temperamental moods — life is not a stream, but a surging ocean where we swim now one way now another."

By 1916, his interest in the European war had intensified to the point where he devoutly hoped the United States would enter it. He flays Woodrow Wilson as ineffectual; he denounces the German nation with a hatred hard to explain in a youth reared on a Texas ranch. He writes Bertha: "Would to God that I were a Savonarola, a Fleury, a Mirabeau to set this country on fire and send its minions sweeping and blazing and, if need be, dying across Europe." Naturally, he found George Bernard Shaw, with his pacifism, a traitor to his country, deserving to be hanged. He fulminates on all fronts. He was terribly hurt that spring when he was assigned to teach English 1 rather than English 2. After an unrewarding visit to Dr. Callaway, Frank sent a tirade to Bertha. Just the night before, two of his younger colleagues had sworn to him that "God intended me to create literature; they often tell me that now." And he wails, "I am the best teacher in the University of Texas; I have more originality than any man I know; I publish nothing; I have no Ph.D.; therefore I am fit only for freshman rhetoric. Curse business, curse politics, curse the materialistic world as I may, there is in it nothing so ludicrously pedantic, unfair and puerilely narrow as the petty jealousies and spelling-bee standards of judgment to be found in academic circles." Following this invective, he adds immediately, perhaps with ironic intent or maybe only for a laugh at himself: "I am now going to church; it is Mother's Day." (By this date he had lost most of his religious convictions.)

He chides Bertha on her conventionality: "By your insistence on formal conventionality you bring more unhappiness on your head than anybody I know." To defy convention, he writes her in May that before going to bed he is "going to walk barefooted on the grassy lawn." He deplores the fact that "conventionality" has removed people from such sensory contact with the earth; few people, he says, still have this elemental primitive impulse. And when he woke next morning, he thought of the grass. "Our back lawn is strictly private; it looked as if it had been sprinkled with the frosty spray of German silver. My feet touched it: the exquisite and ineffable sensations! Barefooted I walked around and around. I remembered my boyhood but my senses are more sensitive now. . . . The *earth* loves us, though the *world* may not. . . . Sweetheart, if you do not understand this new experience of mine, I shall kiss your feet someday to teach you! And sometime you shall walk over the grass, refreshing your feet against the daisies like Nicolette's."

Bertha suggested to him that perhaps he should not marry her but go off to New York to write. He found two flaws in this proposal. One, if he gave up teaching to make a business of writing, the last place he would choose to live in would be New York. "I have no interest in either the Four Million or the Four Hundred, nor am I so far gone in succumbence to Banality to follow the unnumbered herd of sociology — fiction and pornographic — play writers who have made *pediculous* that city with themselves. I should go where the winds blow strong, the blood is red, and the world is new — to the South countries, where even now the revolution of Nicaragua makes the blood thunder in my temples." He tempers this by admitting that there is one other place he would avoid as totally as New York City, namely Beeville, Texas.

Reason number two: "Although I am selfish and hard enough, God knows, I love you and want you more than I want any other one thing or all other things put together. Swift could kill two women because marriage interfered with his business. Ibsen trampled down old friendships . . . for the sake of 'his art.' I may be unable to succeed; I may grievously disappoint you but, nevertheless, I want you, and I am not afraid to try with you."

A few days later, he is still counting on a September wedding date, to coincide with their "day," their mythological totem, the *sixth*. His family has just returned from an outing to the Gulf, at Point O'Connor. "They can come in their car," he tells Bertha, "to our wedding, though I do not suppose that any but papa and mother will come. Bertha, I am worried lest your mother will work and worry herself sick over the occasion."

He became jubilant, with reason, over the financial prospect at summer's start. He went down to Beeville and the ranch when the trimester was over, and confirmed in his letter two days later that "my *mind* is unchanged. . . . I expect to sell the cattle by September," although he may even then be a little in debt. But he is confident that "next year will flow full and fresh for us. Worries will, at least, be aside. . . . Whether we get to New York or not a year or two hence" — he had changed his mind, yet again — "we can at least move about, and that is the next best thing! They can't tie us to one post. . . . Trust to me to extricate ourselves from this predicament." He hated the sense of being fenced in.

He was still jubilant, and still with reason, a week later. He prepared to move his cattle up to the good pasture near Austin that he had discovered through a student. He was so cheered he bought still more cattle, a carload more of cows and calves, but before he could receive them he was offered a profit of $45 on his trade and went ahead and sold them. He sent Bertha the rousing news from San Antonio. Two days before, he had got up at four in the morning, worked till midnight getting his cows ready for loading at Lucas. He found it good to be on the cattle train; four of his good friends were on it, shipping cattle too, and they helped each other with their stock. Frank wrote Bertha that he "slept not a wink, and this morning I feel as fresh as a god." (By morning, he meant 6 A.M.) He had a breakfast bigger, he claimed, than any dinner or any other heavy meal she had ever eaten in all her life. "I think handsomely of myself," he told her, "as to physical durability." In his note, written just after his big breakfast, his euphoria continues: "I like to be down in this country where I know everybody and like people and where I am greeted with 'Como te vas, Pancho?' "

He thought his luck had turned. "I can make money now, and I may go back within two weeks for some more cattle. I had a thousand times rather do this work than teach the stupid summer-school; so do not worry about me." He finishes thus: "Last night as I rode alone on top of the cars, I thought of you. I have a glorious beard, and I wondered if you would kiss me. I love you. Frank." On getting to Austin, he sent further sartorial fact: "I have a wonderful coat of tan, smooth and dark like the furtive glance of some south country murderer and lover; I have on a fresh palm beach suit; and I shall steal a shasta daisy on the way and wear it." He adds that his colleagues at the university now regard him as a special oddity, "this hybrid cow-man, who can outride the natives and outlast them, and a 'professor' in one." This was an "image" that he liked, and one he cultivated all his life.

Over July Fourth he visited Bertha in Velasco. Just before he left, she had last-minute qualms and suggested that they abstain from communication for two weeks. During this time each would concentrate on self-questioning to ensure absolute certitude. After he got back to Austin, he wrote her a ten-page letter to reject the notion of a "brooding" period, as he called it: he was sure of his love, and sure that he could "provide a decent living and command a decent respect."

In an extraordinary letter, poured from his heart in the most intense concentration, he offers a summary of their differences: "You are less of feeling than I am and more of pure intellect, but we can be harmonious. I am not altogether a stupid and there is a wonderful adorable Burbie in you — though you do not always grant it, the finest part of you, the part that is the poet. We have each made the other suffer enough, God knows. Something there is peculiar — when we suffer *together* and I am aware that you are feeling the pathos of things, that we are out of harmony not because of a hardness but because of unyielding nature, then am I in heart infinitely tender to you." He adds an insert in regard to "intellect" in each: "As a matter of fact, I think that I *think* as well as you do, but I do not relatively value pure intellect so high as you do." He has another compensation or good mark for himself: he thinks he loves with more passion than Bertha and is more "respectful" of the "legitimacy and goodness of the bodily appetites," which he regards, when they do not lead to uncontrolled incontinence, as "both desirable and beautiful."

The air was cleansed, the testing over. Whatever doubts Bertha may have had, either of his love or her own, were vanquished or resolved. A week later, Frank began preparing the list of friends and family to whom he wanted to send wedding announcements. He wrote Bertha on Bastille Day that he longed for "the day of affluence" when he could afford a typewriter, a big dictionary, and a rifle of his choice, confessing, however, that "I get along just as well without these articles."

On July 17, Frank was at the St. Anthony Hotel in San Antonio. He decided to take advantage of a train excursion rate for two reasons: to try to contract his cattle to Uncle Jim, and to try once more to get newspaper work on the San Antonio *Express*, at least for the rest of the summer. "The devils of unrest were in me," he wrote Bertha. Another reason was that he was sweltering in a heat wave in Austin. He told Bertha he never got hot working cattle or "chasing" news, but in Austin's summer climate "I smother, I melt, I succumb." He had no luck with either San Antonio paper, and Uncle Jim happened to be in Cotulla. But "San Antonio is a dream of romance — as always."

On his return to Austin, he kept cool by swimming often in Deep Eddy, going there by streetcar. He confided to Bertha that he finished reading Jane Austen's *Emma* only out of "professional necessity" and that he would wait "exactly twenty-seven more years before reading another of the same author." He went to the legislature to hear a speech by Governor Jim Ferguson, and described him as having "the brutal self-assertiveness of a man used to forcing men, because of his financial power, to their knees." He often quotes the Carlyle–Jane Welsh letters as if obsessed by them. Pointedly: "Much ado there was, God wot! / He would love and she would not." But, still, he says, "all the world knows what a mad and sad — yet sometimes glad — life the two led."

One morning Dr. Killis Campbell, the Poe scholar, offered his young colleague some advice on the practical side of marriage. Build a house on the installment plan, he recommended; rent furniture at the start; four rooms would suffice for a young couple. Frank relayed the advice to Bertha, comparing her to Jane Welsh Carlyle. Jane, said Frank, "was a noble woman and brave — like you — and fragile." A note he came across about her set his "ears a-rumbling and his heart rejoicing," because, like Bertha, she was born in the *seventh month* and it is well known that such children, if they survive at all, are generally handicapped for life. But, as Frank observed, marriage kept Jane alive a long, long time. "Oh, Burbie, you shall get *weller* after our marriage, just as Jane W. and Elizabeth B. did. Tell me how you are *now*."

He adds that Bertha's letters are as great as those of Jane Welsh. He has praise for himself, too, not his own. One senior professor told Frank he was the most popular of all the younger men on the staff; and Frank got an unsigned postcard with the message: "Everybody *loves* you." Miraculously, he discovered he liked teaching after all. He wrote Bertha he would much rather be teaching than chasing cows in the thorns of the Brush Country. Ah, well, she had learned to test that by what he would write next week, her impetuous lover who was indeed a man of many and mercurial moods, but who also managed to remain profoundly steadfast and trustworthy, despite all his contradictions. What, for instance, did Bertha think of this: "Sometimes I am possessed of an unspeakable desire to dress like a cavalier and to dandle around in leisurely elegance — the most alluring of all poses"? The cowboy-professor, never without his Stetson, in leisurely elegance? Was this desire a translation of his great enthusiasm at the moment for *Cyrano de Bergerac*? Or was it simply his instinctive flair for the dramatic, a flair he had in abundance? Example: "Well, today I made my exit with more flourish than I have employed since I ended my first year of teaching. . . . I made occasion to end up one class with a reading of Shelley's 'Clouds' — a poem that makes my soul smile always, and tears for its *daemonical* beauty to spring to the portals of my spirit." Followed, after a paragraph break, by "Thursday I shall go in search of a house."

When he went out looking for a suitable house for them to rent, he told Bertha, "I have an expression on the face to make an old woman young." His letters now begin to resemble an architect's, full of the room-plans of both houses and apartments. He regrets their poverty, but they won't be the poorest on the staff: "Clark and Ellis have lived with their wives here in quarters that I simply could not take you to. Sweetheart, I have got to make some money writing." For this, he will buy a secondhand typewriter, with which he can also copy Bertha's thesis. He expresses a sense of guilt about taking Bertha away from her family, "the most affectionate family I have ever known."

On August 14 he triumphantly announced to Bertha: "I have engaged the house; my heart is leaping about like a punch-bag with a boy punching it. . . . It is a place as congenial to your genius as shouting orders across decks 'gay with gore' *would* be to mine. . . . It is the Gray Apartments, the apartments with the great gallery, the trees, the grass; the apartments with hard polished *oak* floors and deep windows, the ceiling high and a wonderful mirror over the mantelpiece of the living room." Frank is impressed with the kitchen, "furnished with a stove – gasoline." And, real delight, fireplaces in both the living room and the bedroom. He turns lyrical: "Good God, Bertha, it is the handsomest, most convenient, most private, most dainty, most ample, most labor saving, most nerve calming, spirit refreshing, likeable, lovable, adorable, bridal flavored and Bertha-Burbie natural set of apartments in the city of Austin." The rent will be only twenty-five dollars a month, and this includes a garden plot; to get that price, Frank volunteered to keep the front lawn in condition – "a pleasurable burden." He boasts: "Nobody else in Austin could have accomplished such a feat. . . . Oh, Burbie, it shall be an event of life to be remembered forever when I *show you* the lodging that I have at last procured. I am so happy that I could cry." Of course, only a week earlier he had written with profound apology that "I am unable to provide that which you deserve and which your husband should be able to provide." But now, he continues, "we have a little garden and *beauty* – and a place to plant flowers in front, behind, around, anywhere. Tell me that you love me a million beautiful palaces of love. I do you, my own darling. Frank."

He kept on buying furniture, despite his assertion he would buy no more till she came. He searched the "want ads," and found a couch that could be opened into a double bed, and a portable set of bookshelves, which he planned to stain "to match the library table we are to get." He bought a Palm Beach suit in a late summer sale; "it pays to buy such goods a year ahead." And he plagued Bertha with precise questions, forcefully suggesting she be sure to answer them. What kind of chiffonier does she want? What kind of bed (the couch was for the sleeping porch)? What shape of mirror, round or square? What kind of wood and color? As for rugs, "the floors are all hard oak, so good-looking that Mrs. Gray has only small rugs in the living room." He needs Bertha's answers; it is the season of sales, and he must save wherever he can. Should he get a rocking chair or a morris chair for their living room? If the latter, he says, "You could lie down in it and go to sleep while I read to you." He offers, when she is "especially good," to build a roaring fire in the bedroom to get up by. They will take possession of the apartment on September 15; he plans to go home at the end of August but will return in time "to move into our house" on the fifteenth, and to engage a scrubwoman to wash windows and make everything clean. There is a grocery store a block away, and the Seton Infirmary is close by. Frank Dobie, a man of decisive action, was enjoying his talents mightily.

This domestic frenzy suddenly prompted in him more understanding of his colleagues and of their satisfactions. One of the professors, Dr. Robert Adger Law, wanted Frank to visit the new Law domicile. Frank was much pleased with it and told Bertha, "Just his pleasantness made me happy; I think that fundamentally I must hunger for love more than nearly any man I know."

In mid-August the Gulf Coast got a hurricane warning. It created some panic, since the storm of the summer before had been devastating to the McKees' beehives, the family business. Bertha wrote Frank, "We simply cannot stand the property loss." She was reminded again of the debt with which she and Frank would enter marriage, and speaks of "the interest on that $6,400 hanging over our heads."

If only he could sell his cattle, he tells Bertha, they could start marriage next month with his being not more than $200 in debt, "and maybe not at all." So, he keeps studying the want ads, the furniture sales. He committed himself to the amount of $91.25 for furniture, on which he made a down payment of half the price, but with an arrangement that the purchase would not be considered final until Bertha had gone by the store to approve Frank's selections. He had bought, on this tentative plan, a dining room table, four chairs, a buffet (fumed oak), a walnut dresser and a walnut bed, a spring and a mattress. All this could be changed, exchanged, as Bertha preferred. He also bought a carpet duster and a vacuum cleaner.

He was in Beeville with his family by August 27, having bought not one but two suits in San Antonio, "at great bargains," and in fact he had bought "only one suit heretofore since returning from New York." He didn't want a black suit for his wedding, so he chose "a kind of blue," a suit he found beautiful and of a fine texture; "I intend to look right handsome in that suit." As usual, he got home in the midst of a church "revival meeting," but he was having plenty of time to talk with his mother and his sister Fannie about "marriage things." Fannie, for their gift, "has worked in linen two pillow cases, large, and a sheet absolutely the most beautiful that I have ever seen." His mother plans to give them either a sectional bookcase or a rug. Meantime, he was selling off the little stock he had left at Beeville and had made about two hundred dollars, leaving him with perhaps a hundred and fifty dollars' worth of cattle there. He told Bertha, "It will seem strange when I have nothing at all in this country, for I have always had a few horses, a cow or so, some little property." He hoped Uncle Jim would buy the cattle he was pasturing outside Austin; if not, Uncle Jim would pasture them on his range. But in a few days Frank decided not to sell his cattle to Uncle Jim: "If he bought them now, for what I need to pay the note, he would simply be giving me several hundred dollars; and I am a charity object for nobody."

Bertha's letters had much information: the wedding would be held at three in the afternoon, on September 20; the minister would be the Reverend C. J. Atkinson of West Columbia; the approaching wedding had been the subject of a newspaper story in the Freeport *Facts;* Lucile had spent fifty dollars buying the newlyweds a luncheon set ("the most wonderful thing my eyes ever beheld"); the piano tuner had already come to put the instrument in shape for the wedding march; will Frank arrive Monday night or Tuesday morning — the kinds of details that make young men suddenly aware that marriage is after all a social sacrament. But there was love as well as information in the quartet of letters. In starting one, Bertha noted, "It is rising time — late rising time — of our blessed last sixth. I suppose they will all be twentieths now." She told him she would go to Houston with her mother to buy clothes, but warned him, or perhaps reassured him, "I am going to have very few." She has pledged herself to the most rigorous economy. And she prefers not to stay over in Houston after the wedding: "I am too wild to see our apartment and get it all arranged." When he got back from Cotulla, more letters were waiting. He estimated he would have time to receive only two more before leaving for Velasco. She wrote from Houston: "At the slow rate the shopping is going, we'll be here until after the wedding." She indulged in one extravagance, a suit-coat, "blue with a big yellow, or rather buff, collar." Wedding presents had begun to come in, and her parents were giving them "very massive sterling silver in a beautiful, simple design: dinner knives, forks, tablespoons, teaspoons, salad forks, sugar spoon, butter knife and pickle fork. I am grateful almost to tears."

Bertha sent him a special delivery letter on August 6, a day with the magically evocative number. The letter was a health bulletin: she was feeling extraordinarily well, her mother fixing for her every day a flip, "containing two raw eggs, four tbsp. of olive oil, cream enough to fill the glass, and sugar and vanilla enough to make the whole fit to swallow."

For the ring engraving, she suggests: "J.F.D. to B.R.M., September 20, 1916," and adds, "I have long loved your initials and *so* shall they and mine be joined one last time. And I like initials for their dignity." It seemed that Frank was wounded by some comment in an earlier letter. She pleaded she could not go beyond total surrender, and that she would love him "as he wanted to be loved."

Three days before the wedding, Frank wrote her that this would be "the next to last letter that I shall write to *Miss* Bertha

McKee." Next to last? Yes, for he planned to write one more, the next day, "that shall come to Velasco on my train." He tells her, "You have written me nearly four hundred letters since the sixth of September 1914," and adds, "All the predictions [that] we should 'get over' daily writing" had proved far from right.

On September 18, he sent this note from Austin: "I shall see you tomorrow; I shall marry you the day after tomorrow — these facts overwhelm all else. Do not be afraid of me, darling little woman. I shall be good to you. Frank."

He got *her* "last letter," as they both thought it to be, on September 17: "This is to be Bertha McKee's farewell to her lover. . . . There is no question that I want to ask you. There is nothing that I have to say except that I love and trust you. Bertha." She did, however, have to dispatch another note, saying in answer to a question he had left to ask her, that "yellow chrysanthemums would be gorgeous" for her to carry. Also, to another question: Yes, he could get his suit pressed in Velasco.

On this practical domestic note, the before-marriage, six-year-long exchange of letters between Frank and Bertha McKee ended, an exchange, so far as this writer knows, unparalleled in the papers of public figures in Texas history.

As it turned out, neither Frank's father nor mother could attend the wedding. His father had been ailing for a long time, and that summer his mother, too, fell ill. He went up to Austin to ready the apartment, and to set out from there for Velasco. In San Antonio, on his way back to the campus, he made queries at Joske's whether he should wear a bow tie or a four-in-hand, whether he would need gloves. He took along from Beeville some books and a deerskin rug.

After the wedding ceremony at three in the afternoon, Frank and Bertha left for Houston, to catch the train on to Austin that night. In their short stopover, they wrote notes to each mother, to assure them of their gratitude and "to send you our good word." Frank wrote his mother of the "beautiful wedding" and of the many beautiful gifts. "Tomorrow night we shall spend in our own apartments — at home." More personally, he told his mother, "I did not get very excited at the wedding, though the ceremony made me feel very deeply." He felt quite handsome in his new blue suit. "Bertha dressed in blue too and looks more beautiful than ever I saw her look. I feel very thankful to God; and the world seems wonderfully good."

It was Frank Dobie's first Great Adventure; it was Bertha's only one.

III

On the tenth day after her marriage, Bertha McKee Dobie wrote a long letter to her mother-in-law. Frank had gone to a nighttime staff meeting; she was arranging "her things from home" that had arrived that day — the wedding gifts, her own possessions, purchases she and Frank had made against setting up housekeeping. She was terribly lonely with Frank absent, but the silver and china and art objects for the buffet looked "so lovely" that she had some respite from her loneliness — and some difficulty in completing her letter because her eyes steadily surveyed and revised her arrangements.

The senior Dobies had given money for rugs as their wedding gift. But the hardwood floors of the apartment were so good-looking, Bertha wrote, that they could not bear to cover them in the living room, except for a few small, and very handsome, Wilton rugs. Bertha confessed they were just getting an "education" in such things, but she thought Mother Dobie would be quite proud of her son's taste "when you see the apartment and the furniture he selected." The mahogany furniture in their living room was their "symbol of grandeur" — and best of all, it wasn't "an extravagance," thanks to Frank's cunning search for a genuine bargain.

Her real "education" at the moment was in cooking. Frank found that although she was having to experiment and was helpless without a recipe book ("which I failed to get before I was married"), everything was good. And among the things that had come in the boxes that day were two dozen jars of preserves from her mother.

Her last paragraph was for Frank's father: "Please tell Mr. Dobie that Frank and I both appreciate very much his advice to be 'lenient with each other but exacting of self' and that we are trying to follow it. He's a perfectly wonderful man to be married to, and we are very happy together."

Their first Christmas together as newlyweds was celebrated in Velasco with Bertha's family. She went ahead early, forgetting to pack a cake knife and a casserole she wanted. Her first letter back to Frank told him exactly where to find them, how to pack them. But the letter was not simply utilitarian; it breathed forth happiness. She told him, "Last night in the dim watches I came to the rare and unusual conclusion that you are an angel." Frank's mother and his sister Martha were to arrive by train in Velasco that night, on the "eleven o'clock Katy." The sense of family, all around, was very strong.

Frank enlisted in the army on May 7, 1917, almost a year after the United States entered World War I, almost eight months after his marriage. The campus had become in part a training camp, with drills conducted for students and teachers alike. The momentum of patriotism and of hatred for Kaiser Wilhelm, "the Anti-Christ," was creating a collective mood in the faculty and the student body. Dobie daily spoke of the war to his classes, wrote letters to the Austin paper, steadily felt it was his growing destiny to take part in the conflict. Bertha, too, who was taking graduate classes, though unable to work hard because she was having much trouble with her eyes, shared this sense of inevitability. She did not want him to go off to war, but she kept silent; the decision must be Frank's, and her duty was to share that decision unquestioningly, and with the absolute loyalty of which she was capable.

He might have avoided active service, and even had a very good reason for doing so. He could not pass the physical examination because of his troublesome varicose veins. He did not allow this to hinder him. He underwent a very painful operation to correct the problem, and after recuperation went on to the army camp at Leon Springs near San Antonio, where he found, of course, both former students and former classmates. Bertha went over on some weekends to San Antonio so that they could be together; on others he caught rides back to Austin, a distance of about seventy miles.

Bertha had to reconcile her mother to Frank's decision to enlist, explaining that he would be training officers in this country and would not be sent to France for at least a year. She also assured her mother of her own total approval of Frank's choice. "If you lived up here where people's blood pulses strong over this war, you would feel that Frank is doing the right, as well as the heroic, thing. Please feel so."

Once Frank and Bertha decided that he could not fittingly stay on in teaching during the war, Bertha summoned all her energies to sacrifice her interests to his without complaint. He insisted that while he was in training camp she should not keep their home, but board at Mrs. Dodd's nearby, and she accepted, though this arrangement was not her preference. She did not want him to worry about her; she wrote him on May 11: "I am absolutely all right, only I feel as if part of me has got lost and I can't find it again. . . . To see you in just one week! I fear that I am not resolute enough to forgo that happiness. . . . I love you more than ever. Aren't you glad you aren't here to witness such a degree? Burbie."

She worried about him, she worried about their relationship — because of her health and her fragility. Two days later, she confided to him that "your concern for my welfare, expressed three times in one short letter, touches me deeply. O, my dear, how wonderful you have been to me." She cannot stress his thoughtfulness enough, adding, "O, my dear, how much you mean to me." And though she admitted suffering from the interruption of their life together, she wrote that she had "a far stronger . . . feeling of joy and thankfulness that these almost eight months have been." Not a year together before external events compelled a separation. She concluded this note, "My two hands want me to tell you that they want to go home."

She distracted herself by working on her thesis for the M.A. degree and by taking a course in French drama at the university. Frank remained at Leon Springs about four months. In late August, Bertha left Austin to spend some time with her parents in Velasco. Her mother, like Frank's mother, and unlike Bertha, was endowed with incredible physical energy. Earlier, Bertha had gone during the summer to visit Frank's mother with him on one of his leaves. The example of those two physically prodigious women filled Bertha with remorse, or regret, for her own frailty. From Velasco, she wrote him, "It is a well Burbie that I want you to come back to. Then I hope there will be no more tears, no more dishes, no more warped views of things, no more of the dozen things that left blighted spots on your first married year."

In early September 1917, Frank succeeded at last in getting transferred to the artillery; there were no openings when he first volunteered, so of necessity he had gone into the infantry. At this good news, Bertha wrote that he had not "been enthusiastic till now," and "when you are not enthusiastic, something is wrong." And: "O, my Cher, I wonder if you know how proud I am of you and how much I believe in you — that is one reason I love you so — what adverb? *ardently, tenderly, passionately, devotedly* — all of them pass in review, but none suits; it is no separable one of them. And your love is my pride!"

She hoped to finish her thesis by Christmas, to be free to follow Frank to other camps. She took time out to have her tonsils removed, and waited in Velasco for news of Frank's expected new assignment. She dutifully followed his advice to walk a great deal ("five miles," one day) and adhered to her milk diet, a gallon a day, a glass every hour from dawn to dusk.

Frank himself continued to write stories and articles in his spare time; he offered to be a military correspondent from the camp for the Dallas *Morning News*, but the paper had already made arrangements with someone else. He was reading proof on an article he had written for the *English Journal*. He sent out a short story, and when it was returned, Bertha offered him some counsel: "You know, Frank, I don't believe you will sell stories until you leave out the supernatural. This is too sophisticated an age to appreciate things that aren't so."

She offered to teach, but that would mean being away from him indefinitely — although she wondered if the army really welcomed wives following husbands from cantonment to cantonment. At any rate, she returned to Austin in late September, her mother accompanying her, in time for the opening of the fall term. She had decided it was best for her to go on with her work at the university. "That way I will have a life of my own; the other, I would simply draw my breath from you." With Frank's advice, she turned down a chance to teach again in Galveston that autumn, and also declined an offer of a thousand dollars a year from Canyon City, the offer having been made over the telephone and requiring a decision "right then." As she was trying to make up her mind, two voices spoke inside, one saying, "Go on, you idiot, then Frank won't have you hanging like a millstone about him," and the other (her "Burbie" voice) saying, "Oh, you won't get to see Frank at all."

But she was troubled because he had had to borrow money, for her. She had really rejected the Galveston offer because Frank had wired her to do so. But her course was taken, and she took comfort in the fact that by finishing her thesis, she could later teach at a better salary.

She thought, however, that something was troubling Frank, and wrote him so, on October 1. "Let me share," she wrote. She must have been very much troubled herself, for she added, with her usual honest canvassing of a situation: "Cher, we want each other, don't we? Do you remember my saying that we weren't very much married because we could each contemplate a life without the other: That seems to me now a most amazing statement. I had thought that this separation would be like being apart when we loved each other before we were married. But it isn't the same. We are bound to each other now." But she concludes, "You know how I long to see you. I think of you constantly, and to-night — it is many hours since I started this letter — with a longing inexpressible."

There were about ten thousand soldiers around Camp Funston. He wrote Bertha that there were many married men at the camp "but not one I am sure loves his wife as much as I love mine, my precious, little, wonderful, perfect woman." He assured her there was "no paradise conceivable" for him without her. One visit to her in early September might, he forecast, be suspended; he felt he would be refused a pass since he had got a "skin [demerit] for having books on shelf out of line." His company had 108 men; he wrote Bertha that the first word he made in semaphore drill was "Burbie." He confided that he believed he had no aptitude for military science, but he was determined to test himself. He added that he was "too *sensitive* for military life," because "I feel too keenly corrections and thus feeling become frustrated."

He had not abandoned his hope to succeed at writing salable stories. He sent one off from camp but got it back soon without even a rejection slip, to his dismay. As their anniversary approached — it would be their first, come September 20, 1917 — he wrote her: "Burbie, I never did love you so much, and being back with you will be sweeter than our honeymoon," but they could not have the day together. He sent a letter, however, to reach her on the twentieth: "You must think on this day that I shall be revolving in my mind how marrying you has been to me the most satisfying and ennobling act of my life; how I love you more than I did before I married you; and how I am always learning to see in you things finer and more beautiful and wonderful — Oh darling little woman, I wish to make my life more worthy of you."

He claimed he was slow, very slow, in mastering artillery problems; he had to study hard, but gloried in his success when he did well on examinations, for the hard work made "victory seem worth while." He was extremely concerned about "qualifying," and wrote her that if he failed, nature and not his lack of application would be to blame.

He wrote almost daily. On November 11, one year before Armistice Day, he told her of a rumor that all married men in his battery would be put into the Reserve Corps. Two days later, he wrote in triumph: "I could talk your head off. I am on the commissioned list of inactives and have a 1st Lieutenantcy." At that point, he stopped his letter to telephone Bertha the good news.

Those who knew him well in the latter half of his life will be surprised to learn that he was not given a captaincy because, as his commander explained, his "quiet nature had been against him" and he was not considered sufficiently "aggressive." Frank himself was pleased enough to be a first lieutenant, and happy to be put on the reserve list. He wrote Bertha they could plan on Christmas together, but a few days later rumors came that the group would be returned to active duty.

Bertha claimed remorse for having been "difficult," because often ill, during their first year together, but he had no complaints at all. Enjoying the warmth of a wood fire, he wrote her on November 15: "The coziest thing in the world is to be near you by the fire. How good and complete and happy the life with you last winter was."

Having "qualified," he returned to his normal self, and wrote Bertha, on November 18, that he had indeed despaired during his first two months in camp. "I suffered such a loss of self-confidence, such a void of personality as I hope never to realize again. I was dogged and cowed."

Later he was to write: "At Leon Springs, in a military life new to me, in which competition was keen, I was pavid and puerile. A certain refined sensibility kept me apart from my fellows. I could not understand the drill regulations, however assiduously I studied them. I had too long soaked myself in poetry and novels. Subsequently, the natural robustness of my nature asserted itself and without losing sensibility I became a match for the hardiest soldier. By degrees the drill regulations became models of lucidity. I began to enjoy the problems of artillery as much as I had formerly enjoyed a novel. With knowledge came power and self-confidence."

That fall, Dr. Callaway offered Bertha a teaching post at the university, to start at once, or if she preferred to finish her thesis that fall, then to start in January. She chose the latter, wanting to be as free as possible while Frank was so near. He was expecting early reassignment. His younger brother Lee was fairly certain to be sent very soon to France. All four Dobie brothers and their sister Fannie, who enlisted for Red Cross nursing service, were wartime participants.

Oddly, Bertha experienced the same disillusionment with what then was considered "scholarship" as had Frank at Columbia, although hers was tempered by a far more balanced view. He took great interest in her reports. Her central statement was this, in a letter of November 3: "I used to wish very earnestly that you would study for a Ph.D., even if it meant your being away from me for three years — I know the meaning of separation better now! But, my dear husband, I would not have you, with your temperament, peg at this stuff for three years if, without such a degree, you would be an instructor at $1,300 all our lives. To do so would kill everything that is you — things much more desirable and much rarer than Ph.D. degrees. I'm telling you my opinion of scholarship so that the cork won't pop out in Dr. Callaway's office tomorrow."

Frank was a relentless taskmaster in regard to her health habits. He believed in a definite program of exercise; he had a number of crotchets about food and diet, most notably the curative powers of honey and milk. Under his stringent guidance, she gained seven pounds that autumn and weighed just over one hundred pounds. She reminded him of his sitting at table and saying, as he ate honey, "Ah, Burbie, I feel virtue going into me." She added, "Often, like that, a memory rises out of the old sweet safe life with the most startling and poignant clearness. Frank, you never do say that you think it was sweet. I'm afraid it is only I that think it was. Frank, it isn't fair that I should say that. Such thoughts arise not from your behavior, but from a profound sense of my shortcomings and regret for them. Please do not refer to this."

She started teaching in January, ceasing, as she said, to be a "dependent creature." She described her health as "rampant"; she weighed 101¾ pounds, slept nine hours a night, attributable in part to his "wonderful" letters that made her "laugh aloud with happiness. . . . You make it a blessed thing to be your wife."

She was not, in her seeming enslavement to Frank's approval, at all indifferent to asserting and maintaining her own sense of identity. While working on her thesis in the university library one day in February, her eye fell on a book left by a predecessor, *Sex and Character*. She looked through it, and wrote Frank that it was by a German who denied to women the possession of "soul," of brains, of aesthetic appreciation. She fumed over it: "I wish the male creature that wrote that book could be living two hundred years from now, when economic, professional, and political barriers will have been removed from women so long that they will compete on equal terms with men, unhampered by tradition and convention." She insisted to Frank that she did have a "soul," and asserts, "I could never have loved a man who did not respect both my mind and my spirit. I love the way — all the ways — you love me. You know that. And however hot my resentment rises against the injustice, the scorn, the tolerance and the patronage with which men have treated women, I am always and absolutely your own Burbie."

On Washington's Birthday 1918, Frank came to Austin before being transferred to Camp Wheeler near Macon, Georgia. Bertha planned to follow him, come summer. She had her classes to finish for the trimester, and her thesis for the M.A.

It was a rough time for him, for his artillery studies required of him a competence he had never had in mathematics. Realizing this, Bertha suggested he write only once a week, not daily. He had become, she wrote, a man of action, adding that "action is your element. I have always known it, yet I have never really seen you in it."

But she still had advice for him: he should try to be more tactful than nature had made him, try to be more deferential to his superiors (in rank) – "please be decently conciliatory." His letters, wherein he could vent his frustrations and vexations with the bureaucratic mind, probably induced her to send similar steady reminders. In one, he asserted, "I am not going to be run over by anybody, I don't care how many gold leaves he wears on his shoulders." She reminds him tactfully that such a comment was written by "the man and not the soldier."

The only "norm" that genuinely existed for him was that of authenticity or genuineness; he had no "side," no Olympian hungers or needs. If on occasion he undertook "role playing" or re-enactment of conventional images of being, as he did sometimes in amusing his classes in Southwestern life and literature, it was out of his fundamental sense of playfulness, and whether he had ever heard of Huizinga's theories or not, he regarded *Homo sapiens* as also *Homo ludens*, man in whom the spirit of play was creative and central, an end in itself, not simply a "game," in a game's nexus of a "winner" and a "loser." (Games, indeed, curiously never meant much to him. When most Texas youths could cite the batting averages of major league baseball stars, such as Ty Cobb, Dobie cared nothing for the national pastime. He was indifferent to football, to golf, to tennis. "Athletics" to him meant three things: swimming, horseback riding, long walks in rural or sylvan settings.)

Their letters, both during their courtship and in the earlier years of their marriage, are studded with French phrases, not for "showing off" but for a gain in intimacy. On April 1, maybe because it was April Fools' Day, she wrote him a long letter entirely in French, and in generally very good French, at that. Its errors in gender and in the agreement of past participles are proof that she ignored looking up the words in a dictionary in order not to sacrifice the spontaneity of this gesture. Her letter of the next day continued the same sense of intimacy. The grandmother in the family where Bertha was boarding arrived for a week's visit, so "I am sleeping downstairs, where I have slept with you. Thus I am made to think and dream much of you and long for you," and she observed a truth they both lived by: "The power of place is a strange thing."

She wrote him every day, as in their courtship days. She assured him that "all our lives" she would be proud of his going into the army. In late April, she mentioned that their friend John H. McGinnis had queried her about accepting a position at Southern Methodist University, in the English Department. Money was an ever present problem. She wanted to buy $100 worth of "Liberty Bonds" out of her "teaching money," but since Frank would have to support her during the summer, she thought he should save that sum to help pay for the pasturage of the cattle Uncle Jim was keeping for him. "It will be safer to keep a little money in reserve." She hoped for an offer from SMU for the fall; Dr. Callaway had told her there was little prospect of her continuing at the University of Texas because he expected a great decline in enrollment.

With her thesis finished, she wrote in May that it now seemed strange to her that she could have wanted the graduate degree with what amounted to a "yearning." Yet she had the temperament of a scholar; perhaps she empathized with his disillusionment in his graduate studies in New York. She added this comment: "Love is the only thing I have ever found the reality of which is more wonderful than the dreaming. You I love and prize increasingly, as you know."

She arrived in Macon on the first weekend Frank would be free. She got there in mid-June, treating herself to the luxury of Pullman accommodations only from New Orleans to Georgia. She wrote Frank's mother on June 24 that by a new reassignment Frank, although a reserve officer, was subject to service in France, so "I may not have even the partial sweetness of seeing my husband twice a week. But I can't grumble in a letter to you, who are the bravest woman I know." She added that SMU was to pay her $1,350 a year. She hated to leave the university in Austin, but "Dr. Callaway isn't favorable enough toward women to give them a decent salary." She wanted to save up something for their home after the war.

In September, Bertha returned to Dallas to take up her new post at SMU. She was able to send Frank several letters to his camp of embarkation (Camp Jackson, Columbia, S.C.), but by October 6 she was using his overseas address: "116th Regiment, 50th Brigade, Field Artillery, American Expeditionary Force, Via New York." Her earliest letters from SMU speak of the epidemic of "Spanish influenza," which had indeed become the "number one topic of conversation." The University of Texas, she wrote, had "closed its doors," but SMU was struggling on, although nearly one hundred students in its two dormitories had come down with the flu. (The Dallas public schools, like the University of Texas, had closed.) On October 12, a Saturday, came the electrifying, but false, news of a German surrender. Joy reigned, briefly. After the report proved premature, attention turned again to the epidemic. Hospital lawns were full of tents where cots had been set up for the incredibly numerous stricken. She learned from a letter received on the seventeenth that Frank himself had suffered an attack of influenza, but had quickly and easily recovered from it. Before leaving the country, he managed to send her a "negligee" and a "sleeping suit." He also sent such a love letter that she called it "the most beautiful" he had ever written her. "Sometimes I pity all the other women of the world because they cannot know what joy it is to be your wife."

His unit disembarked at Brest on October 26, 1918, remained at a camp there for six days, thence on to Rennes and a detraining camp nearby for their scheduled destination, Camp Coetquidou, about forty-four miles from Rennes.

His cablegram of safe arrival reached her on October 30. She immediately urges him in her reply, that if peace came soon, which it did, to "stay on to see something of Europe. . . . I hope you will remain overseas for several months after peace is arranged. . . . You will run no risk of my not understanding if you do not come home on the first possible boat."

She sent him a distressing note on November 6. "My darling, I have decided to tell you about my health after all." One doctor had told her she needed two operations "some time," whereas a second doctor said no, that what she suffered from was malnutrition because, for some curious reason, "my organs are misplaced: the stomach . . . has dropped down, and one kidney . . . floats about at random." These disorders, the doctor felt, could be set right by osteopathy instead of operations. Bertha apologized for telling him all this, but explained why she was doing so: "You can have no idea how much spiritual strength and courage to make the fight your knowing and caring will give me." And, above all: "I am finally convinced that I am not just a whining, complaining person whom nothing really ails. And it is for your sake more than for my own that I want to get well."

The day before the armistice of November 11, she wrote that she wished she had that letter back, but urged *him* not to worry. After three treatments, she felt much better and the pain in her back, which had afflicted her while she was visiting him at camp in Georgia and which had become almost intolerable, had almost gone. Next morning the sirens heralding the peace agreement waked her early in Dallas. She promptly wrote him again that she was eager for him to travel in Europe before returning home. And the next day, her letter assured him that her health was much better: "I am not nearly so ill as I was that summer in Austin."

For the third time, on November 24, she repeated her wish that he profit from the chance to see Europe, and after this insistence, underlined this sentence: "I don't want you to come."

On November 1 he had sent Bertha his address: "Battery E, 116th Field Artillery, A.E.F. (via N.Y.)." One of his first acts was to send her "a right pretty handkerchief of Bretony lace." The Breton countryside filled him with interest and reverence. "My eyes are greedy. . . . We are all quartered in pyramidal tents," he reported, and noted that he had grown a mustache, just as he had done when at Columbia. He said he was enjoying every step of his walks into the countryside. "The hedges break the drainage and they are the cynosure of picturesqueness — an epitome of French poise which combines, interweaves, and amalgamates beauty and usefulness. In this camp itself, the barracks, kitchens, and hospitals exemplify the same character."

On Armistice Day, about a fortnight after his debarkation in Brittany, he wrote Bertha, "Sweetheart, if we are to stay here long, I am sure officers may be allowed to bring over their wives."

He had received her letter saying she had gone to a doctor in Dallas; he was much concerned and wanted complete details of the diagnosis.

In his letters, he remained unshaken in his hatred of the Germans: "My one fear is that the conditions will not be hard enough. 'Vengeance is mine, saith the Lord.' And I think our cause is enough the Lord's to warrant the most terrible vengeance." Many Americans, swayed by the simplistic propaganda of the day, were equally as absolute in condemning Kaiser Wilhelm and his people as minions of the "anti-Christ." Frank Dobie's emotional state about the war may be gauged in this note to Bertha, again at the time of the armistice: "God knows, Burbie, I want to go home to you, but it is bitter to have trained so much and to have come so far, with these *motives and feelings*, and then to be failed of one single battery volley into the Hun ranks. . . . I think I should be ashamed when I get back, never having endured one hardship or fought one fight." This letter concludes: "But, Burbie darling, I am infinitely longing for you tonight, homesick for you. I can shut my eyes and imagine my arms about you and both your dear hands at home. And perhaps you would be in the warm, snug, closed-up things I sent you; but even then a hand of mine should be warm inside. Goodnight, sweetheart. I love you a million-million loves. Do not work too hard, please, and do buy plenty to eat, especially chocolate and grapes and grapefruit. Frank."

The prospect of staying on a few months in Europe struck Frank as a rare bit of good luck. Four days after the armistice, he wrote her that the multitudinous rumors as to plans for his unit, the 116th Field Artillery, at least kept army life from being monotonous. But he had no notion then what disposition of the unit would actually be made. He intended to enjoy himself while waiting to find out. The next day, having taken a drive "over hills high and unspeakably beautiful," he said the roads and the scenery "gave me one ambition — to have you and either a donkey or an automobile for a decade of travel in France." He needed a decade, because his current situation allowed him only to glimpse "what I would not only taste but swallow and feed upon — or rather feast upon and swallow." He voiced a complaint that stayed with him all his life: "Traveling without leisure is a travesty and an anomaly. I wish to linger, to enquire, to be curious, to learn, and to sit at ease and warm my imagination by the embers of history." He concludes the letter with renewed expressions of longing and love for her and her presence.

He got travel orders to join the 131st Field Artillery, stationed near Brest. At parting from the 116th Field Artillery, he wrote, "The Battery gave me rousing cheers when I left," and he received "many compliments." Captain Davis told him directly "that he never saw a man combine as well practicality with a temperament artistic and idealistic," the compliment that Dobie valued the most. He added in his letter to Bertha that he was often "complimented indirectly for that disposition: if there is a beautiful sunset Dobie is called; if someone has seen an old château or a picturesque river, he wishes that Dobie could have been with him."

He had not been on a horse for months, so when horse maneuvers of the battery started up on December 9, "my heart danced like the sheen on a white-rock. . . . The time was short but for that time I was in my element, supreme; it was my battery and I was master of it; and to 'bawl out' a chief of section for not properly executing a command and to gallop down the column waving with eloquent gesture the command for *movement* were alike rare and choice to a savage, an aboriginal of hills and horses."

But this "savage," this "aboriginal of hills and horses," was shocked, as he tells Bertha in the same letter, at the primitive behavior of his compatriots at a "Bazaar" offered the Americans by the French Officers Club. About twenty-five French ladies were present, "and I have never seen so many ladies elsewhere with so much charm . . . the first best society I have really met in France . . . a society that all my life I have read of and admired." But he was revolted at the manners of his comrades when champagne and brandy were served. They drank too much, shouted rather than talked, acted "like boys." He was most offended by their insistence on the superiority of America to France. He is able to end his letter with a soothing thought: "But beyond everything, Burbie, believe me: I know you to be the most really civilized, the most charming, the most adorable being in the world. Goodnight, Frank."

On Thanksgiving Day, anticipating the lag in delivery, Bertha sent him a Christmas greeting, stating again that her health was "fine." "Once I get my health settled, I shall be compelled to work on my character." The strength and source of her will to get well, she said, sprang from her wish to be well when he came home — "so that you may not be troubled or hampered by her who should be your helpmate."

New Year's Day, 1919, however, was to be a revelation to him. He got, as he wrote Bertha that night, within the hour before writing, three letters, in which he discovered for the first time that she had suffered an attack of influenza in the global epidemic in early December. The letters were old ones, in which she told him of an attack and a good recovery. He was glad she was no worse, wrote solicitously, and asked her about her job.

But far from being able to teach, Bertha was nearer death than life. She had had, not only a heart attack, but a relapse of the flu. He did not hear of it, mail delivery being extremely inefficient, until January 25, when he received a cable from Edgar Kincaid, her brother-in-law, at whose house she was convalescing, informing him of Bertha's critical state, but mentioning only "heart," not the flu. He applied at once for a permit to return, cabled her that he was coming, and waited for a reply. After ten days, on February 5, he wrote her that he had heard nothing. "I cannot imagine why I do not get a cablegram from you." In fact, he writes, anticipating immediate news from her, he had decided to hold up his application for transfer to the States. He explained, elaborately perhaps, why, repeating his reasoning when he decided to stay on a few months rather than returning after the armistice with the 116th: he said he would have no teaching post, unless he took hers at SMU, until the autumn, "when I expect to go back to the U. of T." Had he returned at once, after only two weeks in Europe, he would have been discharged and without income for the next ten months. By staying on, he has been able to provide her with his allotment, plus the additional sums he has sent. His decision has been very hard, of necessity based on very fragmentary information. "Darling, if I could but talk to you, I should then know what is best. I seem a million miles away — and I would crawl that million miles to see you. It may be that you will think I am wrong in holding up my transfer. I may be; if so, it is an error of judgment and not a fault of the love that is yours and mine — a love that makes me think of you every hour and look forward to each succeeding hour for some word from the only satisfying and undisappointing *meaning* that life holds for me, you, my wife, my Burbie darling, my Burbie who has her being in every chord of my heart and on every record of my brain. Love me, Burbie, and do not be hurt at me or think I do not want to come now. I swear that I do. If I do not hear by Sunday I think that I shall cable again."

A few days later, he got a card from Bertha, reassuring in that she was able to write it, but melancholy and poignant. She was recuperating at the Kincaid ranch, in Sabinal, not too distant from San Antonio. She had been so ill that she was not sure she would ever be better. He answered with another appeal that she understand his decisions, which had been based on his inadequate information. He also appealed to what he realized was her essential self, her clear-sighted sanity: "Burbie, this month in Paris has meant a great deal to me, and you will see, in the future, that it has made me abler. I was *destined*, in a way, to learn something of the foreign. There was in me a vacancy that, for my work, must be filled with life abroad. It was not a whim, not a child's love of romance, not a fool's paradise of traveling, not a mere gratification of desire for experiences that kept me in France. You will understand this."

He had had the good luck to be transferred to the 202nd Military Police Company ("which is billeted at 31, Rue Montaigne, Paris, France!") before he had received the dismaying cablegram, and had been writing her exuberant letters, under the impression that her health was sound again and that she would be happy to hear at first hand of the great metropolis, of seeing Sarah Bernhardt in *L'Aiglon*, of the Louvre, the Opéra, the Comédie-Française, Notre-Dame, Versailles, the Bibliothèque Nationale. Of Versailles he had told her, "I saw the most formal landscape culture that was ever produced outside of Rice University — though, of course, much more ample."

On March 3, he praised the army's arrangement for sending — at government expense — its officers and soldiers to European universities, "the finest and wisest order the A.E.F. has ever issued." A friend, Shipp Sanders, was already attending the Sorbonne. Frank hastened to take advantage of the offer, mapped out for himself "21 hours per week" of courses in the French language and in French history and literature. "Some of the lectures I can get; some only poorly. But my ear is learning to understand what my eye understands." He assures Bertha that "it will not be difficult to withdraw at any time. In case I learn you are not better, I shall withdraw and seek to go home." He ends this letter: "Burbie darling, we shall never be apart again and each day these days I seem to love you more. I am your own husband-lover. Frank."

A few days later, he wrote that the chance to read Carlyle's *French Revolution* on the spot persuaded him that "above all recognitions, the recognition of geography is the pleasantest I do believe. Would that I had the geography of London in my memory!" But Paris was splendid: "What a city to love is this! what a city to learn and grow in! Three epochs of my life I count as *substantially* memorable: a few weeks in the elation and joy of newspaper work; a few months in the joy and vigor, the hope and pride of commanding a battery that I every whit commanded and trained for the only well defined goal I ever worked earnestly towards — fighting the Germans out of France; and a few weeks of life in Paris, where I have known what it is to love the environment amid which I lived. It seems to me that I shall never grow too old to hope and grow; and I wonder if there will be three other *substantial* memorabilities in the next half of my life. Oh, Burbie, what an adventure life is; and it has cheated you, often, I think with bitterness. And then when I think how brave and fine you are, I am not bitter but worshipful."

Two days after this letter, on March 9, he got the cablegram he had been aching for. It was brief: "Out of danger. Going Sabinal." For a brief moment he was "the happiest man in the world" — until he checked the date of the cablegram, February 1. It had taken five weeks to reach him; but just four days earlier, on March 5, he had got a later cablegram, one dated February 23, sent by "Kincaid." This one read, "Bertha critically ill." All he could do was await now the orders that would take him home. He wrote Bertha that he was trying to take the good news in the belated telegram "as a good omen."

The March 5 cablegram from Edgar Kincaid had taken ten days in transit. Frank wrote Bertha: "Within an hour I was at headquarters with an application for transfer to the United States; the application, with the approval of all intermediaries, has gone to Provost Marshal's headquarters at Chaumont. . . . 'You should hear from it in a week,' were the words of the very considerate and obliging adjutant. 'I am sorry it takes so long.' All my prayers are now that within ten days I may cable you: '*I am embarking.*' I made application to be ordered direct to a port of embarkation, and not through a casual camp." He apologized for being too "sanguine" about her recovery. He hoped his cablegram would reach her within a week, and assured her: "I may not beat this letter to you, but never doubt that I shall follow it close. A thousand times I blame myself for not having returned first with the 116th, and with the 131st. If I were there you would get well quick. Burbie, Burbie, I love you more than I can tell. My poor little Burbie woman, who thinks herself almost abandoned, but who in reality is farther from being abandoned than ever she was in her life."

Two days later, on March 11, he got further word, and replied: "Last came a cablegram that gave me considerable comfort. It seems to have been sent March 3 and says, 'Improving,' though it also says, 'Condition uncertain.' I cannot understand why I have not received a letter for so long a while. . . . Surely my orders will come before this week is over." He added: "I have a class in French two hours every morning and various lectures in the afternoon."

The next day he wrote of having received further reassurance: his mother's news that Fannie, Frank's sister, had gone to see Bertha and found her "not looking so ill as she expected." He had been rereading *Cyrano de Bergerac,* a great favorite of both. He copies out for Bertha, in French, the very long and very famous apostrophe to a kiss. "I thought of you as I think now." He kept on thinking of her, for, writing three days later, he tells her that the balcony scene in *Cyrano* had reminded him of *Romeo and Juliet,* which in turn prompts him to write: "Forever Juliet to me, as she has been for these best ten years, will be the Bertha-maiden I wooed all over Texas. Do you remember how we planned to give to ourselves an amateur performance of the balcony scene? We never did. We composed, all unconsciously, a better scene. We did not need the 'Romeo and Juliet.'"

He had transferred most of his classes to the specially designed courses for the American military offered through the Alliance Française, but he was still going to important lectures at the Amphithéâtre Richelieu at the Sorbonne. He was bitter about most of his American compatriots in the army; they had no taste, no interest in ideas, he judged. He wrote Bertha that American pedantry "combined with our educational system's worship of German pedantry has produced a brutal and unenlightened civilization." At the Centre Apostolique as well as at the university, he met a number of distinguished Frenchmen, and assessed them for Bertha as follows: "They are little, these Frenchmen; they look effeminate; but they are men. They *think;* they aspire — and how gracious they can be." As for the Sorbonne, he wrote Bertha in mid-March: "When I feel myself so happy here, so congenial, and then when I think of the ashen and fruitless days I spent at American colleges and universities, I could cry. One thing I know; that when in the past I have often read history, and reading it desire myself otherwise, I have not desired out of a fool's fancy — but out of knowledge of my own self."

The most important intellectual benefit of his six-month stay in France was probably this reinforcement of his own natural feeling for primacy of the subjective element in all experience, including the realm of thought and ideas, a French heritage and tradition from Montaigne on down, however often challenged and contested by the Cartesian superrationalism also embedded in the French way of life. Montaigne's *Essays* greatly influenced Dobie. He found in Montaigne, as he did in Hazlitt, a reverence for independent and individual thought, neither systematic nor abstract; above all, a way of thinking that was "immediate," that is to say, as free as possible from preconceptions, from the "received" cultural baggage of inherited traditions.

In his brilliant study *Mark Twain: The Development of a Writer*, Henry Nash Smith, who in his early career had been closely associated with Frank Dobie, draws an unexpected parallel between Montaigne and Twain. Smith writes that "provisionally . . . one might say that his [Twain's] highest good was freedom from stereotyped attitudes." He adds:

Yet Mark Twain's perspective is more than a way of thinking or solving problems; it involves the whole personality. When he asserts in the preface to *The Innocents Abroad* that he has written "honestly," the term covers much the same ground as the word "loyally" in the profound and moving sentence which Montaigne — who also lived in a period of cultural confusion — placed near the end of his *Essays:* "It is an absolute perfection, and as it were divine, for a man to know how to enjoy his being loyally." The deliberately vulgar image that follows this exalted declaration conveys some of the tone of the vernacular protest against a stilted and artificial refinement: "Sit we upon the highest throne of the World, yet sit we upon our own taile."

Smith observes that Twain's "intellectual position" approximates the "horse sense" that Walter Blair has traced throughout almost two centuries of American humor. For Dobie, as for his early milieu, "horse sense" largely meant the clear-sightedness not to be easily fooled, particularly by hypocrisy and the tyranny of false "gentility." "Horse sense," which Dobie admired so much in Twain, is very close to Montaigne's goal for education: the shaping of good "judgment" rather than the acquisition of encyclopedic knowledge. But it is also very close to the scientific ideal of *libre examen* or "free inquiry."

Both judgment and free inquiry are required for what Dobie called "knowledge of my own self." Montaigne, with his insistence on subjectivity (*"je peins moi-même"*) — I depict myself), was, like Twain, for Dobie a born affinity.

However restrained Dobie tried to be in reporting his daily joy in just being alive in France, finally knowing that Bertha was too ill to share such exuberance, he could not keep from bursts of exultation, as when he wrote her on March 17 of a "great day at Saint-Germain-en-Laye," where the castle and its noble park with the panoramic view of Paris and the Saint-Germain historical museum gave him, he claimed, a perfect understanding of "la belle France." He enjoyed it all the more, since time there was running out. But the orders that would allow him to return home were slow in coming.

He wrote Bertha on April 1 that he had not written recently because he thought he would beat his letters home. He had been ordered to a departure camp at Saint-Aignan, where he stayed for five or six days, and was then ordered to Bordeaux for embarkation. But, "we found here about 300 officers waiting to go: some of them have been here for five or six weeks. I think it likely that I shall have to wait two weeks or longer." Few boats were available, and the order of procedure was: 1) invalided officers; 2) general officers; 3) field officers; 4) other officers (his group). By way of news, he said he had seen much of the château country and would give details on his arrival. And, of course, he would cable upon embarking.

On April 7, his letter was full of complaints — of red tape, of further delay, of the lack of anything to read at the camp. He was morose, even about Texas. "When I get discharged, I am going to set about making money so that you and I will not have to live amid the banalities of the 'Lone Star State' — the dimensions of which, as the 'crusaders' of that state over here are fond of boasting, exceed those of France." One reason for his gloom: he had applied for a ten-day leave to England, but there were "no vacancies for leaves for this section."

Two days later, his letter opened with cheer. Rumor of the day was that all officers who had been there at camp for four weeks would get out within a week. He would not qualify for that group, but its departure would mean that his group would embark two weeks later. But the gloomy mood hung on. "Infinitely dismal, degrading and disgusting is it to languish thus for weeks in utter uselessness, though well; in utter idleness though drawing the same money as the man giving up his life on the battlefield; in expectation, though wholly powerless to consummate the realization thereof. I think of you at all hours, and Burbie, I want to be by your side more than I can tell. Oh I wish I knew how you are."

There was some relief. He was allowed to travel to Biarritz, but was disappointed when he could not go on into Spain. He did not care for "resort towns."

The cheerful moment was indeed brief. Next day's letter summarized all the problems he had encountered in trying to get out early, before priority. He had tried to pull every string possible, to no avail; he was told that the departures of ninety thousand men had to be scheduled, and *by priority*. There were simply not enough boats available to eliminate the long weeks of waiting. He was sick with disgust.

From Biarritz, he made a side trip to Marseilles, with stops along the border, and finally got to speak Spanish again at Hendaye: "It was pleasant, yea sweet, to hear the Spanish tongue again, to speak it." Even better, his hunger for adventure was assuaged. By chance, he lunched at a restaurant with a group of *contrabandistes*, "a jolly, clean, friendly, spirited bunch they were." When they learned of his disappointment at being denied access when he was at Biarritz, they invited him to go along that night on a smuggling trip into Spain. He went. They came back in the night. He wrote Bertha: "Of that day I could write a whole book. Oh, Burbie, life was on tip-toe. Why did I leave St.-Jean at all? What hosts I had!" But he wanted to get to Marseilles so that he could go to Tunis or Algiers, a wish he had to forgo "because the trip is longer and more expensive than I had contemplated."

Instead, he went on to Nice, to his delight. "My Burbie Wife Darling: — This is surely the loveliest land that there is on earth." Inevitably, he went to Monte Carlo. He set out for Bordeaux again on April 21, telling Bertha, "I am tired of sight-seeing, 'fed up' on it, tired of being a 'Casual Idler'; I want to *work*."

On April 23, he was back at the Casual Embarkation Camp — and the orders came at last. He was to go aboard the S.S. *Moccasin* next morning: "We should be at sea this time tomorrow night." A converted freighter, the *Moccasin* would make a slow crossing.

Frank reached Sabinal, and Bertha, on May 15, 1919. Waiting for him there was a letter she had written him on March 7. In the Dobie archive, one can see the envelope, postmarked at Sabinal, Texas, on March 8, 1919, addressed to Paris; the Paris address is marked through and the letter redirected to Beeville, Texas, U.S.A.; it is stamped "April 13" by the Beeville post office, and marked "For'd Sabinal." She had written it on the day of receiving his letter saying he had held up his application for transfer.

"Had it not been too late, and I too tired to write, I should have written you [the day before] a very bitter letter, in which I should have made use of a certain unpleasant term made famous by Mr. George Meredith. By morning my love and loyalty have somewhat asserted themselves. Probably it is pride that will never let me say to myself for long, 'He cares a thousand times more for experience than for me.' Perhaps I judge you unjustly. Perhaps the cablegram did not reach you in its original form. Then it read, 'Bertha will be ill months. Heart. Recovery expected. Needs you.' If it reached you in that form, I cannot comprehend what explanation you thought you needed. Surely you have known me long enough to know that only the direst extremity could have won my consent to sending for you. Well, I shall say no more. Recriminations are unbecoming." (The present writer has been unable to find this cablegram in the Dobie archive at the University of Texas.)

She continued: "I shall, however, state certain facts. I had thought that your love would stimulate anxiety beyond endurance. But these things now it seems well to tell you." She then enumerates six points: "The heart soon became the least of my troubles. The troubles I told you about in the fall seized their opportunity to lay me low." Second, "better though I am, I cannot so much as bathe myself." Third, she has "the greatest difficulty in digesting food," eating only "baby" food, or Mellin's Food. Fourth, the doctors have told her, "You will make it, if you keep up your morale." But, she tells Frank, he must do that, for "your first cablegram, 'Making all efforts home possible,' kept me going for weeks." Fifth, "Had not Lucile and Edgar assumed a responsibility that is yours, I should not be alive at this hour." And sixth, "there is absolutely no assurance that I shall live more than a few months. We hope that I may. That is all."

A final point: "If I do live, it will be months and months before I can look after myself."

She then draws a line to indicate a break in thought, and adds this: "Perhaps this letter is unjust and too harsh. If it is, please remember that a sick person's mind is not the clearest, and that it is hard for me to remember anything but the incongruous fact that while you are having the most enjoyable days you have ever had, I am battling miserably for life on the lowest terms. When I thought you were trying to come, it was different." She adds in a last paragraph: "O Frank, Frank, cable me that you will come, that you *want* to come, the first minute you can. I cannot fight on without you. B."

But she wasn't finished. She added a very long postscript, which begins: "I do not know whether to send this. I have so firmly acquired the habit of sparing you that it is hard to break it. I know too that you are not altogether at fault — that I have never cultivated in you a feeling of responsibility for me, and that, moreover, I have insisted so upon cheerfulness in messages to you that you have never understood how terribly ill I have been." Further, she says, she knows he is sending her so much money that he barely has enough to live on. "But, oh Frank, it is you far more than money that I need." The same effort at objectivity and justice informs her conclusion: "I hesitate, too, to send this letter lest the worst news should reach you first. That is not likely, but new complications come up all the time and we cannot know. If that should be the case, know that this letter by no means represents the sum of my feelings for you, that you are altogether too much all of my life. And whether there shall be any more of life together for us or not, know that by using your abilities to their utmost good you can make me happiest. B."

Three days after their reunion in Sabinal, Frank wrote his mother the habitual, long Sunday letter, apologizing for not writing earlier on his arrival there. He has been taking care of Bertha all that time, for Lucile Kincaid was "about worn out. . . . And here I want to say that no more generous, ungrudging, unstinted, careful affectionate hospitality and care was ever shown towards a man's wife than that shown by Edgar and Lucile Kincaid. I fear me that I am not nearly so unselfish as Edgar has been; and I am profoundly grateful."

His news of Bertha was reassuring, but the improvement was very slow. Her diet required her to consume six to ten eggs daily, and to drink innumerable glasses of milk. But she was getting "fat" and back to normal (he asks his mother, "Can you imagine Bertha *fat?*"). "Of course, she is still in bed, and it will be a long while yet — in view of previous relapses — before she can get about." The Kincaids would not hear of trying to move Bertha elsewhere; they insisted, and Frank concurred, that she should remain in Sabinal until she "could walk." He would, of course, stay with Bertha; in a week or ten days he would go to San Antonio to resign his commission and get out of the army. "I do not know when I shall get to see you all." He had good news about his cattle: Uncle Jim was arranging their sale. "I find, to my agreeable surprise, that I have enough money to pay off all bills." In a postscript he added that Bertha spoke often of the many, many kind things "you and papa have done for her. She loves you very much. People seem to me very kind and loving and unselfish — my people. You all do too much for me." He added that his article in the *Texas Review*, written two years ago, had been "mangled." It was his first "professional" publication.

Three weeks later, he writes that Bertha is still improving. If it were not for trouble with her teeth — she had to have an extraction — he felt they could leave Sabinal in another two or three weeks. At any rate, he had a sputum test made at the base hospital laboratory at Fort Sam Houston (San Antonio), "which showed there to be no tuberculosis bacilli." He bought a new automobile; Bertha was able to take rides without taxing her strength. But, as was true of so many victims of the World War I influenza epidemic, she was to be vulnerable to yearly attacks for the rest of her life.

3

The Western Side of a Train

I have tried to give significance to the natural things of the Southwest and to emphasize its cultural inheritance. Yet I combat provincial-mindedness. After teaching "Life and Literature of the Southwest" for years, I came to the conclusion that the Southwest needs perspective on itself and the rest of the world, as much as it needs knowledge of its own past.
— From *Some Part of Myself*

F RANK DID NOT ENJOY his return to teaching that autumn of 1919. Uncle Jim Dobie, over the years, had steadily urged him to make a career of ranching. The wartime demand for beef, mostly for the military, had briefly but spectacularly galvanized the livestock industry and spurred big profits. Now Uncle Jim desperately needed a man of Frank's experience to manage his Los Olmos ranch near Cotulla and the 250,000 adjoining acres he had under lease, plus various holdings in Mexico across the border. He found it unbelievable that a young Dobie could possibly prefer "schoolteaching" to ranching. Though skimpy, as Frank complained, the $150 monthly salary he offered his nephew was almost half again the university's, for Frank was being paid at the same rate as bachelor instructors. Because of Bertha's ill health, the Dobies could not dispense with domestic help.

Frank was readily tempted, and impetuously accepted his uncle's offer. Since no suitable ranch house was available at Los Olmos, they bought a house eighty miles north, in San Antonio, where Frank planned to spend the weekends. He was immensely apologetic for this new separation, and in October 1920 wrote her from Eagle Pass, on the border, that this was "about the first time I ever went to a new place without enjoying it. I am too homesick for you to enjoy anything." Bertha was then taking a health cure at Fredericksburg, a pretty German settlement in the Hill Country. Meanwhile, Frank readied the San Antonio house as best he could, with considerable help from both families; and they moved in late in the month. Bertha told him of an aunt's fear that she "would always be an invalid" and insisted, "But I'm not, Pange dear." She had recently cooked a roast herself, and assured him that she counted on doing most of her own work by spring, when she would be "your real, well, wife."

But by the spring of 1921 it was plain that they could not hope to live together on the ranch. Bertha's back pains had made her dependent on the help of a San Antonio osteopath, and Frank had arranged with a nearby garage to provide her with weekly "taxi" service to and from his office. That summer found her in Fredericksburg again for a protracted cure. Most of this time, she was running a continual, slight fever.

Frank's letters voice his constant concern for her health: was she eating honey? And her happiness: had she walked barefoot on the new grass? ("The feel is only equaled by the picture of Aucassin [or is it Nicolette, the girl, I mean] coming, her feet white in the night-shaded grasses.") From the ranch, he sent her the venison and quail she loved, and the young kid roasts known as *cabrito*, in such oversupply that at times she cried "calf rope!" the jargon of the ranching country for "enough, enough!" Though his ranch chores often made it impossible for him to come to her on the weekends, she benefited from a stout nexus of family relationships, receiving visits and help from both the Dobie and McKee families, and from more distant kin in the San Antonio area.

At this time she wrote him a number of quite candid, quite reasonable letters about their life together. In all of them she stresses that her constant frame of reference was the ensuring of Frank's happiness. The extent of her surrender of her own temperamental inclinations to those of her exceptionally vital and healthy husband seems remarkable, for she was a decisive person in her own right, with sharp contours to her personality. She was in no sense the rather standard feminine ideal of the mores of that time, the "clinging vine." She clearly judged Frank Dobie, as she often wrote him, to be an uncommon, even a unique, man; she clearly meant to find her own fulfillment in the process by which he would find his.

This was the underlying, and unstated, sense of sacrifice she brought to their marriage, but the surface problems on occasion drove her to untypical outbursts of vexation, some small, some serious indeed. One problem was the possibility that Frank might have to go back to teaching. His year of managing the ranch revealed to them both that the economic depression following

World War I and the awful siege of Texas droughts might drive Uncle Jim into bankruptcy — a possibility that weighed heavily on their minds. Bertha, especially, longed for some stability in their lives, some sense that the idea of "couple" outranked the fulfillment of the individual. When, inevitably, Frank foresaw their return to Austin, she agreed but with a stipulation. She wrote him, to Los Olmos headquarters, that she was perfectly willing to make any move he wanted — but she could not again endure, as she had in his year of teaching upon returning from the war, his endless "belly-aching." She mentioned the "thousands of fits of anger" when, once home, he railed against his colleagues and his "situation." Accept the good with the bad, she proposed. They could not live in a perpetual state of anger with other people, indeed with destiny. As she was to discover over the years, *he* could, and suffered almost a compulsion to do so. But he was a born crusader, and his need to set an imperfect world back on the right track was fueled by high optimism that vigorous action would solve all problems. He lacked the ability to temper righteous indignation, which many human beings feel about destiny, by "philosophic" stoicism. If ever there was a stoic, in Texas, it was Bertha Dobie.

"You are bringing me health, and I am happier than I have been since the first year of our marriage. And you know how happy I was then." Quoting one of her own earlier letters, her postscript adds: "I love you, 'so happily, so kind of serenely, and yet so profoundly.'" And again, despite his earlier "*command*" not to do yard work, "the plants want you too. They are looking forward to being considerably dug around. I have hoed a good deal myself, especially about the new roses, which have thanked me with fine growth. Your Bertha." At moments she wrote poignantly of their separation: "How terrible that two people who love each other as much as we do have to live apart," and in giving Frank the news that her sister Lucile is expecting soon (Lucile, so often irritated by children's noise, when Bertha loves them so much), says sadly that a child of their own would have softened the hurt. But, "I suppose there is no hope for that now." A few years later, Bertha did go to Houston for the Baldy-Webster operation, which was then thought to offer hope to barren women: a demarche which seems to contradict a persistent underground rumor that the Dobies had what the French call a "white," that is, unconsummated, marriage.

Frank's constant letters respond to her moods and reflect his own in all their variations:

"Though there is never an hour when you are not in my mind, I have not anything to say. I am about to conclude this long, long 'history' of *The Adventures of Philip*, and it is really the best love story I have ever read. As I read it, all our own period of courtship, which has not ended yet, comes to my heart, and I have done what perhaps I never did before — shed tears over a love story. I can't see that this novel is in any way inferior to what are generally reckoned as Thackeray's greatest works. Reading it makes me love you more, and I see all the plainer, your bravery, your nobility, your good sense, your unselfishness. Burbie, it seems to me very often that I have made for you a great and tragic mess of life, but I am trying the best I can. For myself, little matters, but I *so* want to bring health and happiness to you.

"Often I see light ahead and if it helps you to know that I believe in you as I believe in nobody else in the world — I mean believe in your personal powers — then you should be infinitely helped." He concludes: "Burbie, I love you with all my soul. You are the most wonderful woman in the world and you are the end of life for me. A fair good morning to you. I hope that you are sniffing the freshness of the south wind right now. Frank."

Or: "I do not know whether I enjoy reading more or riding alone horseback. I positively care nothing for riding in an automobile; its sole use is to *convey* me promptly. I mildly enjoy riding with the cowboys after cattle occasionally. I am mighty proud of roping wild hogs. What I like best is going out alone, best with the dogs, taking my lunch, unsaddling and enjoying the lunch all the more for watching the horse enjoy his. There is the country to look at: the hills, the brush, the cattle; there are some deer; perhaps some rattlesnakes (I kill two or three every day); maybe a wild hog. I was alone yesterday, without dogs, and I roped, marked and 'cut' two immense wild boars."

"I never saw a finer country," he had written on his first visit to Uncle Jim's Mexican ranch, Las Rucias. "Corn grows 15 feet high and yields six or seven ears per stalk." The spread was 100,000 acres, rich valley land backed by mountains; it had dozens of fine springs and good streams, plus several well-irrigated fields. But Uncle Jim was trying to sell it, being hounded by blackmail in regard to title, and by "rascality," chiefly of Americans in Mexico. On that early trip, Frank had been able to thwart the ranch's boss in his effort to abscond with $14,000, though the man did get away with $2,000. Frank's letters reflect his pleasure in his own competence, in the earthy details of dipping thousands of head of cattle, of doctoring calves with chrysillic ointment (he was afraid his letter would reek of it), of supervising the building of a concrete dam. He even gave the camp cook a lesson. The men had captured a wild hog, but having no bacon to grease the pan, Frank took some fatty scraps of boar meat, sliced up a kershaw (a large squash), and after "seasoning with sugar and salt, baked the stuff in a camp skillet. It was as good as any kershaw I ever cooked. The men devoured it like hounds; they had never tasted real kershaw before." Another day, he caught a coyote pup, finding it "the *cutest* animal I have ever seen." He thought he'd bring it with him to San Antonio to let Bertha see for herself, and then to give it, if he wanted it, to the young lad next door who mowed their lawn.

In the spring of 1921, he says he is working on two essays he hopes to sell, one on Robert Louis Stevenson, the other on Mexican folklore. He may have found some inspiration for the latter in the talk of a new friend, an old Mexican vaquero employed by Uncle Jim, named Santos Cortez. Bored by the cowhands' chatter in the evenings around the campfire, Santos was apt to seek out the "boss man" for serious conversation on a ruminative, even philosophic level. Frank was later to write of these talks: "During the year I spent on Los Olmos ranch, while Santos talked, while Uncle Jim Dobie and other cowmen talked or stayed silent, while the coyotes sang their songs, and the sandhill cranes honked their lonely music, I seemed to be seeing a great painting of something I'd known all my life. I seemed to be listening to a great epic of something that had been commonplace in my youth but now took on meanings."

For Frank, this "illumination" from the past was a signal for his personal future. It was in that year that he relinquished his intermittent dream of ranching as a primary vocation. Because the state of Bertha's health might never be equal to ranch life, because her illness imposed a constant strain financially, the end of the cattle boom in 1921 — demonstrating ranching as an unacceptable risk

— was decisive. The boom expired so quickly that Uncle Jim indeed faced bankruptcy. For cattlemen, 1921 was as catastrophic a year as 1929 was for bankers. In this disaster, Uncle Jim advised Frank to return to the modest security of the academic life.

Early that summer, with the cattle business at a nadir, Frank received a sudden and fortunate offer from the university. Promptly deciding to return, he wrote Bertha that he knew she would be glad "to be settled forever in Austin." As for himself, "while I am in one world it is forever my fate to hear the music of the other: in the university I am a wild man; in the wilds I am a scholar and a poet. It is terrible for you to be married to such a man, for I am plainly not a success."

Though perhaps disappointed at having to leave ranching, he knew he had had a "learning year." And he was now ready for the "revelation" that had come to him from the companionship of the old vaquero. Although he had claimed, at the time of joining Stith Thompson's Folklore Society of Texas in 1914, never to have heard the word *folklore* before, he was even then an admirer of the work of John A. Lomax in collecting cowboy and other ballads.

Lomax was already a good friend. He had tried to supplement Frank's income at the university two years previously, by paying him for a monthly column on faculty activities for the former students' monthly, *The Alcalde*. Lomax was also an example. "One day," Frank was to write of that decisive summer, "it came to me that I would collect and tell the legendary tales of Texas as Lomax had collected the oldtime songs and ballads of Texas and the frontier. I thought that the stories of the range were as interesting as the songs. I considered that if they could be put down so as to show the background out of which they have come, they might have high value."

While Bertha was undergoing another summer's rest cure in the cool of Fredericksburg, Frank sold their San Antonio house, rented a room in Austin, near the campus, and packed up their belongings and furniture. Though, as he wrote her on October 2, he missed her so much that he could hardly keep from going after her, they were both agreed that she had better stay on until November. They would take their time deciding whether to buy or build a house in Austin with the $5,000 proceeds of the sale in San Antonio.

In that year, student enrollment for the fall term was about four thousand, about one-tenth of Austin's population at the time. (It is now forty thousand, the size of the city in 1921.) Most of the senior faculty was composed of scholars trained outside the state; and it was perhaps natural that they should set a high priority on bringing local standards up to the criteria of excellence prevailing in the great universities of the world. These criteria, influenced by the rigor and precision of nineteenth-century German scholarship, were rigid indeed, as was the Texas faculty's insistence on the Ph.D. as a certificate of fitness for senior appointments.

Confronting his superiors, head-on as usual, the "wild man" may have been thinking of their comeuppance at the hands of John A. Lomax. As an undergraduate at the University of Texas, Lomax had shown his embryo collection of cowboy songs, words and melody, to Professor Callaway, who told him forthwith to forget such trivia and to turn his attention to *Beowulf*. Disconsolately, the farm boy from Bosque County held a small private bonfire. Nevertheless, when the faculty had a distinguished visitor interested in the region, Lomax was summoned to sing his songs. Immediately aware of their significance, George Lyman Kittredge later arranged that Lomax come to Harvard on a fellowship.

Wishing to incorporate the range inheritance into the realm of literary study, and to do so in his own way, Dobie resisted all pressure from the university to resume graduate studies — their way. His response was to assert that Texas students ought to read about mesquite trees and coyotes and wild turkeys instead of weeping willows and yellow daffodils and nightingales. He was warned that, without the doctorate, he would not be in line for promotion; and this never failed to bring on fulminations. Something in him loved to be outraged, to let his indignation rip.

Bertha, who wrote her master's thesis under Professor Callaway's direction and who was well aware of the virtues of formal scholarship, nonetheless "rejoiced," as she wrote Frank, that he had "entered upon folklore." In her opinion, "these legends are a big thing, much bigger, I think, than Mr. Lomax's 'Cowboy

Songs.' " And she herself "entered upon folklore" with him, becoming such an authority in her own right that in future years, when hay fever drove Frank away from Austin at cedar-pollen time, or when he needed solitude to write, she would take over his courses. Despite her poor health, she taught regularly for several years so that he might go "prospecting" for legends; and again and again she offered him her savings to take a leave and go off for further study. For some years after his decision to quit ranching full time, he periodically reconsidered his refusal to pursue the doctorate: Chicago might be the place, he would say, or Harvard. Or Columbia, perhaps, or the University of Mexico; but never Austin. In any case, it never came to pass.

His disdain for the shibboleths, labels and rank-orders of the scholarly profession may have been motivated in part by injured vanity. It is noteworthy that his most carefully documented work, *The Mustangs* (which was also his masterpiece), was written after a stay, during World War II, at Cambridge University in England, where the dons received him with the utmost respect and adulation. Meanwhile, he was understood, helped and appreciated by Bertha. She wrote him once, "Indeed, sir, I know very well the impudent egoism that constitutes a quarter of your charm and perhaps two-thirds of your driving power and that is such a trouble for me." Without his intransigence, an artist like Frank Dobie might never have realized his creative potential.

Long before he "found himself" as a researcher, teacher and writer, Frank was sure of one thing: that he wanted "to be independent and original." There were no precedents in Texas then for the work and the persona he found and developed; in his search for himself and his destiny, he learned along the way to amalgamate his cow-country origins, his Methodist ethics, his nostalgia, his practicality, and his imagination; he could never have reached his full scope without a certain orneriness. As Bertha told him, the most characteristic thing he ever said of himself was "I always ride on the western side of a train." That comment, she said, was "a whole biography."

She knew him well. She studied him. Their letters offer a remarkable contrast between her steady concern to define his character — which was, after all, the "given" around which she had

Frank Dobie and Bertha McKee as seniors at Southwestern University, Georgetown, Texas (1910). Bertha McKee's almost Japanese likeness is deceptive; she was a campus beauty, but very much in the style of the young Quaker, as Frank called her, whose parents moved to Texas from Pennsylvania before she was born. Frank Dobie was described a few years later by a student in his early classes as "the kind of ethereal, beautiful young man women fall desperately in love with."

Frank Dobie as a first lieutenant in World War I (1917). *Courtesy of Edgar B. Kincaid, Jr.*

In the Sierra Madre of northern Mexico, a region that lured Frank Dobie back for personal refreshment and for "story hunting" time and again between 1928 and 1958, until poor health halted such rigorous journeys. In a land of great horsemen, Dobie was judged by Mexicans to be one of the best, *un jinete magnífico*. (Dobie is wearing the Stetson, not the sombrero.)

In the Brush Country: with two javelinas. Frank Dobie lost his taste for hunting in later life, but never for the camaraderie of hunting-trip campfires. *Photo by Boone's*

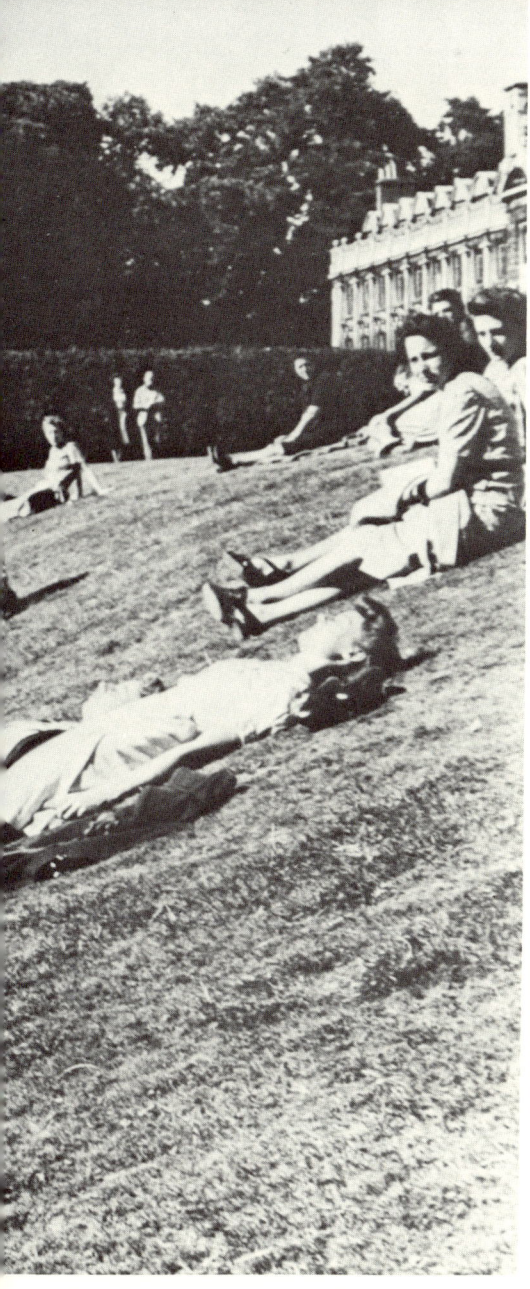

In a posture typical of cowmen, Dobie enjoys a favorite diversion, talking with friends, on the River Cam when he was both a visiting professor at Cambridge and "an ambassador at large" (1944). *Courtesy of Edgar B. Kincaid, Jr.*

When friends asked for a photograph, Frank Dobie liked to send this one — after all, he lived a good part of his life outdoors, and horseback riding, like swimming, was a lifelong pleasure.

Writing in the guest book at the Holland McCombs ranch on the Pedernales River in the Texas Hill Country, July 4, 1949. The summer heat explains the untypical headgear. (Rattlesnakes explain the boots.)

As good a listener as he was a talker, Dobie's face was often questioning. *Photo by Russell Lee, courtesy of Edgar B. Kincaid, Jr.*

According to Lawrence Clark Powell, Dobie's grin was "one of the most famous grins in history. When Dobie's weathered face cracked with amusement, the atmosphere around him was charged with good humor." *Photo by Russell Lee, courtesy of Edgar B. Kincaid, Jr.*

Frank Dobie and Lon Tinkle "on location" (1959) at the filming of John Wayne's movie *The Alamo* on Happy Shahan's ranch near Brackettville, Texas. The herd of longhorns in the background was put together and held together, here, by Bill Daniel, a Texas rancher and former ambassador to Guam. Dobie and Tinkle appeared briefly on a TV special, made by General Motors, about the filming. *Photo by Bernie Abramson*

Frank Dobie sometimes had to redeem his impulses toward making large gestures. Here, in characteristic white suit, he meets a friend's challenge to prove that his bank would "cash any check he wrote" by using a shingle as a check. The bank complied — with photographers and public relations staff at the ready. Dobie, known as "the best copy in Texas," was the newspaperman's delight. *Photo by Horace Evans, courtesy of Mrs. Catherine Evans*

One of the last photographs of Bertha McKee Dobie. *Photo by Frank Armstrong*

to organize her life — and his way of evoking her presence according to his mood, as, for instance, when his joy in a field of bluebonnets recalled to him her "lovely smile."

"Those hard-heads won't do any more than they have to for a man without a Ph.D.," she wrote him from her summer rest cure in 1923, in reply to a letter announcing that the university had given him a raise in salary. He had been there two years. He should have got a promotion too, she wrote. "Well, you'll wring it out of them." In fairness, she added, a teacher without the degree "should offer a good deal of proof that he is worth promotion. The degree is itself something." In the same letter, she sent him full details from Fredericksburg about his mother's health. Mrs. Dobie was then convalescing from a "hemorrhage," and Bertha was anxious that she be kept from doing too much when she returned home. Her letter also contained instructions for his care of the garden in Austin. A following letter, written in the late summer from Velasco, is as serene as a pastoral poem: "We went to the farm, where we saw corn ten feet high and the loveliest grapevine bowers, and high, glorious pecan trees — with no pecans on them, the trees having bloomed as usual at the time of the April rains. We got a gunny sack of roasting ears and came back by Lake Bend, which is more beautiful than I have ever seen it." Later they drove along the hard fine beach to the San Bernard River: "I went bathing, and we collected shells. . . . There are plenty of fish for eating raw, and I certainly enjoy them." Her father went upriver to extract honey from his beehives, a job that might take a couple of months because he had to load the six-hundred-pound barrels onto a barge alone, most of the local hands being afraid of bees. "There was never so much honey before of such light color. . . . He is rather proud of his strength." And, teasing perhaps: "He says not one of his sons-in-law could load the barge." Frank, too, was enjoying a fine vacation at the Los Olmos ranch. "I rode, roped horseback, cut cattle, trailed wild hogs, burned sacawista [that is, *sacahuiste*] and killed the biggest buck that I have ever killed. He was a noble fellow with twelve points on his velvet antlers." Bertha had written him rejoicing in the "health and utter content" of his letters from the ranch.

Reading on, she came to the unwelcome information that he

had hastily accepted an offer hastily made. President R. G. Tyler, of the Oklahoma Agricultural and Mechanical College in Stillwater, had offered him the chairmanship of the English Department. In the emergency, pressed to accept on the spot, Frank had done so without consulting her. As Bertha had written him a few years before, she was "the sort of person to whom change is the most trying and difficult of all earthly processes, and who can be happy only when putting down roots." Stillwater was a prairie town of five thousand people, and Frank's new job, though carrying an increase in income, meant that she would have to abandon her own work in Austin. She did not want to leave, and she was to be miserable in Stillwater from the start.

She wrote to him: "You were right, I think, to take the place. . . . We feel alike, of course, about leaving Austin and the university, but I suppose it is unwise to let sentiment overrule advantage." It would be good for him to get away from Austin's cedars, which caused his hay fever. Since her father was still upriver and her mother ailing, she must stay on at Velasco; but she had useful suggestions to make about the packing, which Frank would have to do. Perhaps the new post would allow them to save enough the first year to pay off Frank's indebtedness to his mother, "and enough the next two years to start a home or visit the city of Washington or some other highly desirable thing. When will your cattle be sold?" Evidently vexed at not having been consulted in Frank's decision, though aware that he had been given almost no time to make it, she concluded her letter by saying she was proud to be the wife of a "department head."

While awaiting Bertha's delayed arrival at Stillwater, Frank worked long hours trying to reorganize the English Department; he taught four courses (though he had to drop one), and took a few side trips, to lecture and to see the Texas State Fair. His letters were cheerful and appeasing; he was taking good care of her potted plants, he loved her "very, very much," and of course she must stay and look after her mother. He was going to speak to the Poetry Society of Texas on folklore ("I am building a reputation on these legends and I am not going to relinquish it"), the country was lovely, and he was working very hard. "I am going to make Law and Callaway eat out of my hand yet." A collection of folklore he was editing, *The Legends of Texas*, was nearing readiness for the press. He had so far published only four articles, in regional and academic magazines, as a college teacher.

II

Though neither Frank nor Bertha was happy in Stillwater, the two-year exile in Oklahoma was packed with formative influences and friendships that would continue to manifest themselves, often most unexpectedly, over the years — as when Ralph Johnston, whom they met in Oklahoma, bought Frank's ranch, Paisano, after his death, thus assuring its use as a Dobie Fellowship Memorial for the University of Texas and the Texas Institute of Letters. And it was in Stillwater that Frank met E. H. Taylor, editor of the *Country Gentleman*, the magazine that gave him his first nationwide audience. They met through Frank's friend Ed Hadley and, indirectly, through Walker Stone, one of Frank's best and favorite students at Oklahoma A & M. As editor of the student paper, Stone started a column called "Firing Line," which prompted Frank to send a note at once. He congratulated the young editor on his courage and observed that, as chairman of the Department of English, he had found the paper heretofore devoid of critical thought, in fact "an almost uninterrupted paean of praise . . . more suggestive of mental torpidity than of any mental activity." Stone and Ralph Johnston (who was his classmate), and the noted Oklahoma writer John Joseph Mathews (an Osage Indian), were probably Frank Dobie's most cherished deer-hunting companions in later life.

The summer of 1924, following their first year at Stillwater, was a very good one. Thinking of applying for a teaching post in Austin that fall, Bertha spent much of her time there, studying, and made some family visits. Frank crisscrossed Texas in search of legends. "I wish that I could take a year off," he wrote to his friend John McGinnis, "to do nothing but collect legends and write them down. I can smell a legend as far as a buzzard can smell a dead cow, and the moment I cross Red River my nostrils are a-quiver with the delectable odor of legends of my own soil." He wrote to Bertha from Los Olmos, where in two days he had helped burn off a thousand acres of sacahuiste grass, that he would like to write a book called *Sacawista Country*. Still thinking of doing doctoral work in the East, in the field of indigenous legends and regional history, he wrote her from San Antonio: "I am getting material easier and better than I ever did. I know now that my field is Southwest Texas. . . . In fact, I am at the stage where I can hardly work unless the work is where my heart is."

He was gaining confidence and becoming known. In Santa Fe, he gave a talk at a librarians' convention, and confessed, "Burbie, I made the hit of my life there." He also made a new and remarkable friend, Mrs. Maud Sullivan, librarian at the El Paso Public Library, "the finest lady I have met in years, the most charming, the most cultivated, the most interesting." Through her, Frank was later to meet friends whose presence in El Paso ultimately endeared the city to him, though he disliked it on that first visit, and had only the worst to say of Juárez, just across the border. "The best argument for prohibition is a visit to Juárez," he wrote, scandalized by the drunks he saw. Drinking in Juárez, he pronounced, was "not the free-hearted expression of the strong as it was in the Old West; it is the sickening make-believe or else impotent retreat of the weak!"

It will be noted that by this time Frank had outgrown the fervor for temperance of which he used to boast to his mother. But he was a man of decided preferences, for bourbon over tequila, among others. Once when he was managing Uncle Jim's border-country ranch, only a day's ride from Mexico, a bootlegger came to the ranch afoot, after dark. The custom was to bring the tequila across the Rio Grande by pack mule, then off-load it onto trucks in the Brush Country. The bootlegger's truck had got stuck in a boghole created by a recent heavy rain, and he was in search of men and horses to pull it out. Frank told him to go down to the bunkhouse and "tell his bad luck story there." The man had no trouble getting a sympathetic ear; and he sent back six bottles of tequila to Frank by the rescue crew.

It may have been thanks to that tequila that Frank found his first national audience. Always alert to luck, and a devotee of Conrad's *Chance*, Frank had intended to tell the story in his autobiography, reserving it for a chapter to be called "Chance," which he did not live to write. It seems that he had a "civilized" and "somewhat sophisticated" student in Stillwater, who had financed a private printing of the notorious *Conversations in 1601*, which Mark Twain had excluded from his collected works. The student was careful to see that Dobie got a copy. That fall of 1924, when Frank and Bertha returned to Stillwater, Dobie's friend Ed Hadley told him that a former newspaper colleague, E. H. Taylor of the *Country Gentleman*, was in town and would like to see *1601*. Frank still had two bottles of his bootleg tequila, and he told Hadley to bring his friend "around to our house on Duck Street, which always seemed to me a very appropriate name for a street in Stillwater, about five o'clock and we'd have *1601* and tequila together."

They came on time and Frank had the refreshments ready, the tequila mixed with lemon juice and sugar and ice and water. "Neither Hadley nor Taylor seemed averse to it." Before long, Taylor was inviting Dobie to write an article on cowboy songs for the *Country Gentleman*. Frank said that he didn't know much about cowboy songs, but was strong on cow people and the legendary tales of the Southwest.

Taylor was firm; he didn't want legends, he wanted cowboy songs. Frank knew he could write an acceptable piece — he was a friend of the foremost authority, John A. Lomax, and had reviewed a reprint of Lomax's famous collection in 1920 for the *Texas Quarterly* — but he was too modest to ask about the payment. And he had never heard of the *Country Gentleman*. When he asked Taylor to whom he should send the article, Taylor replied, "Oh, send it to me." Frank asked for the address, and Taylor answered, "*Country Gentleman*." So Frank had to ask where the magazine was published. "Why," said Taylor, "Curtis Publishing Company, Philadelphia, Independence Square."

Frank wrote the piece, as he says, with care and he thought that "it sang like a fiddle." In his letter accompanying the manuscript, he told Taylor that the Old Trail Drivers of Texas were soon to have their annual meeting in San Antonio and that he would like to write about them.

Taylor answered by telegram: the article on cowboy songs had been received "with enthusiasm" and would he write *two* articles on the trail drivers. Frank went to President Knapp and got a brief leave of absence (Bertha, as usual, would teach his classes) to attend the Old Trail Drivers convention in San Antonio, where he had "one of the bully times" of his life. Having quickly polished off the articles, he got another wire from Taylor: "Articles on trail drivers very interesting. Want more from you." A check for four hundred dollars from the magazine came in time to be a Christmas present. Frank commented to Walker Stone: "And none of the Rockefellers ever gave anything more bountiful." He had already got two hundred dollars for the article on cowboy songs.

And to Stone, Dobie drew the moral: "If it hadn't been for Ed Hadley I never would have met E. H. Taylor, and if it hadn't been for E. H. Taylor, I might still be writing my Ph.D. thesis on 'The Influence of Agricultural and Mechanical Colleges on American Literature.'" But the chain of luck had started farther back: if it hadn't been for his leaving Austin to manage Uncle Jim's ranch, if it hadn't been for the nation's experiment in prohibition, if it hadn't been for the rain that left that providential boghole, if it hadn't been for his preference for bourbon over tequila . . .

At any rate, Stillwater that autumn of 1924 was full of good auspices: besides the encounter with Taylor, which was to prove so profitable, Frank had made a real estate deal in Beeville, and in September, when the land was sold, found himself with a profit of three hundred dollars. He was spurred to other ventures, at least in thought, and wished he were in South Texas "to trade in cattle this fall. The opportunity was never better." Like his mother (a far better manager than his father) Frank was canny about money and always alert to a good trade; and he was to make a side line of small deals for the rest of his life. Bertha, whose only fault, according to Rucker Stanford, was her frugality (he also mentioned her being "very hard to please" and exigent, but not as a fault), was shrewd herself.

Oklahoma A & M had grown considerably that year; Frank was excited to note that the freshman enrollment in September was half again the size of last year's. His department now had ten full-time instructors and was sure to add one more, a post Bertha promptly asked for. She may have been reacting to a line from one of Frank's letters: "There are twenty or so American Literature papers waiting for your corrections. They can wait." She returned to Stillwater in time for Mrs. Dobie's planned visit in November and, while Frank escorted his mother back home, taught Frank's classes. En route he wrote her: "It does not seem fair that I should have all these trips of freedom and you none. You were very homesick with us leaving for Texas, I'm sure. I love you very, very much. I cannot tell you how much. Goodnight, Frank."

Another good auspice in that (academic) year was the fact that the book Frank had edited and (with help from Bertha) partly written for the Texas Folklore Society, *The Legends of Texas*, was reviewed early in January 1925 in the *Nation*, the *Saturday Review of Literature*, and other national periodicals. In that month, too, Frank's first article for the *Country Gentleman* appeared, though he thought — and wrote, vociferously — that it had been badly edited. Bertha agreed, writing him that it made her "sick to her toes."

She was then convalescing from the operation, performed in Houston at Christmastime, which was then thought to offer some hope to childless women. Their correspondence at that time is gay, full of love and teasing. She wrote Frank that she had heard from a friend who had seen him in Santa Fe, sporting, of all things, "a sombrero and a bandana." He wrote her not to tire herself out with visitors. "And you *let the visitors do the entertaining*. It always does take energy to entertain — especially strangers." He concludes: "Burbie, take life easy and as a matter of fact. I love you very, very, very, very, very, very much." Six verys — his magic number. She thanked him for *Green Mansions:* "The romance seems unreal and strange enough to a woman; but the book makes and leaves in the mind a melody like that of Coleridge's book. It is a melody compounded of style and spirit, and quite independent of the occurrences." He responded by sending on Hudson's *Purple Land*. When he told her of a Stillwater colleague's kind offer to relieve his bachelor solitude, she wrote, "I laughed at your saying, apropos of the Solbergs' invitation, that you could not understand the psychology of a comparative stranger who proposed his society as an agreeable substitute for your own."

She thanked him for writing so faithfully to her mother, and in particular to her niece Ray Pearl: a letter which Bertha thought perfect for a child, and one which — as she told Frank — she had asked her sister, young Ray's mother, to save for Frank's "biography." No sentence could have been more flattering, confirming as it did Bertha's faith in his future. Another powerful boost to his ego followed almost immediately: President P. W. Horn of Texas Technological College in Lubbock offered him a position paying $3,600 for nine months in Tech's opening year.

This afforded Frank some leverage in his maneuvers to get back to Austin. He wrote Horn to ask for extended time in which to make a decision, and wrote Bertha reassuringly that he "intended to get back to Austin sooner or later." Bearing in mind her resentment over his decision to go to Stillwater, he added, "I'll take you into council this time before I make 'ary' a move." He then wrote his close friend Leonidas Warren Payne, Jr., of the English staff at the University of Texas, for advice.

A great admirer of Dobie's, Payne urged him to consider returning to Austin instead of going to Lubbock. He thought he could manage to get him an associate professorship. "I have wrtten Dr. Payne tonight," Frank told Bertha, "to cry 'Ho' and turn the dogs loose. A few disgruntled professors of English would not phase [sic] me; the campus is big and I have as much right there as they have and I know that I have more inside of me than most of them have inside of them. Friction has spurred me to do whatever I have done, and my sides are so tough from so much spurring on the part of opposition that I would hardly know how to pace without spurs."

At the same time, Frank wrote — out of superstition, perhaps — but did not mail that night, a letter to Horn accepting the job at Texas Tech. He also asked Horn — as his letter to Bertha reveals — to employ her as well as himself, and described her as "an unusually careful scholar" who "taught with rare effectiveness." He went on: "I made clear the injustice of your being deprived of employment merely because you were married to a man who has employment." He was not sure, of course, that Horn would or could guarantee a position for Bertha. So, she must decide whether to take her chances in Austin or in Lubbock. At any rate, in Austin, for the first year "the orthodox crowd would probably extend their dislike of me to you. That is the only reason that I dislike their dislike. The fact that they would extend it proves their littleness. Do you think that you would like to go back to Austin?"

After Dr. Payne urged him to return to Texas, Frank wrote

Bertha that he told Payne he would willingly forgo Tech's offer if he could get as much as $3,000 at Austin. He was a long way from disdaining money, he who had very little of it, but he loved the land even more. And his attachment to the landscape of Austin bordered on a mystique, beyond rational explanation. This has been true, incidentally, of a great many Texans and even outlanders. No amount of bulldozing fine old stone homes and grand mansions, no amount of highways and expressways and up-to-date shopping centers, has yet spoiled the charm of Austin's rumpled hillocks and undulating vistas.

President Horn improved on his original offer, upping the salary to $3,750, and proposing, if he could put it through, to give Frank a leave of absence the first year so he and Bertha could do research in Mexico or, as second choice, graduate work at the University of Chicago. Frank admits to Bertha that he has not been wavering in the face of such blandishments but that "I have been pulling wires in Austin." He had a sensible reason. The new school at Lubbock had the disadvantage of having to start from scratch in building up a library. Frank pointed out to Bertha that "as my work is *Texas*, of course a considerable advantage lies in living in the state — but no books!"

Sometimes as thorny as a cactus, he bristled when Bertha ever so tentatively questioned his reestablishing himself in Austin without the Ph.D. so dear to the old guard in the English Department. Frank rejoined: "Well, I have faith in my ability to do just that, and I do not believe that I incline to overestimate myself." When he was invited back, no matter how much he wanted further graduate training, with his stubbornness he would never have admitted it. His frequent caustic opposition to the Ph.D. requirement was not seriously aimed at scholarship; it was a part of his program to prove himself what he early said he wanted to be: "independent and original." As Harry Huntt Ransom has shown, *The Longhorns* and *The Mustangs* certainly display the long perspective and meticulous research that characterize high scholarship. And indeed the notes to those two books are almost exhibitionistically exhaustive.

For a sick woman, convalescent after a serious operation, away from her husband by five hundred miles and recuperating in her sister's home, Frank's gyrations about the immediate future posed problems in understanding. He oscillated between sticking with the challenging situation at Oklahoma A & M, going off to Chicago to work on a Ph.D., returning to Texas for possible posts at either the University of Texas (first choice) or the new Texas Technological College at Lubbock or at Southern Methodist University, or to devoting full time to free-lance writing.

Misunderstanding between Frank and Bertha could hardly be avoided, as an important letter she wrote from her Houston convalescence on February 2, 1925, shows. It deserves quotation in full:

"My dearest husband: I intended not to write you again for several days, but there remains a thing to be said. You spoke of my having little confidence in your ability to get back to Austin. You understand, don't you, that I have the greatest confidence in you and your future? Did I not tell Emily to keep your letter to Ray Pearl so that we might have it for your biography? You will chide me and say that I'm silly, but you will know that I do not think lightly of your ability. It is true that I do not think that you can override the English department at Texas and go back in their *despite*. If you can do another thing as good as *The Legends of Texas*, I think they will want you. Please don't go to Lubbock because you are out of sorts with Dr. Knapp and Stillwater. If your judgment agrees with your prejudice, very well. To love either place I cannot promise, but I can promise not to feed my dissatisfaction as I have done. I think it is because I was so unhappy that I have disliked Stillwater rather than the other way around. But now I mean to be good in whichever place we live, and think that I can."

Two days later, she was equally candid, accepting defeat, it seems. She writes: "Since the battle is joined there is nothing for me to do but wave the flag, is there? If you can go back to Austin, I shall be glad. You would not mind cold behavior. Dr. Payne deserves your eternal gratitude, winning or losing. 'Bucking the system' is no holiday pastime. Of course you know that if you lose you will have destroyed the possibility of Austin for either of us forever. Perhaps this is as good a time as another to make the trial. Here's to the venture."

The battle was indeed joined, and Frank proved to be victor. Against strong opposition in the English Department, he was invited back to the University of Texas at Austin on terms he could accept.

In these maneuverings, Frank benefited enormously from the able and skillful groundwork laid by his friend Professor Payne. Payne was a man of rare integrity, even of nobility. Not a native Texan, he genuinely felt that Dobie would write books all Texans would be bound to read, and just as genuinely he felt that for Frank to do his best work he needed the discipline and the association of being at the University of Texas.

Payne's task of persuading the powers-that-be at the university to reengage Dobie was greatly furthered by the distinguished historian Eugene C. Barker, a man who would twenty years later be involved in a quarrel, and major university upheaval, over the worth of contemporary American writing, most notably in regard to the English Department's inclusion of John Dos Passos on its required-reading list for sophomores. Payne was also helped by the enlightened mind of President Harry Yandell Benedict. There was no need to persuade Dobie at all; he found the president of the Stillwater college intolerably opportunistic and hypocritical, and, as he wrote to Bertha, they both "loathed" working there.

President Horn at Lubbock wanted a decision from Frank by February 15. Bertha's stout reply to his charge that she doubted his ability to reestablish himself in Austin gave him the stimulus he needed to make up his mind. Since she really was only suggesting caution and a full canvassing of the prospects, not doubt about him, he replied to her good letter: "You make me feel so powerful that I believe I can go or do nearly anything that I determine on." Payne advised Frank to make formal application to Professor Robert Adger Law of the English Department, which he did, telling Bertha, "Now, if the fight is lost there will be no accusation of underhand methods." To his surprise, he got very cordial letters from both Professor Law and another peer, Professor R. W. Griffith, nationally esteemed as a Pope specialist.

Frank was committed to teach in the summer session at Stillwater. Bertha, in need again of a health trip, would join her mother at the resort of Siloam Springs, near Fayetteville, Arkansas, selected for them by Frank after a trip of personal inspection. He chose well. In late June, he reported to her that the temperature at Stillwater was 106 degrees. Arkansas was cool.

Before leaving Oklahoma, he drove over to the Cherokee Strip, through which the Chisholm Trail ran, to interview Oscar Brewster, secretary of the Old Cow Punchers Association of the Cherokee Strip. He got "wonderful material," he wrote Bertha, and he got an experience of atavistic or Jungian memory. He talked with range cooks, trail drivers, buffalo skinners. And at one point on the "Dodge" Trail, seeing "the corrugated land, not yet plowed up, where the trail used to run," Frank writes: "I saw my father, many uncles, Grandpa Dubose, old Joe Cloud, Joe McCampbell, Eli Boatwright, Julien Verdeau, Rafael Rodríguez and many another ride by. And I tried to picture them as they were in youth and primy manhood." He never spurned the uses of imagination.

Until the 1920's, the only writer in Texas history with any national reputation was "O. Henry," who was not really a Texan anyway. Though some of his stories owe something to his Texas experience, one thinks of him as essentially a New York writer. The Texas Folklore Society, although founded early in the century, published little before 1920; and it will be remembered that Frank claimed never to have heard the word *folklore* until his friend and coinstructor at Austin, Stith Thompson, asked him to join the society in 1914. Succeeding Thompson in 1921 as editor of the society's publications (a post he held for twenty-one years), Frank served as editor of its second "bulletin," Publication Number 2 (1922); the third, the society's first publication in book form, was *The Legends of Texas* in 1924.

On his trip that year to the librarians' convention in Santa Fe, Frank was delighted with the place, where an artists' colony was already flourishing. Not many of its members were native Southwesterners, but it was there that the new doctrine of Southwestern regionalism — promoted especially by the remarkable Mary Austin — took strongest root.

One hears sometimes of the "Southwestern renaissance," whose two major voices in the twenties and thirties were Frank Dobie and his friend John H. McGinnis of Southern Methodist University in Dallas; the prefix *re-* is misleading, though. It was not a second birth but a first one. Without friendships like Dobie's with McGinnis, the *naissance* might never have taken place. An artist needs some kindred spirits, and some precedents as well.

Always caring intensely what sort of figure he cut, Dobie cherished his reputation for competence and manliness, in the cheerfully *macho* tradition of the region. In Texas in the 1920's, it took audacity to adopt a writer's persona, and more audacity to look to writing as one's means of support. By refusing to pursue his doctorate, and by taking frequent leaves of absence to look for material, Dobie had committed himself and Bertha to a very modest income, one which he had to supplement with his publications. Even when his work came to command high fees from national magazines, Dobie was loyally to send the best of it to McGinnis's little quarterly, the *Southwest Review;* and, moreover, he made substantial financial sacrifices by publishing his early books through a new regional press.

Dobie had known McGinnis casually as a member of the faculty – though not as his teacher – in his years at Southwestern. When the Methodist Church decided to locate its second Texan university at Dallas, McGinnis followed President Hyer and other Southwestern staff members to the Southern Methodist University campus. (It was he who had been responsible for Bertha's invitation to teach there in the fall of 1918, when Frank was in the army. Bertha and Mrs. McGinnis had long been close friends.)

The two men were in many ways dissimilar; and McGinnis's arrogant, sardonic manner had annoyed Dobie in college; but their special devotion to the Southwest in an aesthetic sense, and their common need, as professors who wanted to make their way as creative writers rather than as research scholars, bound them for two decades in close friendship and association. McGinnis's father had been a professor before him, and McGinnis specialized in Shakespeare; he was not a maverick in the academic world as Dobie was. But Dobie respected his brilliant mind and shared his passionate admiration for Mark Twain, first as the originator of a native American style and second as a thinker. Both men were enchanted with the vitality and creativity manifest in the painting and literature of the new cultural commingling at Santa Fe and Taos: Indian, Spanish, Anglo and "modernist" art blending into a new Southwestern esthetic and sensibility.

For nearly two decades, Dobie and McGinnis were able to make the *Southwest Review* into a fraternal forum, even a common bond, for most of the major writers and artists of the Southwest.

Looking back on their long association, Dobie wrote to McGinnis on his retirement from teaching, book-page editing and magazine work: "I often think of you with affection and glee. As I reflect in quietude, it comes to me that you have contributed a great deal to civilized living in our part of the world. You have certainly made living richer for me, made it more of an art, and contributed concretely to the craftsmanship that I hope I shall still be trying to master when I die. For a long time, a very long time in the lives of men, we were partners in a way. Perhaps like the Doctor of Physick and the Apothecary in Chaucer, 'each made the other for to winne.'"

Frank's close friendship with McGinnis — and it is a question which man more influenced the other — began in 1923, when George Bannerman Dealey asked McGinnis to add a side line to his teaching, the establishment of a respectable "Literary Page" for the Dallas *Morning News*, at that time the one "statewide" newspaper in Texas. McGinnis leaped at the chance to exercise power in favor of good taste and of cultural enlightenment; his success was signal.

This success was in very large part due to the help he got from writing members of the University of Texas faculty. Chief of these was J. Frank Dobie, who quickly became McGinnis's "contact" in Austin and who soon had Walter Prescott Webb, Leonidas Warren Payne, Eugene C. Barker, Howard Mumford Jones and others contributing lengthy reviews to the paper.

For Dobie, the matter of reviewing books was not at first tempting. He wrote McGinnis on July 16, 1923: "Mack, about reviewing books for the honor of it, I am not very enthusiastic. I am getting tired of writing for glory. . . . However, if I can help out let me know."

Dobie then began the work of propagandizing McGinnis, who, after all, was not born in Texas or reared in it, who taught Shakespeare, and who hoped Dobie would line up for reviews the university's famous specialists: Professors Griffith and Law and Campbell and Battle. For McGinnis, a new book on Alexander Pope — which would command Griffith's attention — or on Poe — obviously for Professor Campbell — was more important than a new novel by Sinclair Lewis or Theodore Dreiser.

The alliance was really launched in the summer of 1923, when

McGinnis sent Dobie a new novel about range life by Emerson Hough, *North of 36*. This book galvanized Dobie. Here was a sample of what could be done with regional material.

Before sending in his review, Dobie sent McGinnis an article about the Texas Folklore Society, with the hope that it was not too much "like propaganda." He added: "I am going to have a hell-firing good book on Texas legends next year — the only thing like it in America, and I am powerful anxious to get interest in the matter stirred up. I say I; it is the society's publication, though I conceived the idea and am conceiving most of the legendary off-spring. . . . I wish you would do a little missionary work among your high-browed confreres."

Then, on August 1, he sent the review of *North of 36*. Unpaid for it, he was exchanging it for the propaganda about the Folklore Society. Much more importantly he was paying another debt. "To me," he wrote McGinnis, "it seems that this novel is more important to us of the Southwest than a new book on Shakespeare or a sensational tin-pan beating by H. L. Mencken. . . . I have had a lot of ideas since I saw you. Why not feature sometimes Texas stuff, as you spoke of featuring American poets? I know a man here, my good friend Webb, who would be glad to write a feature article, say, on 'Literature of the Rangers.' . . . Webb is getting his Ph.D. in history on the subject of Rangers; at the same time he is popular enough to have sold articles to *Scribner's* and to an oil magazine on the same subject. . . . Call on me for anything that I can do." He suggests Robert Adger Law and Howard Mumford Jones as Texas colleagues for reviewing. He volunteers generously that if McGinnis doesn't know what to do with a book, to send it down, and "I will get some person either of eminence or of sense, occasionally of both, to review it."

Dobie's review of *North of 36* was printed on August 5, 1923; it occupied nearly a fourth of the entire book page. "It is," he wrote, "a truly (and the word is used with calmest deliberation) great historical novel . . . a story of the first Texas herd of cattle trailed north after the Civil War . . . tinctured with that sense of fatality that the winds and the waves, the mountains and the prairies give their children."

Dobie rehearses the faults of the standardized and meretricious picture of the Old West and its people then current in the books of Zane Grey and a dozen others. He certifies that Emerson Hough falsifies nothing, is as true as Charlie Siringo and Andy Adams. But Hough adds something else: "The subject is epic. Emerson Hough in his treatment of it is no less so. . . . History alone, no matter what its fidelity, will not make a novel. There must be character." And Dobie judged that the characters in *North of 36* were "ample men" of the sort the Old West produced under its spacious atmosphere. But steadily he assured his readers that he was not speaking of the kind of picturesque fakery that informed the mistaken notion of what the range and its people were like.

Dobie quotes with approval Hough's assertion that the cattle and range tradition "is our first and only true American tradition." And Dobie adds, with proper tributes to Andy Adams and others, that Hough's is the first great novel of the range. He is careful to note that he is taking into account Owen Wister's much-praised novel *The Virginian*.

After an impressive display of mastery of the literature of the Old West, Dobie concludes with a lyrical and personal final paragraph: "When I read it, the hot blood came to the back of my head, and tears of sympathy scalded my eyes. I was reading the first great chronicle of my own people."

Obviously, it was quite an experience. Dobie later came to value the novel much less. But the review tells us a lot about Dobie himself.

McGinnis was bowled over by Dobie's piece. His wife's family lived in Georgetown, thirty miles from Austin. McGinnis, having gone to Georgetown with his family for a weekend, as he often did, went on over to Austin to tell Dobie in person how much he admired the account. Later, he sent an amplifying letter. Dobie replied that such praise "warmed my very marrows." But he had achieved more. He had opened McGinnis's mind to the Southwest. The reader should know that, ironically enough, McGinnis (the only legendary teacher Southern Methodist University has ever produced) trained such great names in contemporary English scholarship as Henry Nash Smith, Herschel Baker, and Claude Simpson.

Brimming over with the discovery of *North of 36*, Dobie wrote to McGinnis that the novel composed as a kind of "chronicle" seemed to be just the right mold. Both men projected works of fiction. Dobie at least composed a title: *Down the Nueces: A Chronicle Novel*. He was also greatly interested in the play form, no doubt an echo of his newly discovered love for the theater when he was at Columbia in 1914 and had the playwright Hatcher Hughes as a fellow graduate student. Later he mentioned an emerging desire to write short stories.

In May, Dobie was in Austin tending to last-minute details, his visit happily coinciding with a folklore meeting. He asks McGinnis to speak to Dallas booksellers, to whom he is sending the publication on consignment. The society also wants to order an "ad, four or five dollars' worth of space on your page the day that the review of the *Legends* comes out." (McGinnis was affronted by advertising placed on his page, even book advertising, and would never run a review on the same day an advertisement for the book appeared; Mr. Dealey faithfully supported him in this holier-than-thou ethic.) Dobie concludes with an interesting correction to a sentence: "It is heavenly to be in Texas again. I have a thousand friends here that I love." He marked through the typed word "thousand" and wrote above it the word "dozen."

"I did not fail to run the Texas Folklore Society several miles in debt on these legends," he confesses. But at last he was an author. He was thirty-five.

Walter Prescott Webb told Dobie that he would like to review *The Legends of Texas* for the *News*, but McGinnis had already assigned it to Hilton Ross Greer, poet and member of the *News* staff. The review pleased everybody. *The Legends of Texas* sold unexpectedly well. There had to be a second printing of fifteen hundred copies.

Along with the *Country Gentleman* and McGinnis's Dallas book page, the *Southwest Review* became a third channel for Frank Dobie's "propaganda." Until World War II, it was the chief voice of the so-called Southwestern renaissance, led by Dobie, McGinnis, Mary Austin, Witter Bynner, Paul Horgan, Walter Prescott Webb, Stanley Vestal, and others who met in its pages and often in person.

Like his academic colleagues, and unlike the members of the Taos and Santa Fe colonies, Frank's mind was still fixed on the past. He was pleased to have found, unlike most of the academics, a good commercial channel for what E. H. Taylor called America's "great legendary literature," though he could snort at Taylor's claiming for himself "the zeal of a crusader." McGinnis, who was something of an intellectual snob, chaffed Dobie about being a professor and a writer for a slick Curtis publication like the *Country Gentleman;* but Dobie took it in his stride, observing that the income was allowing him to pay off his debt to McGinnis's brother Karl, who held the lien on the Dobies' new Austin house.

In the summer of 1926, Taylor suggested that Frank shift to fiction, paid his way to Philadelphia to discuss it, and guaranteed him $10,000 for each serial accepted.

Dobie thought at once of the story which was to become *A Vaquero of the Brush Country*. It was the life story of John Duncan Young, whom he had met fifteen years ago in his year of teaching at the Alpine High School, but with whom he had "never actually conversed," an extremely colorful ranchman with a picturesque and far-ranging career. In common with a great many Texians, Young was as interested in selling and trading land as in ranching it. He was at this time a real estate dealer, and he had grandiose ambitions. He wanted to build in San Antonio a marble hotel "where the cow people of Southwest Texas would be at home." To finance this project, he counted on making money out of his reminiscences — and the man he wanted as "collaborator" was J. Frank Dobie. Dobie was much interested.

Young's life could represent a vital history or chronicle, of the greatest authenticity, of the development of ranching in the West at the very point where it had a central origin in the skills and techniques and practices of the Mexican vaqueros of the Brush Country. Dobie realized how important such a book could be, and after some exchange of letters and visits, entered into an association with the memory-laden range veteran. The association did not "fully satisfy" Mr. Young, either financially (the marble hotel for cow people required an oil well instead of a book for its funding) or personally or professionally, since Dobie emphasized the "sociology" of ranching far more than Mr. Young's individual experiences — and also eliminated a great deal of one kind of material Young valued but which Dobie considered to be "bucolic humor." In a revelatory passage, Dobie confessed that in this book "without my knowledge of the fact — for I have never been analytical of self — I was moving toward the point of view that everything is kin to everything else."

When the manuscript of *A Vaquero of the Brush Country*, Frank's first book that was all his own, was finished, McGinnis suggested that Dobie consider offering it to the new publishing house just launched by P. L. Turner, former manager of the Dallas store of the Methodist Publishing House. This was the first major venture to establish a self-supporting commercial publishing house, publishing in all fields and for the general public, in the state. The idea was ahead of its time, but the venture was a worthy one.

P. L. Turner loved the artifacts of Texas, its history, its landscapes, its mystique and its mythology. He also loved money, and while managing the Methodist bookstore, he had invested both his time and talent in outside enterprises connected with the world of books. He wanted to be a publisher, and in the midtwenties persuaded his bosses, the Methodist Publishing House Board, to publish what became a "classic" in Texas historical writing: Professor Eugene C. Barker's *Life of Stephen F. Austin*. The considerable success, regionally, of this masterwork of the University of Texas' leading historian persuaded P. L. Turner that he could successfully launch his own publishing house, the P. L. Turner Publishing Company, which he later named, on McGinnis's advice, the Southwest Press.

In 1927, Turner issued his first formal catalogue (written by the present writer, who went to work for Turner upon graduation from college, thanks to McGinnis's maneuvering) with more than a dozen respectable titles, including fiction, poetry (Stanley Babb, Grace Noll Crowell), history (*The Mexican Side of the Texan Revolution* by Carlos E. Castañeda), range-life memoirs — a really impressive collection, including an anthology, edited by Hilton Ross Greer, of the best Southwestern short stories. Turner was banking heavily on school-book adoptions. He did not have much capital, but he had the know-how and the connections — with bookstores, printers, university professors, schoolmen, and writers in general.

Quite naturally, McGinnis, who was serving as a sort of midwife to Texas culture in his triple role of professor, book-page editor, and editor of the *Southwest Review*, recommended him to Dobie. Turner was elated at the prospect of having Dobie on his list. He had in mind a "reader" for school-book adoption in the state, a book on Texas legends. As soon as he had contracted for *Vaquero*, he began outlining to his new author the financial prospects for a fourth-grade reader. At first Dobie resisted; he had other uses for his time. But he was never indifferent to money. Their first correspondence took place in June 1927. Dobie agreed to read proof on a reprint of *The Life of Billy Dixon* that Turner was bringing out. Always a canny bargainer, Turner paid for Dobie's services by crediting him with one hundred dollars' worth of stock in the pending incorporation of the business. And they both meant business. Turner sent Dobie his first contract on April 7, 1928, involving three books. On the fourth-grade reader, Turner agreed to pay a $500 advance against royalties on receipt of the manuscript, royalties to be fixed at 8 percent. The other two books were actually an arrangement with Dobie and the Texas Folklore Society: for a two-volume reprint of *The Legends of Texas*. For each volume, there was to be a $500 prepayment against royalties on receipt of the manuscript, but the royalty would begin at 15 percent on the first fifteen hundred copies and would jump to 20 percent thereafter; 75 percent would go to Frank Dobie and 25 percent to the Texas Folklore Society. As it turned out, this part of the project died aborning.

By December 6, 1928, the P. L. Turner Publishing Company had become the Southwest Press. Turner envisaged school-book adoption as his anchor. He wrote Dobie on that date, on the new letterhead: "When we can get your *Vaquero* and *Lost Mines* [their working title for *Coronado's Children*] on the list, I believe we will be headed for success and a permanent Publishing Company in the section."

Seven weeks later, on January 30, 1929, Turner urged Dobie to complete the manuscript of *Coronado's Children* by September 1. Amazingly to present-day ears, he said he could have the book out, in that case, by November 15. (Artwork would be chosen and executed during the summer.) Of course, *Vaquero* was still in production. The color proof of its jacket, in fact, did not reach Dobie until late July. Turner had been very ill all the spring of 1929, and had in fact "nearly given up." But he had submitted *Vaquero*, though without success, to both the Book-of-the-Month Club and the Literary Guild. One person Dobie particularly wanted to have an advance copy of the book was Carl Sandburg, who had become a friend when he came to lecture at Oklahoma A & M in 1923.

By the time the first royalty statement was issued on *Vaquero*, on December 31, 1929, the Great Depression had hit and Turner's financial situation was precarious. Of the first printing — two thousand copies — all but sixty-one had been sold. According to the agreement between Dobie and John Duncan Young, whose "memoirs" Frank had used as a source, Dobie was to get the $500 advance, which Turner had been obliged to pay in four installments in May and June. Dobie had himself bought fifty-five copies, royalty free, and Young had bought two hundred copies, royalty free. Nobody made much money on the first printing. Turner claimed that his net profit was only $382.58. He urged Dobie to find investors in Austin for the publishing venture. The future looked bleak. In June of that year his young "editor and general flunkey" resigned, with three months of salary in arrears. The literary life in Texas was just on the point of a considerable harvest, but customers were few.

Dobie was committed to making a "regional" press succeed. Turner was hardly responsible for launching his press at the worst possible moment, financially speaking, and he was certainly, as time showed, right in believing that a genuine literary ferment was at work in the Southwest.

He tried to do right by Dobie, but he was financially strapped, the banks were ultraconservative, and he had to delay payments to Dobie or make them in dribbles. Dobie was vexed, but cooperated generously. He very much wanted the Southwest Press to survive, not for selfish reasons but out of a sense of dedication to regional significance. He did not mind waiting for payments, but he was disappointed that sales were not vigorously pursued. Turner had, of course, put *Vaquero* into a second printing, and by May 1930 this printing had sold nearly fifteen hundred copies. Furthermore, Turner was taking advance orders on Frank's second book, *Coronado's Children*, and he reported that these were coming in copiously. He cited as one example to Frank that on May 29, 1930, he got an order for fifty copies from Venables (bookstore) in Oklahoma. Turner could also take pride in a new addition to his staff, young John William Rogers of Dallas. Scion of a wealthy and prominent Dallas family, Rogers had graduated from Dartmouth and had gone into the publishing world in New York, working for the newly organized Literary Guild along with W. E. Woodward and other notables. Turner was much encouraged at the prospect that Rogers might be able to persuade the Literary Guild, burgeoning in its first success, to make *Coronado's Children* one of its selections. Rogers had already enlisted the support of Woodward.

Dobie was pleased with all this, but he might have preferred receiving the overdue advance royalty on the book, which Turner had to defer. Still, Turner's enthusiasm was catching. He predicted that *Coronado's Children* would "sell ten where *Vaquero* sold one." He was right, but *Vaquero* was selling steadily. The December 31, 1930, royalty statement showed that it had sold 836 copies, and it sold nearly as many in the next six months. As his share of a serialization in the Fort Worth *Star-Telegram*, Dobie got seventy-five dollars.

By the time Dobie was well into *Coronado's Children*, the Depression had paralyzed Turner's plans for the Southwest Press. Dobie knew he had an important book in *Coronado's Children*, and he wanted it to be presented to the public in a proper format. He found the illustrator he needed in Ben Mead, a Texas artist. Candidly, he wrote Turner on May 11, 1930, to ask: "Considering how hard pressed you are, can you finance the publishing of the book now?" He said it was a "good book" but an unusual one that would require special promotion. He had some good news about that: "The Texas Folklore Society will take 300 or 400 copies off the bat, provided we can get royalties on our purchase — and we will shove sales and advertising."

He was so eager for Turner to agree to make the book something special in format that he added a bit of boasting, saying that he expected this book "to keep my memory green." And, "Without boasting at all, I doubt if you'll get another chance to print a book as good as this."

Dobie expected to have the manuscript ready by June 1, when Turner would arrive in Austin for a visit. But he allowed himself some leeway. "You have no idea how much time one line — one word — one name can take for one who yearns to have a book perfectly written." He was equally sanguine about sales: "The more I go over the state and see people, the more do I realize that there are thousands of people hungry for literature about the Texas soil. The potential buyers of books that graphically portray old Texas are enough to keep a big publishing house up. Of course, I'd like to have money, but the honest truth is that I'd give my life to make the heritage of my soil a living part of the people existing on it. I have some great plans, some of which I expect to live to execute." Further good news he gave Turner was that he was not going to teach the next year, and so "the other book" would be ready in 1931 — "and it will be a book for the schoolchildren of Texas."

He did ship off the manuscript by June 19, writing Turner that he "felt dazed," and could not analyze his emotions "now that I am parting with 'Coronado's Children.' For ten years I have been writing it. I doubt if I shall ever produce anything else that will have so much of *me* in it. These stories and the people in them are far more real to me than any stories I ever read or the people with whom I associate daily. I know that I should feel elated at ridding myself of them, but I don't." He was delighted with Ben Mead's work and felt that "it is going to be the best illustrated book dealing with the West since Remington." And in a final burst of pride and enthusiasm: "It will be the best dealing with the Southwest ever printed."

The contract for *On the Open Range* called for a school-book edition and a trade edition, that is, a book for the general reader. It was a "juvenile" and Dobie wanted this to be clear to the public. There was no question concerning the school-book edition, but when Dobie discovered that the trade edition, delayed to coincide with the publication of the school book, was identical, he wrote Turner angrily: "You have not, I think, dealt fairly with me." He had a strong point: the school-book edition contained some material from *Vaquero* and *Coronado's Children*, since schoolchildren, unlike buyers of the trade edition, would not presumably have been purchasers of those two works. But the trade edition did not need the duplication and Dobie had sent in new copy as a substitute. He insisted that Turner present the trade edition to the public as a "juvenile" and that the duplicate twelve pages from *Vaquero* and the thirty-eight pages from *Coronado's Children* be replaced with the fresh material.

Following the success of *Vaquero*, Dobie worked very hard on his next book, *Coronado's Children*, again dealing with venturesome spirits and their adventures in the Southwest. Bertha Dobie had the greatest confidence in the worth of the new project, drawing as it did so heavily on the earlier Folklore Society anthology *The Legends of Texas*, of which Frank later said her name should have been on the title page beside his. Bertha found in Henry Adams's *Mont-Saint-Michel and Chartres*, which she regarded in 1929 as "the most civilized book" she had ever read, a sentence she thought profoundly adaptable to Frank's purposes in the new volume: "For us the poetry is history, and the facts are false."

She wrote him the sentence from Velasco, where she had gone to take care of her sick parents that summer. A week or so later she also cautioned him not to take time out from his manuscript to write something with sure-fire sale for the *Country Gentleman:* "You can't afford to." She assured him that "the thing for you to do is to push on toward the publication of *Coronado's Children*, which I am confident will, if it can be brought properly to the notice of the public, make your fame." She warns him not to make the book too long: "What will keep the stories of buried treasures and lost mines from being tiresome, like the Paul Bunyan stories, is their rich background of place and historical event, and the diversified, yet in some way unified, characters. As for me, it is the people and the way their minds work that interest."

Whether he owed this perception to her or to his own innate similarity of values, *Coronado's Children* exemplifies the justice of this notion that the people in the story, and their motives, count for more than the surface excitement of action and random circumstance. Throughout the rest of his writing life, he maintained that people and their inner drives were more interesting than their contingent involvement in external events. In his savage criticism of "Westerns" and of movies and radio serials derived from such fiction, he deplored the loss of human traits in the welter of ritualized "shoot-outs" and conventional simplifications.

Coronado's Children created a genuine stir. Edwin L. Sabin, in the *Saturday Review of Literature*, called it "a rich and fascinating volume," and he announced that in selecting it as its February offering, "the Literary Guild distinguished not only Mr. Dobie and his Texas publishers but also itself." R. L. Duffus in the New York *Times* wrote that it was "entrancing, a book in which the romance and glamour of the Southwest are, seemingly without effort, preserved." Attention was national; in Texas, L. L. Click, a colleague of Dobie's, wrote in the Sherman *Democrat:* "The Southwest has never before had a living book to come more directly out of the heart of its earth. Nor has it had a more vigorous and original one."

The amount of time, energy and thought Dobie dedicated to the problems of Turner's publishing venture is astonishing. At the height of Turner's troubles in 1932, when McGinnis and Smith spearheaded a salvaging or rescue party, Dobie very sharply accused Turner of misstatement about Turner's own salary. Turner claimed not to be drawing any salary at all, but Dobie wrote that the audit of the press's books by Smith's father revealed that Turner had not merely drawn his salary but had "overdrawn it by one thousand dollars," and had never cut his salary back to meet the "stringent circumstances."

Turner's financial plight caused great concern to John H. McGinnis and Henry Nash Smith, as well as to Dobie. Smith's father was a well-known Dallas accountant. He and a lawyer, Thomas Knight (a close friend of McGinnis's), and the Dallas bibliophile–oil man William D. Wrather and several other patrons of the *Southwest Review* came to Turner's rescue when he agreed to a reorganization of the Southwest Press and to a transfer of power to this group of backers. As Frank Martin, Turner's second-in-command at the time, wrote Dobie, it was "a trying time" and everyone involved was grateful to Dobie for "all his consideration and help."

Smith also wrote to Dobie that he and his father were appalled at how much time and energy they had all wasted in the proposed reorganization and at how Martin and Turner displayed an irritating strategy of putting pressure on their new backers at the wrong time. In June of 1932 Smith felt it was a stalemate, probably a lost cause. Dobie, too, wasted much time. Hoping to salvage at least the royalties due him, he came up to Dallas in 1932 for several conferences. By June, he could no longer control his anger. On the ninth he sent a bitter note to Turner about monies due him. Turner replied in kind, and in spades, for in addition to rebuking Dobie for being critical of the way he conducted his business, he delivered an insulting blow: if he had not engaged John William Rogers to sell *Coronado's Children*, the Literary Guild, through Carl Van Doren and Milo Sutliffe, would never have considered the book. "If they were asked why they took the book, they would say simply because Rogers presented it in person." He adds that all the profit he made as publisher from the sale to the Literary Guild went into promotion of the regular bookstore trade edition, on which he "never made a penny" of profit. "Royalties paid you and the Folklore are over $6,544.00."

On this letter, Dobie made this notation: "Not one cent have I received from *On the Open Range*. The Literary Guild paid $13,500 for *Coronado's Children*. I got only ⅓ of it — should have got ½."

A month later, Turner sent a rather pathetic letter to Dobie, admitting that the reorganization plans had "fallen through." He intended to offer a new plan to his creditors, offering them stock in the newly reorganized press in exchange for debts owed. But if the creditors rejected this proposal, he told Dobie, his only recourse would be bankruptcy. He admitted, for the record, that he owed Dobie $2,369.60. Dobie did not return the form enclosed, whereby he would agree to exchange this debt for stock in the new venture. After a five-day lapse, Turner wrote again to complain of Dobie's silence. An enclosed statement about stockholders in his publishing firm, as of July 26, 1932, included himself at $21,000, Frank Dobie at $1,500, John William Rogers at $1,250, his associate F. O. Martin at $1,000 and the Reverend E. L. Shettles at $100, for the "common stock"; in addition, there was a sum of $6,850 in "preferred stock," of which Frank Dobie held $1,000 and his colleague at the university, Professor Eugene C. Barker (author of *The Life of Stephen F. Austin*), held $500.

A great wrangle then developed between Turner and Martin. Rogers wrote Dobie that all the blame lay with Martin, who was trying, said Rogers, to get the creditors to force receivership. He warned Dobie that if Martin succeeded, they would never get their money back. He invited Dobie to stay at his home when he came up for a meeting of the creditors.

As it turned out, Martin decided to pull in his fangs, for there was a sudden prospect of a good contract for the school-book adoption of a speller in Georgia. Additional good news came in October, when the state of Texas finally adopted *On the Open Range* for the seventh grade for the academic year 1933–1934, "at a 55¢ price." Turner wrote Dobie that he could not say at the moment "just what the sale will amount to."

All the uncertainties crippled Turner's health again, and he was seriously ill, bedridden, for several months at the start of 1933. He and his firm both just barely managed to survive. He was up again in June, weary and defeated. He wrote Dobie in September that sales of *On the Open Range* to the state on a one-year contract amounted to twenty-six thousand copies. He had no intention of seeking readoption because he could not make anything on the contract price. "At the price made to the state of 55¢, they could not be manufactured." Part of his pessimism may have been to ward off Frank's insistence on payments due. In November, Turner was still having to stall off meeting his royalty payments to Dobie. The final amount Dobie made from the school-book contract: $1,219.82.

When Turner at last declared bankruptcy in July 1935, Dobie sent a very sharp three-page, single-spaced letter to Frank Martin, "Receiver," saying he felt sure the Southwest Press legally owed him several thousand dollars that he knew he wouldn't get, but that he would accept, instead, the copyrights on *Vaquero* and *Open Range* and the plates of the latter. However, he sanctioned Turner's republishing *Open Range* when Turner reorganized in 1936 – because Turner had the prospect of an adoption in the state of Oklahoma.

Rogers did succeed in persuading the Literary Guild to select *Coronado's Children* and wrote a very useful brochure about it, titled *Finding Literature on the Texas Plains*, which also included the selection of Southwestern books that Dobie recommended for his classes in "Life and Literature of the Southwest" at the university. This was the first time, Rogers wrote Dobie on October 3, 1930, when selection by the Guild was virtually assured, that either the Guild or the Book-of-the-Month Club had gone out of New York or Boston "for a book from a publisher." To Dobie's delight, Rogers added that Carl Van Doren was very much excited about the book.

An undated letter has Turner writing Frank to say that at last the check has arrived from the Guild "today." "I am enclosing one dated today for $2,361.64, one for $2,000 not dated." The reason for leaving the date open on the second check was that he hoped Dobie would hold it for a week. Dobie got the Texas Folklore Society to enter an agreement with Turner to act as agent in selling *Coronado's Children*, an arrangement that netted the society $901.88 on the royalty statement of January 1, 1932. Frank's royalty on that statement amounted to $3,607.52, and he had already earned $1,048.50 on the preceding statement. Sadly, however, he notes on the statement of 1932 that he had received only the following payments: "Sept. 9, 1931 — $500; May 2, 1932 — $200.45." Meantime, the school-book reader, *On the Open Range*, had been published, but the local adoptions of the state-wide recommended book were far below anticipation.

The Southwest Press was adjudged bankrupt on July 17, 1935, in "the Honorable Fourteenth District Court of Dallas County, Texas."

Frank's later insistence that Little, Brown, his ultimate publishers, keep all his books in print arose from his early experience. In the autumn of 1933 he complained to Bertha that good orders for the Folklore Society publications were coming in, but "the trouble with us now is that Vols. II (the first I edited), III (*Legends of Texas*) and VI (*Texas and Southwestern Lore*, with your long article in it) are all out of print."

Dobie always claimed that he lost thousands of dollars from his involvement with the Southwest Press. Turner's dream was too far ahead of its time and too fully afloat in the financial disaster of the Great Depression. He rallied after the bankruptcy, and in 1936 started publishing again under the old name of the P. L. Turner Company. But he had had all he wanted of dealing with creative artists; he confined himself mostly to school-book and commercial contracts. This brave episode in regional publishing was a flash in the pan, but its history deserves more than a footnote in the cultural annals of the Southwest.

III

After the resounding success nationwide of *Coronado's Children*, and with a Guggenheim grant in his pocket, Frank Dobie set out for Mexico in the autumn of 1932 to gather tales for a book on legends of Mexico. Bertha went ahead to Mexico City for the long stay of eight or nine months, intending to write a book herself on aspects of Mexican life. Frank planned to work his way to the capital, searching for stories as ardently as Coronado's children sought buried treasure; his major interest was in the folklore of northern Mexico, familiar to him in a degree from the tales and talk of the Mexican vaqueros on his father's ranch and on Uncle Jim's, and from the Mexican families living in the Brush Country. He and Bertha planned to rendezvous at intervals.

His starting point was to be Raymond Dickson's ranch on the Rio Grande, near Del Rio, Texas. Through Dickson, an old friend, Dobie made at the outset the most helpful acquaintance of his entire trip, a distinguished Mexican rancher of Coahuila, General Alberto Guajardo, aged seventy-four, the author himself of unpublished works on the history and the lore of his region. As Dobie wrote Bertha in his first exultation at this "find" so early in the project: "If I do not get anything else out of Coahuila but Guajardo, I shall be enriched." His admiration for and enjoyment of Guajardo increased daily. Guajardo secured a "guide" for him, a man, Dobie wrote, "as honest as the general himself." Guajardo was so honest that after the revolutionary wars were over he paid out of his own pocket everybody from whom he — as an officer — had taken horses, goats, corn and other troop necessities. Landrich, the general was in money terms now poor.

In the *modo mejicano*, Dobie agreed to pay his guide twenty-three dollars for the first week-long leg of the trip along the Mexican side of the Rio Grande, and to supply the food and buy it in advance; the guide would provide a mule for Dobie and two pack mules, and if he wished, he might bring along another helper.

After this first venture, a new "trade" would have to be made for further trips. Once they came into Ojinaga, Frank would cross the river to pick up mail in Presidio, Texas, before beginning the long journey into the interior. Back in Ojinaga, he would take the train southwest to Chihuahua City, then another train north from there to El Paso, again for mail, and back to Chihuahua. The initial week was in country rich in game, and the plan was to make game the primary source of food.

Frank hoped also to shoot a bear, but he wrote Bertha that whether they got game or not, he was certain to have the pleasure "of being in the society of animals." He had a qualm, he confessed, about how little the first "exploration" would cost him. "When I think of 2 men and 5 mules spending 2 days getting to me; then 7 days taking me; then 8 or 9 days getting back home, all for $23 — the man's own price — I am almost ashamed; but he will be that much better off than he would have been without me, for both men and beasts are idle, I suppose."

In early November he got a superb story, the now well known tale of Juan Oso, half man, half bear; then he hit a dry spell for a while. From Chihuahua City he wrote Bertha at the Casa Alvarado in Mexico City to urge her to meet him in Durango to make the pack trip across to Mazatlán. A woman graduate of Southwestern University living in Chihuahua assured him it was safe; a young American bride she knew had just recently made the trip. Another Southwestern graduate and a classmate of Frank's, Lem Newberry, was also living in Chihuahua and put Frank up in his home. One wonders how Frank found time, on such an arduous and busy trip, to write Bertha such long, long letters. True, the letters were a kind of rough draft of a manuscript, but the energy involved is impressive. Before Christmas, he wrote her that he was gnawed by a fear that the material he was gathering was not going to yield as good a book as *Coronado's Children*. "Maybe when I can get still and get settled I can enlarge them and *englamour* them." One detail that pleased him was the corroboration he got from hunters that W. H. Hudson's Pampas accounts of the lion's friendship for man, guarding him in case of danger from other animals, were true in the Mexican experience of lions. (Teddy Roosevelt had challenged Hudson's testimony.)

In addition to writing Bertha the "rough" draft, he was hoping to write articles for the *Saturday Evening Post* and the New York *Herald Tribune*. He had got, before the Guggenheim grant, a grant from the Rockefeller Foundation; but the poverty of his early youth still haunted him. Since Bertha was so wonderfully set up as a paying guest in one of the most elegant villas in the city, Frank wrote that this gave him the deepest satisfaction and that perhaps the best thing would be for him to come on to the city and make trips out from that center. But he had to return to El Paso for a lecture in mid-December that he had long ago accepted.

While there, he was a guest in the home of El Paso's famous mayor, Tom Lea, Sr. Lea had served as a lawyer for President-General Huerta during the Mexican Revolution. Frank liked him greatly and in his letter to Bertha he mentioned that Mr. Lea had a son "who is an artist; his home is an art gallery and a museum, particularly for guns and Casas Grandes pottery — some extraordinary things. He is one of the most daring and original and interesting men I have ever met; he is an avid reader — and he thinks *Coronado's Children* the most gripping book he has ever read."

Their travel plans suffered little modification, but the plans for the book *Tongues of the Monte* did. Only a month or so after beginning his research, or search, he wrote Bertha that "like you, I think I'll have to modify the book from a pure book of tales to something of a chronicle of observations." He was not finding the wealth of surefire "stories" that he knew existed. He realized more and more that he would in a sense have to "invent a great deal." "For instance, I want a ghost story as good as any in *Legends of the City of Mexico*. To have one I might weave several I have into one pattern."

He complained to Bertha in several letters in December that he was finding fine *animal* material, but not what he really wanted. Writing on the day after Christmas, from a ranch near Chihuahua City, he observed: "If I were writing *scientific* folklore, I could go home and publish my notes. I'm after, as you know, drama, pictures, romance. I'm going to keep after it until I find it, but I hope I'll be with you by the end of February anyhow." He was leaving the next day for a ranch fifty miles away to see a missionary doctor and his wife renowned for their repertory of ghost stories. As he said, "Nobody can say I'm not searching."

A week later, at Parral, he met an American mining engineer, a graduate of the University of Texas in 1906, who had so admired *Coronado's Children* he was planning to send Frank a story. With glee, Frank wrote Bertha, "I know that Foster is my man — the man I have been searching three months for." Another stroke of good fortune happened a week after that, when Raymond Bell invited Frank to his ranch, Hacienda de Atotonilco, Yerbanis, Durango, "the most delightful hacienda I have ever been on." Bell was one of many Americans who had stayed on in Mexico after the 1910–1911 Madero Revolution. He told Dobie that before that revolution there had been about twelve hundred Americans living in the state of Durango, engaged in ranching, mining, lumbering. A fine neighboring estate was up for sale; Frank toyed with the idea of trying to form a company in Austin to buy it, but then dropped the plan.

He wrote Bertha that a letter from his sister Martha gave him great pleasure, "about the best I ever read of hers," and he berated himself for being such a poor correspondent — except with Bertha, since "you are the only person nowadays that I ever expand to in a letter." The lifetime correspondence between them is, on both sides, incredibly voluminous and rich.

One example: While "on camp" in the Sierra Madre in the autumn of 1932, Frank sent Bertha, in Mexico City, an "average" letter of about two thousand words, the length of at least one full newspaper column in those days when the use of white space and magazine-style display were spurned. The letter recounts details of a four- or five-day trip in "about as God-forsaken a spot as there is in northern Mexico." He started the letter after lunch, and had already spent the morning making notes, for the book, on his past three days. He was keeping a diary, and estimated he already had fifty pages of notes.

He was far from having inactive days with nothing to do but gather yarns and set them down. While his mozo and assorted nomads — the latter attached themselves for an hour or two or even days to the traveler and his outfit — watered the three saddle horses and two pack mules, often going eight miles or more from camp to the nearest springs or watering holes to water the animals and to fill the canteens and the two-gallon water barrel carried along, Dobie left camp to kill game, which yielded not only venison steaks for the day but dried "jerky" for the rest of the trip.

Time-consuming and unexpected nuisances occurred, as when a mule ran away after the mozo had carelessly unhobbled it at the wrong time, or when fresh mounts had to be engaged at a rancho on the trail; if the mozo did the packing poorly, stops had to be made for doing it over. Wanderers over the mountains found their way to camp to be offered hospitality and a supply of matches. Frank arose about five in the morning; he looked out of his tarpaulin (the nights were very cold at that high altitude) to see the morning star and to watch Gustabo, his mozo, work the fire for breakfast. With deer meat for dinner, breakfast was equally un-Spartan. Gustabo prepared bacon and cornbread, which Frank greatly enjoyed with his coffee and dried fruit. On the first day out he killed "an enormous black-tailed buck, as fat as a mutton." Although the days were warm in the sun, the meat kept well because of the altitude.

Other distractions also took time. Caves abounded and had to be explored; Dobie found one with Indian pictographs on its walls. He gorged on wild cherries on a lucky day when they struck a thicket in fruit.

In Durango, at the start of the New Year of 1933, he borrowed a United States–made typewriter from the American consul, a former student at the University of Texas. Ellis Bonnet was helpful in other ways, introducing Frank to a German naturalist, reared in Mexico, "whose talk was a great help," and to a Texan who owned a ranch near the Promontorio Mine. The latter knew "the very right man" to be Frank's mozo and guide, and was delighted to supply Frank with pack mules and other help.

Frank planned a two-week trip out of Durango, but would not leave until he found out if Bertha was all right (she had been struck by illness just after Christmas). While waiting for the telegram, he met, again through the consul, the family of a Confederate general who had come to Durango in 1865 and whose daughter was "the best oral historian" in the region. Other Americans who had settled in the picturesque city were helpful. At a Mexican wedding dance he got some good songs, and he wrote Bertha — of significance for those who have read *Tongues of the Monte* — that he "met a señorita whom I propose to put in my book. She wanted to dance the *jarabe* with me but I couldn't dance it." He added: "I am counting on buying a beautiful set of silver even though it costs one thousand pesos. I don't know of anything we should both enjoy more and enjoy it all our lives."

Out of fear that Bertha was not suffering just from the normal tourist affliction but from her inveterate enemy, influenza, he suggested that she join him in about two weeks at Mazatlán or Guadalajara, both of which had climates of "perpetual springtime" as claimed. He knew she wanted to travel out of the city toward Veracruz in order to see the famous gardens in Jalapa, and advised her to hold to that plan if she preferred, but he could make it to Mazatlán in a few days. He told her in a postscript: "If you are down with the flu, I am going to you. I could come back later to the Sierra Madre." Bertha wired back, "Am well," so he spent the next two weeks going out to mining towns in the Durango area.

By February 1933, he wrote Bertha that he had all the "stories" he needed. "What I want now is heart-blood." For this, the Sierra Madre country was his real affinity, and he planned to return to it after a trip to be with her in Mexico City. But something held him away from the capital; its life was too complex and multisided for the book he had in mind, as he well realized from the remarkable letters Bertha was sending him. Thanks in part to the "contacts" the consulate in Durango had provided, each of these supplying still others, he was immensely pleased with his stay in the neighborhood of Durango. He wrote Bertha that he had been given "a priceless sense of accord" with the Mexican way of life "in that area."

In mid-February Frank wrote Bertha to meet him in Mazatlán on March 2, and sent her his itinerary so that she could get in touch with him if she needed to (she would make a trip to Veracruz meanwhile). "In case . . . you arrive before I do, go to the Hotel Belmar and await me." He himself left on Washington's Birthday for Mazatlán, with a mozo who wore the kind of native sandals called *guaraches*, for, as he told Bertha, "I have laid down for myself the iron-clad rule to engage no mozo who wears shoes."

After their enjoyable visit to Mazatlán, Frank went on to another famous Pacific Coast resort (though it was far from famous in 1932), Acapulco, and then cut across southern Mexico, with two American companions, to reach a place he longed to see: Oaxaca, a mecca that did not disappoint him. The three travelers drove a car that often had to be pushed along the inadequate roads or up difficult inclines, as when they spent four days out of Oaxaca riding over the mountains, at one place reaching a point thirteen thousand feet high. This scenery was far removed from the harsh grandeur of the Sierra Madre range of northern Mexico, but it provided Frank with a fascinating example of how environment creates contrasts in the way Mexicans live.

He preferred the north, "which, despite its bleakness, remains *for me* the most interesting part of Mexico." Few travelers before or since have shared that predilection; but for him, the Sierra Madre region was kin to the Brush Country of South Texas in sparseness and harshness and bleakness, in its solitude and space, in simple ways of living and its dedication to ranching, and its "feel" touched his reservoir of profound early memories. Northern Mexico did not possess such awesome artifacts of a very rich and varied Indian civilization as the remains of Mayan and Zapotecan and Aztec and other cultures. To these temples and pyramids of the past, Dobie confessed to Bertha he was at the moment indifferent. He wrote: "Now that I am in Oaxaca, I suppose I shall go out to Mitla and Monte Albán, though I am truly sorry to say that I have no great interest in them." For the moment, he was in single-minded pursuit of the material that would fit the book he had already formulated in his mind.

But with the ever "open" nature of his personality, he changed this point of view somewhat when he met in Oaxaca a famous Belgian scholar, Paul Van de Velde, an expert on pre-Columbian Mexico. This was the first "intellectual," it seems, that Dobie had had a chance to converse with at any length since the start of his trip. He wrote Bertha of his pleasure in Van de Velde's company, finding him "the most enlightened man I have met in a long time." Then Dobie came up to the capital by way of Puebla, and he and Bertha were back home in Austin by summertime. But he was by no means through with Mexico, and planned to go back as soon as Bertha returned from a visit to her parents in Velasco, when he would make a mule-pack trip with Henry Nash Smith.

It was not simply the search for more material that drew him back to the Sierra Madre. "I discover within myself a very strong subconscious feeling of freedom, of personal liberty in Mexico, that I don't feel here," he wrote Bertha while she was with her parents. In the same letter he made a comment that he was later to belie almost totally (this was on July 30, 1933), "I have no use for Roosevelt and no use for his plans." Politically, he was still oriented to the Texan mystique of "rugged individualism," at least as it was understood at that time.

Two weeks later he returned to Mexico. He and Smith stopped overnight at a favorite old hostelry of the Dobies, the Hotel Arizpe Sáenz in Saltillo, where Frank renewed acquaintance with American and Mexican friends. Among them was an author and physician named Stoker, whose house in Mazopil Dobie hoped to use. It was not offered. They went on to Mazopil by train anyway, and there received a welcome offer to visit the great Los Cedros Hacienda, one and a half million acres now owned by the Transcontinental Rubber Company but for many generations earlier the property of the marqués de Aguayo and his heirs. Perhaps the finest short story, in the usual sense of that term, Dobie ever wrote he owed to this stay at Los Cedros: the well-known "Saga of the Saddle," about the marqués's legendary horseback ride to achieve "blood revenge" — and without punishment. The manager of the Transcontinental Company, stationed in Torreón, arranged the visit.

As Dobie wrote Bertha, he and Smith were good companions, but he paid her a proper tribute: "I had rather be with you than with anybody I know. I have seen no scenery better than that we saw together — on this trip, I mean. The trail from Concepción de Oro to the Promontorio Mine was spectacular, but you rode as good. I have wished for you, honestly, hundreds of times. In the morning I am going to Flohulilo, at the end of a short branch line north of here; it is two days by horseback, I think, from there to Sierra Mojada. I'll go east to Monclova and thence to Piedras Negras and Eagle Pass. I still expect to get home by September 10."

Meanwhile, Bertha was working away at her book of essays on life in Mexico City, and finished one on *la gente pobre* (poor folks) that fall. Frank was so keen on it he sent it off to *Scribner's* magazine. But Bertha had no luck selling manuscripts that season.

In collaboration with a colorful sort of "soldier of fortune," C. B. Ruggles, whom she and Frank greatly liked, she "edited" Ruggles's autobiographical story "In the Light of Freedom" and hoped to sell it to Harry Maule, a friend and former Texan, now an editor at Doubleday, Doran in New York. Maule turned it down, but Bertha did not give up seeking a publisher for it, more out of loyalty to Ruggles than to her own investment of time.

The new owners of Uncle Jim's Los Olmos ranch issued Frank a standing invitation to hunt there any time he liked. He assured Bertha, who was still nursing her ailing parents in Velasco, that he would hunt there without fail in Christmas week. "When the time comes that I can't go down there to hunt, life will be a lot less rich." He was teaching that autumn of 1933, but set out to organize a Dobie family visit to San Antonio, where the Witte Museum was staging an important exhibition of the Monte Albán jewels. Clearly, his encounter with the Belgian scholar in Oaxaca caused an about-face in his professed indifference to pre-Columbian culture.

He was working very hard, up at six every morning, shaving and cutting a little fireplace wood before breakfast, teaching and writing both, and he was usually in bed soon after ten o'clock. With Bertha in Velasco, he was not much involved in social life, but everybody he knew, it seemed, wanted to write a book — after getting Frank's advice and help first. He complained to Bertha of the time thus consumed, but could do nothing about it; some of the projects or manuscripts he found worth publishing, and all such requests from friends he felt were legitimate claims on his attention. As he wrote Bertha on several occasions, "I have not been hoarding myself."

As in the days of their courtship, he wrote to her nearly every day, though sometimes only a brief note to express how much he missed her. He concluded what he regarded as a dull letter with this explanation: "I have been grading themes all afternoon when not watching the leaves and just wanted to say a word to you. I love you. Frank."

For Christmas of 1933 he and Bertha sent out to friends "separates" of his *Southwest Review* article on Juan Oso as a Christmas greeting. For many years their Christmas salute was a brochure of some essay by Frank. In 1933, he included a Christmas poem he had composed the year before while in camp in the Sierra Madre, working on *Tongues of the Monte*, a short poem of a score or so lines celebrating "all tellers of tales."

At that Christmas season he went hunting on the Los Olmos ranch with Elrich; while in Cotulla, they saw a local performance, lasting three hours, of the famous Christmas pageant traditional with Mexican folk, "Los Pastores." He found it extraordinarily interesting as evidence of how "Mexican" South Texas was in feeling and spirit, all the more vivid to him after his year in Old Mexico. He also had a good visit with Santos Cortez, who gave Frank one of the "very best" coyote stories Frank had ever heard. Santos, he wrote Bertha, claimed that "I once saved his life — *quién sabe como*. . . . He had written me and sent all sorts of words to see him." Another pleasant reencounter on the hunting trip was a visit to Eagle Pass to see the remarkable General Guajardo.

In late January of 1934 he was again on the road, fulfilling a lecture contract with a professional lecture agent in Denver for a one-week series scheduled in a Denver hotel. On his way home, he had speaking engagements at colleges in Colorado Springs, Greeley, Las Vegas (New Mexico) and Albuquerque. He often said that "Nature puts something into man," meaning an unconscious and spontaneous sort of chemical working that seemed spiritual; certainly, an audience drew out of him a similar sort of magic-making, however much he deplored the expense of energy. Bertha, an indispensable help, again finished his classes for him and gave the final examinations that he had prepared, an arrangement not infrequent in the hay-fever season. Frank carried with him on the trip term themes to grade.

The lectures in Colorado Springs were "stage" appearances of a sort, like Mark Twain's, like Will Rogers'. The agency advertised the series and printed a large mailing piece headed "Theodore Fisher Presents That Unique Figure FRANK 'PANCHO' DOBIE" . . . (He was sometimes nicknamed Pancho.) "Pancho" was billed as teacher, folklore editor, cowman, writer and Guggenheim Fellow. The initial lecture, a social event in a private home, cost $1.10 admission, and was followed by a series of four lectures in the ballroom of the Shirley-Savoy Hotel at a fee of

$2.50 for the four. Students benefited from a special price of forty cents a lecture. The five lecture titles were "Tales of the Southwestern Soil," "Talks on the Southwest," "Cowboy Literature," "Old Mexico," and "Trails and Tales of the Sierra Madre." This was Frank Dobie functioning in the role he liked best: oral storyteller. His success at it was satisfying to him in a deep-down way. And while in Colorado Springs he took advantage of the chance to visit again with Andy Adams, whose *Log of a Cowboy* Dobie judged to be a classic of frontier writing.

Bertha meanwhile sporadically pursued her own career as a writer, trying to sell the manuscript on her experiences in Mexico; and she hoped to get her syndicated newspaper articles on gardening gathered into a volume. She went to New York in the summer of 1935. While she was there, two manuscripts, rejected, were returned to her in Austin: the manuscript of C. B. Ruggles's memoirs, which she had edited and worked on as partial collaborator, and an article she had tried to sell to the *Atlantic Monthly*. Frank wrote to her that while in New York she should "see the world and get acquainted with as many book and editor people as possible. Some of the Garden City folk should be interested in garden articles you can write."

In that year, Harry Maule of Doubleday, Doran published *Tongues of the Monte*, which Frank had originally meant to call *The Hacienda of the Five Wounds*. Maule had simply written in 1934 to ask to see the next manuscript, and almost as casually as Frank had signed up with P. L. Turner, he had signed a contract. The book failed to arouse much interest in either the critics or the public, which considerably dismayed Dobie. Had the book missed because it was a mixture of fact and fiction in perhaps unhappy union (this was Bertha's view), or because the material itself lacked vital appeal, or because the publishers failed to discern the book's proper market? He kept a very special fondness for the book, and allowed a later edition to be published in 1942 under a supposedly more attractive title, *The Mexico I Like*. But this venture, the idea of his friend Donald Day who was then running the *Southwest Review* and the Southern Methodist University Press, faced the problem of World War II and its paper shortage — only a small edition could be printed in the circumstances, and this was quickly sold out. Dobie always felt that the book had suffered originally from a title that was perplexing to American readers, and that it never recovered from bouts of bad luck. He allowed himself a lyricism in the book he did not risk again, and exhibited in it an artistic sensitivity to structure and to style that clearly established his kinship with the temperament of W. H. Hudson. He also displayed in it both a gift and a yearning for writing fiction — a longing he had to satisfy later by "telling tales."

Here is a sample of his lyric vein: "At this instant I happened to glance towards the mountains to the east and, although dusk was approaching, the sun having disappeared, I saw one of them aglow with a soft yet brilliant blanket of light, rose and amethyst and golden, misty like a veil and at the same time pellucid, surpassing in beauty and strangeness and effect upon the imagination any light my eyes have ever beheld."

Inspired by a work of critical scholarship that made a signal impact on the academic world when it was published in 1927, John Livingston Lowes's *Road to Xanadu*, a study of the sources of Coleridge's "Kubla Khan" and "Rime of the Ancient Mariner," Bertha Dobie made a detailed analysis, for her enjoyment and Frank's, of *Tongues of the Monte*. Her study, based particularly on Lowes's chapter "The Deep Well," is handwritten in a "Journal" that Bertha started keeping late in 1929. She explains on the first page: "Frank Dobie, my husband, having given me this dummy of his book [*Vaquero*], I can think of no more fitting matter to fill the blank pages than stories about people — which he loves above meat and drink, and many of which will come to me from his lips." She even gave the dummy a title: "People and the Stories They Tell." This record of their social and professional life she kept sporadically for the next five years; it is a fascinating chronicle of faculty life in Austin at that time, recorded with wit and irony.

Why she chose to record her study of *Tongues of the Monte* and its origins in this sort of diary perhaps sprang from a wish to make it a special sort of reminiscence, rather than a methodical analysis. Nonetheless, it is of small-book length itself. Her purpose seems to have been to prove to herself and Frank that his talent lay not in fiction but in synthesizing and structuring external material, *external*, not *subjective*, experience.

The tone is set by an early observation: "Frank is one of the most acute listeners I have ever known." She cites scores of phrases that Frank overheard and then used, most often in dialogue. One instance: "In September 1934 we attended my first and only bullfight, in Chihuahua City. It was a most farcical fight, since neither the small, poor bulls nor the *matador* had any desire to fight.... One spectator yelled, when the matador hung back from killing the bull, 'Shoot him with a quince seed!'" "But by no means," she stresses, "has all the phrasing come from Mexicans directly or indirectly and books about Mexico. Many, many slight allusions, some of them conscious, some probably unconscious, are out of the years when, a very young man, Frank plunged himself into English classics. The whole tone of *Tongues of the Monte* is expressed in the line from *As You Like It*, quoted in the description of days at the hacienda Las Cinco Llagas, 'Lose and neglect the creeping hours of time,' which is underlined in Frank's old Arden edition." She adds: "The wells of English literature and childhood on a ranch, with Mexicans for playmates and mentors, are for Frank deep, deep wells. It is because those wells are deep that *Tongues of the Monte* is a rich book. Yet mostly he knew when he dropped the bucket in."

She emphasizes that the material for the book was collected "from wide sources over many years, much of it blown out double, a bit of wool carded and spun into a long, strong thread. ... Almost nothing occurs in the book just as it occurred in reality." Rather offhandedly, without mentioning the señorita who wanted to dance the *jarabe*, she indicates what she thinks of the love episodes in the book: "Frank says that [W. H.] Hudson got him into the Dolores-Lupita episode. He refers to the escapades with women in *The Purple Land*."

Bertha's assessment of Frank's writing strength is defined in her judgment on the character of Inocencio, "a compound of all the mozos Frank ever had and a product too of the imagination.... Inocencio is but one instance of the writing skill, care, and ingenuity in fitting parts together — comparable to the skill, care, and ingenuity employed by a worker in the leather mosaic of fine bindings." Or: "In Frank's case, it seems to me that invention is chiefly synthesis, the fusion in the imagination of many disparate elements into an imaginative whole.... Out of the heart the mouth speaketh.... Nothing, I believe, comes out that has not gone in through one of four avenues: observation, experience, conversation and reading." Rather unexpectedly, she concludes that the book "has the truth of fiction rather than of fact."

But by far the most interesting observation she has to make about Frank Dobie in her Journal concerns the man rather than the writer. It follows an observation she cites from Carl Sandburg, who was lecturing in Austin in March of 1935, and in whose company she and Frank spent much of several days. Bertha noted that Sandburg used his voice as an instrument, much as he used his guitar, and she found his storytelling skill matchless ("he has the power to separate the ambience of the anecdote from that of the room in which it is told"). In a letter following his visit, Sandburg characterized Frank in a way Bertha thought "hit close enough to a true description of [him]."

Sandburg wrote: "You are the salt of the earth I was going to say but while thinking of you as made of the same plain red clay as the general run of Texans I had a flash that the hand of the Potter felt experimental and threw in honey kindling phosphorous H_2SO_4 ashes sheepguts horseneck ironore coal radium songs thongs horizon blue rainbows maps documents disguises chile beans jumping beans much else saying: we will see what this piece of humus can stand and not go under."

Bertha then comments: "Never of Frank could it be said, 'The elements were so mixed in him.' They are not mixed at all, but separate, warring. In my simpler analysis than Mr. Sandburg's, I should say that in Frank pig, charging bull and mule together make a half, and that the other half is *humanity at its very finest*."

Three other notations in Bertha's Journal, at least three others, cry out for attention. In her discussion of *Tongues*, she says her favorite chapter is "By Sun Time" because "it best expresses the lingering, enjoying habit of life that so belongs to both [the] Mexican temperament and to Frank."

The second notation followed soon after the Sandburg visit. "Last night Frank came from Town-and-Gown, which all its members say is the best club in Texas, in fine fettle." He had opposed the talk on art and the discussion that followed. He told Bertha: "I was fierce; I don't rib myself up to being fierce; I am just naturally fierce about anything I am against — and when I am fierce I am interesting."

In her entry of June 9, 1935, she quotes him again: "People have always tried to tag me and they can't do it. When I was at Leon Springs training for a commission, they said I was too academic; at the university they have said that I was a ruffian — Callaway said, 'I should think that you would have played football in college, Mr. Dobie'; at the ranch [Uncle Jim's Los Olmos] Lee Keithly said I was too much a bookworm to make a good ranchman." Bertha adds: "I realized then that all his life has been a protest."

Of many others still worth attention, one final observation of Bertha's, regarding one "hilarious" story Frank included in *Tongues:* "Thinking he had been held in all his life, first by his God-fearing parents and then by me and feeling in thorough revolt against any tightening girth, he put the anecdote in. I think he contributed some of the Rabelaisian detail himself." To find any Rabelaisian detail in *Tongues* requires a more powerful microscope than most readers possess.

The relative lack of success of *Tongues* was a turning point in Frank's career. He abandoned thereafter attempts to fulfill himself in what is usually called the writing of "creative imagination," and overmodestly tended for a while to call himself a "chronicler." He was fated to be what he wanted most to be, "independent and original," even as an artist. In time, he came to insist that he was far more than a chronicler, that he used the faculty he most admired, imagination, effectively in the form and structure he gave his later books, and that this sensitivity to "form," however unconventional, likewise encompassed the "form" of a sentence, with its cadence and tone and rhythm as well as its content. He was, in short, a "shaper" as well as a chronicler, deeply concerned with the overtones that a feeling for beauty added to his respect for seriatim facts. A man who admired and who knew by heart as much Wordsworth as he did could hardly be indifferent to the vigor and power of "poetic condensation."

His disappointment at the reception of *Tongues* haunted him for a year, or until he began to realize that his absorption and interest in the tales for his next book, *Apache Gold and Yaqui Silver,* promised the same excitement in creation as had *Coronado's Children.* He went off to Kerrville in December of 1935 to work on some folklore material — and to avoid the plague of hay fever

— but he confessed to Bertha that he received a long document from a man in El Paso about the Tayopa Mine that set his creative juices to working beyond any spur he had got from "this piddling with legends": "It set me off on that track and I thought how much I had rather write something like that." It also revealed to him how dissatisfied he was with his productivity. "I have worked but I'll swear that I don't see how I can spend so much time doing so little." He felt that he did more work with less advantage to himself financially "than any other man of my powers in America."

He made an important decision. His career as a writer, he said to Bertha, required a practical revision. It was essential for him to go to New York, perhaps to get a literary agent, but certainly to "get acquainted with publishing tricks and learn something about my own game." He wanted to get article assignments, for a special reason. This most popular of teachers was in a very real state of depression at the time: "I loathe the prospect of going back to teaching students and trying to make them learn when they don't want to learn and would not be any better off if they did learn." He had a built-in compulsion, maybe a part of his need for independence, to repulse, intermittently and briefly, nearly everything he profoundly loved. It is a matter of record that his students in the years after this outburst did not find him lackluster or remote or pessimistic. In the survival wisdom of writers, Frank Dobie was already at work, enthusiastically, on a new project — a return to the "matter" of *Coronado's Children* — to temper the disappointment over *Tongues*. He went off to work, in January 1936, on the new manuscript at a "retreat" offered him by his friend Raymond Dickson at the latter's Caballo Ranch in northern Mexico. He was convinced, he wrote Bertha, that only in solitude could he write at his best: "the only way for a man exercising his imagination is simply to get away like this — away from everybody and everything. . . . Monday I worked from early morning until midnight. Tuesday I worked until four o'clock and then rode alone out in the hills until after dark. Today, Wednesday, I worked until nearly six o'clock; then I talked with Joe Bridge [foreman of the ranch] and a high class *ranchero* here for about two hours, our conversation being carried on mostly in Spanish." From the Caballo, he was going to Chihuahua City, "there to begin the search for Tayopa."

In his Sunday column for February 25, 1951, "Fires and Fireplaces," Dobie repeated the theme frequent with him, the need for anyone wanting to write to withdraw, or as he often said, "You have to have the cream of your own time for good writing." From the column: "I have read and written in many places but in none quite so genial as the Caballo Ranch, owned by the Hogg brothers and my friend Raymond Dickson, down in Coahuila, Mexico. It was wintertime while I was there. I had an enormous room with an enormous steer hide on the floor for [a] rug, an enormous bed, an ample table, a fine kerosene lamp, and a wide fireplace. I was writing a book on Mexico. I would write all morning, ride horseback for hours in the afternoon, eat a bully supper, and then after some talk go to my own fire. A Mexican kept a big pile of mesquite wood on the gallery just outside the door. After I had worked maybe two hours and then read past midnight, I would get in bed and watch the fire die out. I did not want to go to sleep, the fire was so delightful."

4

Mr. Texas

The Texas longhorn made more history than any other breed of cattle the civilized world has known. As an animal in the realm of natural history, he was the peer of bison or grizzly bear. As a social factor, his influence on men was extraordinary. An economic agent in determining the character and occupation of a territory continental in its vastness, he moved elementally with drouth, grass, blizzards out of the Arctic and the wind from the south. However supplanted or however disparaged by evolving standards and generations, he will remain the bedrock on which the history of the cow country of America is founded.
— From *The Longhorns*

I*n a brief questionnaire* that he returned to *Town & Country Review*, London, after the success of *Coronado's Children*, Frank asserted that "I wish Texas were still a republic and I bitterly resent the obliterations of the culture of the American soil through the productions of Hollywood and the sidewalks of New York." He described himself as a "rebel" in his vocation of college teacher and adds that his favorite pastime is "riding with a pack mule into the Sierra Madre." He was finding the role he finally was to play, and most of the time to his great delight: that of "Mr. Texas," a public personality. He inaugurated in 1932, on January 11, a radio program called "Longhorn Luke and His Cowboys," sponsored by the Portland Cement Company on Station WOAI in San Antonio. He got twenty-five dollars for each program, plus expenses to and from Austin. His part in the program lasted only five minutes. His first topic was cattle brands. That year, the New York *Times* carried a news story stating that one picturesque institution of the old range days "has been revived as a modern business venture by a group of Texans, headed by Lt. Gov. Edgar Witt and J. Frank Dobie, master of southwestern folklore." The "institution" was that of the chuck wagon, which the *Times* called "the ranch dining car, with its barbecue and sonofagun stew." The venture was launched in Austin, the old chuck wagon transformed into an up-to-date lunch wagon and sandwich stand, "specializing, however, in the oldtime foods." The "pilot" installation was, according to the promoters, only the first of a chain they planned to establish throughout the country. As in many other Dobie financial ventures, but most certainly not in all, anticipation far outran fulfillment.

He had reason to plume himself. He was being published in the

Saturday Evening Post, the *American Mercury,* the *Nation* and the *New York Herald Tribune Magazine;* he was making more money from his writings than from his teaching.

The Austin *Statesman* on April 3, 1936, carried two banner headlines, in boxcar type and one just below the other, the top one announcing "Bruno to Die," in the Lindbergh kidnapping case, and the second one — in the same size of type — "Dobie Works Out Traffic Fine," the latter with a subhead: "Jail Is Preferred over $2 Payment." Just below these two was another headline, ironic to those in the know: "Callaway, UT's Noted English Prof, Dies," a one-column headline over a one-column story. The center picture on the front page showed J. Frank Dobie, seated and holding his pipe, defying the court's orders and protesting to reporters the deplorable notoriety the incident had received. Poor Dr. Callaway should have lived another day to revel in the latest unorthodox behavior of the "Cowboy Professor" whom he had so valiantly tried to discipline and to initiate into the virtues of conformity. Dobie, of course, feeling himself a second Thoreau, was reveling at having his day in jail. And at home, Bertha Dobie was enjoying a good laugh.

She knew the episode had not turned out as her impetuous husband expected, even though it had its "larky" side. In reply to a summons to pay three accumulated traffic tickets, Frank had written the judge that he would only pay one, since the other two were foolish. Now, as Bertha cheerfully told reporters, "he could do nothing but go ahead with his pledge." She added that in the future "maybe he will be more careful of what he says."

He was allowed to work out his fine in the traffic department office, where he typed up, as ordered by the chief of police, some reflections on traffic safety for the use of the officers on the staff. When he finished that chore, he whiled away the rest of his six hours of detention by performing some of the routine office chores of filing, writing up accident reports, and best of all, giving an impromptu lecture on the history of Texas to a traffic-safety class then in session. About four o'clock in the afternoon, Chief of Police R. D. Thorp decided that Dobie had worked off the two dollars he owed (most of the time only one dollar a day was allowed for persons who chose to work out a fine instead of paying it, but Dobie's rate was doubled because of his "qualifications").

What had happened was this: twice that spring Dobie got one-dollar tickets for overparking, though in the afternoon when there was no traffic congestion and when, Dobie maintained, his car ticketed for parking over the one-hour limit was the only one visible on either side for half a block. He ignored the conventional summons to appear to explain his violation of the law; any man of sense could see that the rule in these instances was stupid. But a third infraction he could not defend, nor did he propose to. He got a ticket for running a stop sign at ten o'clock in the morning ("although there was no car in sight"), and when this ticket prompted a summons for all the cards in his file, he wrote a personal letter to Judge Maxwell. He was willing, he said, to pay the three-dollar fine for running the stop sign, which on reflection he thought to be a good law, but the same kind of thinking compelled him as a responsible citizen not to pay the stupid fines for "illegal" parking where there was no traffic problem whatsoever. He wrote: "If I am fined for parking . . . I will not pay the fine." When Judge Maxwell read this letter, he commented to officers around him, and evidently to some reporters, "The hell he won't!" In his letter, Dobie had offered to "go to jail and lay the fine out," although he preferred, as his letter said, to "work it out." In short, he accepted the fact that he might be punished, but he wanted to protect the rights of the individual against indiscriminate rule making.

Somehow, Dobie's letter got to the press. Judge Maxwell himself called Dobie to express regret that the personal letter had been made public. Neither he nor Police Chief Thorp knew how the disclosure had happened. The general assumption was that some alert reporter had heard of it, and of the comment "The hell he won't," and had stolen the letter from the police chief's desk. Dobie appeared early in court the next morning, when his case was on the docket. He wanted to make certain that his stand was clear.

On arriving in court, he was handed a "pledge" in regard to good driving, which alleged traffic offenders were urged to sign. Dobie read it, but told reporters he would not sign it. It had one stipulation he thought silly, a pledge that upon turning the driver would always check in his rear-view mirror. "No," said Dobie. "I prefer to turn and look at what's behind me." He was militant, of course, and told Judge Maxwell and Chief Thorp, "I'm a man of my word, and when I said I won't pay that fine, that's exactly what I meant." The judge threw up his hands, shrugged, and turned him over to the marshal.

Perhaps beginning to feel a bit sheepish, Dobie would consent to being photographed in court only if reporters would promise to use as a caption this statement he composed on the spot: "I am a sight more concerned with not having any more of Coppini's monstrous statues, some of which now litter up the Texas landscape, placed as Centennial memorials than I am concerned over having to pay a fine for traffic violation and being committed to jail for overparking." Later on he was to consider his rebellion, in this case, to be as ludicrous as the rule he was protesting. But he took himself seriously as a crusader against bad statuary.

In the previous autumn, he had been asked to serve as a member of the Texas Centennial Commission, a legislature-established group to organize the state's celebration in 1936 of the hundredth anniversary of the Texas "War of Independence" from Mexico. Dobie served on a committee authorized to spend half a million dollars on highway markers. Two other members were his close friend (then) J. Evetts Haley, a historian at the University of Texas, and Lou Kemp, one of the acknowledged authorities on Texas history. Because a federal grant increased this initial fund by $200,000, something memorable for the state could be achieved. Conflict soon arose. Local patriots on the Centennial Commission were concerned more with local grants than with historical significance.

In his minority report, Dobie insisted that the purpose of the celebration was to exalt "heroes" rather than communities, and to recognize past history rather than current parochial vanity. Although most of the 254 Texas counties were unformed and unnamed and unpopulated at the time of the "War of Independence," they did not agree with him. Local vanity was buttressed by the desire to grab any kind of governmental handout. Dobie acknowledged in his report that a single heroic figure might very well symbolize some idea or deed, as in a statue of Justice or of the Goddess of Liberty. On the other hand, certain picturesque Texans lent themselves to sculptural representation, when some good men much respected by Texans did not.

He contrasted Thomas J. Rusk and Jim Bowie: Rusk was a "nobler man" than Bowie, even though Bowie died in the Alamo, and contributed far more to civilization in Texas than Bowie did. "Yet," Dobie wrote, "I have recommended $14,000 for a monument to Bowie and $8,000 for one to Rusk . . . because of the relative values for sculptural representation. We may esteem a man without finding him very interesting. Jim Bowie, riding alligators, wielding the Bowie knife, making love to Ursula de Veramendi, fighting Indians and looking for a fantastic lost mine at the same time, and then dying in the Alamo a death as brave as his whole life — this Bowie could be immensely interesting in bronze."

He refused to side with the committee members who wanted to restrict memorialization to those whose fame rested on laurels won in battle or politics. He wanted to honor those who had contributed to "the culture and the civilization of the state," such as a naturalist "whose name is attached to scores of wild flowers of Texas" and whose life work made Texans more interested in "nature around them," and to honor "a man worthy to be called the 'Father of Texas Literature,' " or a pioneer historian who strove to perpetuate the history made by others. Naturally, he wanted to memorialize those factors in nature that had shaped Texan ways of living, such as cattle and cotton.

But his principal concern, he stated, was not so much the subject matter chosen for celebration, whether Texas Rangers or vaqueros or frontier Indian fighters or episodes in the official history, but first and foremost "what effect our dedications will have upon those people who look upon them. . . . If you wish human beings, whether young or old, to regard history, then touch their imaginations. Literal catalogues of fact and literal statues will not kindle their interest."

To clinch his point, Dobie cited Ewing Cameron, a "hero" executed by the Mexicans for his part in the Texan raid across the Rio Grande on the town of Mier. Texas' southernmost county, with Brownsville as county seat, is named for him. "He was, it is true, as brave a man as ever stood against a 'dobe wall; in his fearlessness, his gay recklessness, his generosity, daring and energy he was altogether admirable. But a single statue of him standing up in the vacant air could never express a hundredth part of what

Ewing Cameron means. . . . He captained a company in the Mier Expedition — and it is the story of him *and* this strange and mad and glorious episode in Texas history that the monument should tell. There is nothing else like it in the history of North America." In his campaign to make Texans conscious of their unique heritage, and to live in harmony with it and with their landscape, Dobie protested the University of Texas' first skyscraper, a new main building that was virtually a slender twenty-seven-story tower, built in 1936.

Dobie stormed forth with the argument that the university owned two million acres of land (under which, out there in West Texas, lay enough oil to make the state university the second richest in the world) and owned half a section (320 acres) in the Austin area. Therefore it could reasonably take the high-rise tower, lay it on its side, surround it with a gallery, and have something both distinctive and truly Texan. For him, skyscrapers were not only unnatural but inhuman. When he carried his opposition so far as to refuse to move with the rest of the English staff into the new tower, maintaining his picturesque office in Old B Hall, he was accused of role playing. He replied that the new offices all "looked like steam lockers in a laundry"; certainly, his office paraphernalia of Western relics would have been as out of place there as the inscription on his door, written on the thighbone of a cow: "Office Hours: Irregular." Not to mention his longhorn skulls, deerhide rugs and rawhide chairs. He roared as loud at the landscaping of the campus by a Kansas City firm, but was grateful that a few unplanned mesquite trees came up anyway.

His sharpest wrath and ridicule he saved for a statue on the campus executed by an Italian sculptor then resident in Texas, Pompeo Coppini. This resulted in a long feud, with Coppini ultimately publishing a "vendetta" attack on Dobie, telling most Texans what they already knew, that Frank Dobie had a powerful thirst he loved to assuage with Jack Daniel's bourbon. Coppini's statue, still standing at the south entrance to the campus, stirred Dobie to scathing satire: "It is a conglomerate of a woman standing up, with hands and arms that look like the stalks of a Spanish dagger; of horses with wings on their feet, aimlessly ridden by sad figures of the male sex; and of various other inane paraphernalia.

What it symbolizes probably neither God nor Coppini knows."

Even more fierce was Dobie's verbal lashing of the sculpture commissioned from Coppini by the Texas Centennial Commission for a plaza in front of the Texas "Shrine of Liberty," the Alamo. Of this "cenotaph" Dobie wrote in one of his most famous Sunday columns that it looked like a "grain elevator," and that the androgynous figures supposedly representing the major Texas heroes could not be distinguished anatomically from the accompanying female figures supposedly symbolizing angels of mercy and justice. The cenotaph, too, still stands, to the dismay of all Texans either aware of the history of the state or gifted with good sense or good taste.

He knew what he did want, too. In 1939 he worked hard to secure for the university a planned sculpture of mustang ponies by A. Phimister Proctor. Proctor and his wife came down to Texas in March. Frank got them settled in Austin, then took the sculptor to study live mustangs in action at Tom East's ranch near Hebronville, a ranch that reminded Dobie very graphically of the countryside in which he grew up. He personally helped "cut out a bunch of mares for models," and told Bertha he felt sure the work would go forward. It could hardly fail; Proctor was both a remarkable man and a remarkable sculptor.

The statue was not unveiled until 1948, when Dobie took his friend Tom Lea, the artist, to see it. (Lea was the son of a contemporary of Dobie's, Tom Lea, Sr., who was mayor of El Paso and known there as Don Tomás.) "Tears filled Tom's eyes," Dobie wrote, "and his voice was choked — not only for the beautiful bronze but for the inscription chiseled into the granite pedestal. 'Frank, it's so beautiful,' he cried."

What Dobie demanded of painting and sculpture was fidelity rather than mere verisimilitude. He made the distinction lucidly in "A Summary Introduction to Frederic Remington," writing that "Remington toiled too furiously trying to satisfy the demand for naked action to linger and let things soak into him. He knew more than he understood. In this respect he is not the equal of Charles M. Russell, although he may have had some advantage in craftsmanship. I cannot say. As a reporter through eye and ear, through drawing, painting, and writing, Remington habitually got and gave the right words, but less frequently the right tune. Sometimes even his soldiers seem to me clever imitations of Kipling's." With characteristic generosity, Dobie concluded: "It is to be remembered that he understood the crouch of a panther, the howl of a coyote, and the gesture of the medicine man. If few secrets of the invisible passed into him, he translated the drama of the visible into an astounding variety of pictures that do not fade in interest or power."

"The facts of life," he observed in another connection, "are not life itself."

Of Russell, whom he considered a great artist, he wrote: "He not only knew this West [the Old West], he felt it. It moved him, motivated him, and gave him articulation, as a strong wind on some barren crag shapes all the trees that try to grow there." Comparing him with Tom Lea, whom Dobie admired enormously and who was to illustrate many of his books, Dobie wrote: "Tom Lea is at home in a cosmopolitan world of change, whereas Charlie Russell was at home only in a West that had ceased to exist by the time he arrived at artistic maturity. Tom Lea grapples intellectually with his world, is a thinker; Charlie Russell evaluated life out of instinctive predilections. Vitality, that 'one thing needful' to all creative work, shows constantly in the work of both."

Dobie wrote the above, a preface to a Russell portfolio, in 1950, when he had gained in perspective and felt himself very much a citizen of the world. In the thirties, though his self-conscious Texanism was never simple-minded, nor his ideas of regional art dogmatic, he had not come so far. His evangelical zeal for Southwestern "culture" burned in nearly every thought he had in public — or private. Typical is a paragraph from an introduction he wrote for Carl Hertzog's catalogue of the work of Tom Lea:

These pictures are the expression of a man who understands a vast land peculiar to itself, a land with a culture of its own that he burns to reveal and make the dwellers in that land understand as their own inheritance. The only art and literature worth an Indian fig that the Southwest will ever have will be an art and literature growing out of the Southwest's own rock and soil, burned on by its own suns, sifted by its own winds, given perspective by its own spaces, and humanized and dramatized in the personalities that have made up its own population — people who belong, like Tom Lea, to the land.

Dobie later disavowed this phase of incantatory rhetoric. It had a relevance for its time. In the late twenties and the thirties, there was an impressive artistic vitality, quickly discovered by the Eastern tastemakers, manifest in the Southwest. Santa Fe and Taos had been discovered by D. H. Lawrence in 1922; his enthusiasm brought in its wake Aldous Huxley and many other British intellectuals and artists. American immigrants to the region included such primary figures in painting as Georgia O'Keeffe, John Marin, and John Sloan. In writing, the high priestess and theorist of regionalism was Mary Austin, greatly appreciated by Carl Van Doren and other literary critics of the time. She loaned her house for a while to Willa Cather, who wrote *Death Comes for the Archbishop* there: a novel about the great French priest Joseph Lamy, who shaped Southwestern culture almost as significantly as the Spanish conquistadores, whose dominion he succeeded. Mary Austin, dynamic and brilliant, gathered around her a host of talented people — painters, writers, anthropologists, philosophers. True, most of these were not natives but expatriates from other regions, such as the poet Witter Bynner, a graduate of Harvard who brought to his home in Santa Fe his priceless collection of Chinese art and his cosmopolitan way of living. During World War I he had been notorious for his refusal to fight for a cause he did not believe in.

In 1929, one nationally respected journal of the arts had predicted that the next "renaissance" in American culture would occur in the Southwest. H. L. Mencken had declared earlier that the South was "the Sahara of the Bozart." The Southwest, of course, was beneath notice. But no longer, after D. H. Lawrence announced the importance to him of his experience of northern New Mexico and its unique landscape.

The region also benefited, in national political interest, because of its close ties with Mexico in its historical past. The Madero Revolution, which deposed Porfirio Díaz in 1910–1911, was almost identical in time with the Sun Yat-sen revolution in China, and its success stirred international attention to the possibility that the "indigenous" culture of Mexico might be restored. Until then, it had been dominated in one way or another by "imported" ideas and, economically, by foreign powers. "Indianism" became a battle cry, a *grito*.

National interest in the "indigenous" was dramatized in the one year 1930. Oliver La Farge, scion of a long-distinguished New England family and a student of anthropology in Mexico, won a Pulitzer Prize for his novel *Laughing Boy*, a tragedy of the mismating of Anglo and Indian ways in New Mexico, all the advantage in the author's eyes lying in the Indian way of life. Marquis James, born and raised in the Cherokee Strip, won the Pulitzer Prize in biography for *The Raven*, his life of Texas' most dramatic hero, Sam Houston. Katherine Anne Porter, reared near and in San Antonio, was acclaimed for *Flowering Judas*, her first volume of short stories. J. Frank Dobie's *Coronado's Children* was chosen by the new Literary Guild, at that time dedicated to the publication of new and original American talent. Stanley Vestal, Indian-reared and a Rhodes Scholar from the University of Oklahoma, was credited with enlarging the techniques and the aim of biography in his life of Sitting Bull.

The Southwest, in prompting such national interest, had suddenly become very self-conscious. When Dobie first proposed a course on the literature of the Southwest to the University of Texas English Department, he was told by several of the full professors that there was no such thing. He replied, "Well, there's plenty of life in the Southwest, so I'll just teach the life." By the time the course was first offered, in the spring term of 1930, he could muster considerable evidence that the Southwest did indeed have a literature as well. Aside from that, he was shocked by the fact that "some of the departments here have no more sympathy for the life of the Southwest than they have for life in Patagonia." He thought the Southwest was entitled to its sense of identity.

He was fighting, almost single-handedly in Texas, a battle familiar to historians living in the West, who steadily pointed out that colonization of the Southwest had preceded by far the Pilgrims' arrival at Plymouth Rock. These historians were not claiming equal importance in the shaping of the nation, they were just insisting, "Look, we too belong to the American destiny — and have belonged for a very long time." In its first seventy or so years, only two of the seventy or so presidents, elected for one-year terms each, of the American Historical Association have made their careers west of the Mississippi — and only one of these two was reared west of that dividing line. He, fittingly, was Walter Prescott Webb of the University of Texas, author of *The Great Plains* and *The Great Frontier*. Webb and Dobie were close friends, mutually helpful in each other's difficult winning of respect and prestige with their colleagues at the university.

He had begun to collect Western objects and artifacts; and in 1933 Victor Lieb gave him an old longhorn head and horns, bought in the Brush Country from a Mexican vaquero. Elated, Frank wrote Bertha that he had seen much longer horns than these, but the gift horns are "massive, shaggy, rough, gnarled, mighty, weathered by all the drouths and knocked against by all the thorny limbs that the Brush Country of Texas ever knew. . . . I doubt if you can realize how much they mean to me. I don't think I'd trade the head for the half dozen rarest Western and Texas books in the world that my library does not contain. I am glad the horns are not polished or mounted. I don't know where I can put them — certainly not downstairs — but I have them. Praise Allah."

Dobie's extreme championing of what he considered to be the "unlike" culture of the Southwest must be understood not only in terms of his personal struggle but also in the context of the interest in the region at the time. Small wonder that for a brief while he thought of himself as a public lecturer who was blending the showmanship of both Mark Twain and Will Rogers. No wonder many of his colleagues thought he was overplaying the part of "Cowboy Professor." No wonder he himself agreed with this judgment years later.

It was at the height of this period in his life, the time when, he later said, he was too much in love with "the pageant of the past," that he met Tom Lea. Tom Lea was emotionally rooted in the rock-hard, dusty, desertlike and beautiful sun-drenched country of the Rio Grande around El Paso as profoundly as Frank Dobie was in the Brush Country of his boyhood. Tom Lea felt that his home region was entitled to tell its story; he was recording it in paintings and drawings, and reaching out to augment the telling in words. The association of the two men, their collaboration, was immensely rewarding and enlarging to both.

Dobie knew that Lea should illustrate *Apache Gold and Yaqui Silver* (1939), just as he felt that Tom would be the ideal illustrator, or collaborator, on his next major book, *The Longhorns*. And his new publishers, Little, Brown and Company, agreed. His working program was the same as it had been in the past. He sought out isolation, going this time to a coastal ranch on Saint Joseph Island, near Corpus Christi Bay, belonging to Sid Richardson, the Fort Worth oilman and collector of Russell's paintings. The only access to the island was by barge; Frank stored his car in the mainland town of Rockport. He was six miles from a telephone. He worked at his book in the mornings, part of the afternoon and sometimes at night. He wrote Tom Lea: "I ride a bully horse about three hours every evening, seeing deer and turkeys and birds by the thousands, picking up bottles along the Gulf Shore and feeling something like a free man." He also felt like his favorite essayist, Hazlitt; he liked his own company.

In September he sent Tom Lea a letter of a dozen or so single-spaced, typewritten pages, praising with immense pleasure Tom's drawings for the book and correcting some details in the illustrations. Both praise and the stated criticisms were strong and straightforward, the criticism having nothing to do with the artist's execution but with inaccuracies of observation. This openness and directness set the tone for what was to be the strongest friendship Dobie had for the next two decades. In Tom Lea he no doubt found the son he might have had and trained, for Dobie was a born teacher, as his success steadily proved. Indeed, as usually happens in strong father-son relationships the pattern was not complete until the fledgling flew the nest to establish his own identity and independence.

In the artistic sense Tom Lea was a "fledgling" only as a writer; he was, when he and Frank Dobie met at Tom Lea Sr.'s law office in El Paso, already an "arrived" painter, with credentials from Santa Fe, the Art Institute of Chicago and study in Rome. He was in his early thirties, he shared Frank's vigorous gusto, and shared his feeling for the Southwest as a cultural (in the anthropological sense) entity. Theirs was a true meeting of both minds and temperaments, both fiery-tempered and exacting perfectionists, full of vivid enthusiasms and violent dislikes, both cheerful and optimistic, both somewhat bellicose when crossed, full of animal energy and human delight in the physical world of the rugged sunlit Southwest, where sky and space were unlimited, unfenced, free, natural, as — in their minds — life ought to be.

In the spring of 1939, when Dobie was working at Sid Richardson's island ranch on the longhorn history, he encountered a young artisan of a type very rare in Texas — or anywhere for that matter. Richardson had built a ranch house designed by O'Neil Ford, a young Texas architect with a touch of genius who had been trained mostly in Dallas, where he associated with "young intellectuals" on the *Southwest Review;* he later established his own architectural firm in San Antonio. His brother, Lynn Ford, was a craftsman in woodworking and carving, with a talent as big as his more flamboyant brother's. (At this writing, O'Neil Ford has recently been called by Wolf Eckhardt, architectural critic of the Washington *Post,* "probably the best architect now practicing in the nation.") Dobie wrote Bertha that the most interesting person on the island was Lynn Ford, whom he had engaged to stop off in Austin sometime to mount Frank's cow horns on some mesquite wood with rawhide. From then on, the Fords were important friends of the Dobies'. After studying the horns in the Amon Carter collection, Frank wrote to Lea:

The loveliness of the colors — shadings — in the horns came to me as never before. You will never again perhaps see the time when you can find as many Spanish cattle in the yards at El Paso as now — varieties in color, dew-lapped, stag horned, etc. Don't leave for Missouri until you have gone out there and drunk in memories that will keep as long as you live. The sun is going down on the old breed. You have a chance to see it set. Go to both stock yards, Gilroy's and the other. I wish to God I had had more time, much more time to watch the light on the horns — not very long there — the colors of hair — many little features. Something is always driving me on and on. If you have to delay getting off from El Paso 3 or 4 days, don't mind. You'll never see cattle in such quantities again. Study *dew-laps,* color formation. Your friend, Frank.

That summer, Frank went to Kansas City "to check on the record of Old Champion, who once belonged to my Uncle Jim and who seems to have had the champion spread of horns for all time." On his way home, he stopped in Bonham, Texas, to make the acquaintance of Erwin Smith, whose early-day photographs of range life constitute a remarkable record (Dobie later helped them into publication by the University of Texas Press).

When he got home, he found the August heat so intolerable he slept at night in the backyard on a bedroll, as he often did during heat waves. But he had enough energy to start a new enterprise, one that remained very dear to his heart: a weekly newspaper column, meant for syndication, to be called "My Texas." The Houston *Post* and the Dallas *News*, however, "sewed up the whole state on the series excepting El Paso." The first column appeared on the first Sunday of September 1939; he kept it going for a quarter of a century, even during long absences abroad. He at first wanted the column headed by a drawing of a longhorn, but then decided he didn't want to identify the column with either the longhorn or the Lone Star State only. He had more "philosophy" now, he wanted to roam afield. He told Tom Lea that *The Longhorns* would allow him his "final say" about the Brush Country. "I know more than when I wrote the *Vaquero* and have more philosophy, though less of something else I wish I had still."

It is possible that the German invasion of France had stirred him to think beyond regional concerns, to be discontented with his narrowness. That would be like him: just as he prized literature for what it told him about himself, anything he felt deeply he incorporated and thereby changed and grew. One of his principles about experience, and about his own rhetoric, he expressed thus: "All interesting things cohere." Or as he sometimes put it, "Everything is kin to everything else." He was basically a romantic relativist.

Though much distressed by the war, he felt good that autumn, for he expected to finish the longhorn manuscript by December 1, and much of what he had done gave him great pleasure. He was satisfied that one chapter "describes the Brush Country in a way to curl the whiskers," and "another is just as good." Curiously, he adds a strange sentence in this note to Tom Lea, dated November 11, 1939: "There will come a time again when I will hate them [these chapters] and have a contempt for this kind of writing, but I am feeling mighty well toward them these days."

Why the hate, why the contempt? Was it the fact that he, a veteran of World War I, was writing on Armistice Day and suddenly felt the limitations of writing that depended so much on regional context, that dealt only indirectly with universal man? Or was it a corrective modesty to soften his bragging? At any rate, we know that he rarely returned to read himself, never even felt the urge. Once a book was finished, he was drained of response to it, and was fairly indifferent to its critical reception. He made a point of stating that he very rarely read the reviews of his books, and when he did, he was almost invariably bored by the reading, finding in them nothing to interest him. This was not superciliousness or protective coloring, but a genuine comment on a kind of mental activity that left him blank. Nonetheless, he did a lot of reviewing himself.

His reward for finishing *The Longhorns* by the first of December was to be a deer hunt, after which he and Bertha would go to his family in Beeville for Christmas Day, and then to Bertha's family in Velasco. Luckily, he was not scheduled to teach the next semester, for the annual siege of Austin hay fever was more than he could face that season. He wrote Tom Lea, "I suffer the torture of ten damned souls wadded into one." Occasionally he lapsed into Spanish when writing Tom, whose command of this second language greatly surpassed Frank's in correctness if not fluency. On December 17, Frank resorted to Spanish to tell Tom he wasn't quite sure he would finish up the manuscript before Christmas (*"cositas y cositas entren como hormigas"*).

But by mid-March of 1940, the "things and things that kept crawling in like ants" had returned his doubt about the virtues of the longhorn manuscript. He wrote Tom that if all the chapters were as good as the Brush Country chapters, fine, but he realized that the others were not. He tried, he wrote, to ride two horses in the book: to be factual and to be interesting. He was well aware he hadn't always succeeded in his double intention. Cattlemen, he thought, would value the book, but the general public, he feared, might not like it at all. "I determined in the beginning to give the full story of the longhorns — the facts. I wanted the facts to be interesting. I doubt the general public will read the book." The editors at Little, Brown shared his doubts. They thought the book would be a commercial risk, and with the illustrations it would be an expensive book to produce. They proposed, and Frank agreed, that he accept a royalty of 8 percent on the first five thousand copies, instead of the usual 10 percent. Tom Lea accepted a fee of $600 for the illustrations.

Dobie's first book, *A Vaquero of the Brush Country*, was in a way a trial run for *The Longhorns*. But the emphasis in the first book was on the life of the cowboy; in *The Longhorns* Dobie has matured into a philosophic social historian. As the cattle were compelled to domestication, and eventually to being supplanted by more practical breeds, the free life of the oldtime range had to yield to fences, railroads and urbanization. But the new could not replace the myths of freedom and self-sufficiency and courage that were quite literally part of the historic truth about the Old West. *The Longhorns* is regarded by some critics as finer than the masterpiece of Dobie's maturity, *The Mustangs;* stylistically it is more crowded and cross-hatched. Dobie had not yet achieved the assured, easy rhythms of his most self-confident years. But to Texans, especially, it came as a revelation. Harry Ransom wrote him a typical, and characteristically sensitive, letter of appreciation: "The way you get from facts and reminiscences to deep truth is your best feat. I like the freedom that you leave your reader. I like the quick introductions to ideas that might have been labored. I like the noises you make in some passages, and the stillness in which you have written others. . . . I like the big impulses everywhere. . . . I understand the over-plus of meaning in the book. . . . It will outlast bound volumes, it will keep running through what you have said until the meaning goes out of Texas."

"*Cositas y cositas*" were indeed a plague. Much as he and Bertha both loved their two-story, white-frame home on Waller Creek, they found they were too accessible. Bertha's garden, a sort of living museum of Texas wild flowers and plants, was a constant lure to tourists. Her syndicated newspaper articles on gardening had given her a statewide audience; the garden was mostly on a long pie-shaped lot between the street and the creek and the house, its blooms and glory immediately visible to passersby, on foot or by car. Frank Dobie, of course, would never have agreed to fence it in. Dobie's Sunday newspaper column and his radio program and his books had given him a fame far beyond the campus. He was a symbol of the state, like cattle and oil rigs and cactus and the Alamo. The trouble was that although he raged at the inability to work in Austin, he delighted in these spontaneous visits. If his temper had been sour instead of sanguine, word would have spread that he was an old bear, and people would have left him alone. But the frontier tradition decreed that a man's first responsibility was to be neighborly and hospitable; Dobie honored the creed by the compulsion of loyalty and by the impulsion of temperament.

He was as generous with his time to students as to friends and visitors. The writer Maurine Block, who was in his class about then, says that "despite the critical eye with which he regarded his pupils, they flocked to join his classes. Like a frontier wagon master whose lore and expertise were unexcelled, as he guided his wagon train of students over his beloved Southwestern terrain, he instilled a memorable sense of place." He permitted no note taking, ranged over all sorts of terrain, and was famous for his pithy dicta: *Realism without spirit is literalism. Romance without realism is sentimentality.* "His discourses on the flora, fauna, literature or people of the Southwest" were "frequently interrupted with angry explosions on such matters as the folly of planting Chinese elms instead of mesquite trees and the choice and execution of statues on the campus," Maurine Block reported.

It must be remembered that Dobie was the first Texas-born member of the University of Texas English faculty to have been made a full professor: in 1933, after the great success of *Coronado's Children* had made him a national figure. Some of his Texan chauvinism was surely the natural response of the "prophet" too long without honor.

Another former student writes of Dobie's class in the forties, when the outbreak of a second world war in his lifetime had liberated him from the narrow regionalism he was ready to outgrow. This witness is Professor John Deschner of the Perkins Theological Seminary of Southern Methodist University:

My reminiscences of him are those of many of his students. They are modest in extent, but his influence was very large indeed. He was one of the great teachers I have had — along with Paul van Katwijk, Richard Niebuhr and Karl Barth.

He used to tell us that a civilized man was one who could look with understanding upon the world he lived in. Dobie opened my eyes to the Southwest, the world I grew up in, and helped me understand a bit why I loved it so much. But he taught me more than that.

The year I met him, 1942–43, my father was pastor of the First Methodist Church, Beeville, and when I went home I would see his aging mother at church and plenty of people who looked and talked like Dobie. So I knew he was real. One old ranch hand would shake Dad's hand after church and say: "Well, preacher, you're hangin' the fodder high, but we can smell it."

My first encounter with him was at long distance, but woke me up in a hurry. My first paper in his course, on the political campaign techniques of Davy Crockett, came back with an A on it from the grader, Frank Goodwyn. (What happened to him? His *Magic of Limping John* got the front page of the New York *Times* Book Review Section a few years later. They compared him with Mark Twain. I've not heard of him since.) But that thin-ink grade had been heavily penciled out and replaced with a D—. And the margins were full of the same pencil's question: "What do you mean?" "What do you mean?" I was lucky. Many got F's.

The results were salutary. I worked like a hound from then on. My term paper, on "Northers," more or less exhausted the reliable and the other kind of sources, and he liked it. He called me in and said we ought to publish the best term papers, and showed me some mimeographed copies with linoleum block covers, of "Lazy E 346" — I guess it was printed " LU 346" — of earlier years. The name came from the course number.

I got Jack Maguire, who is now secretary of the alumni association, and some others together and we organized the project. We chose and edited about a dozen papers and had illustrations drawn for them. We found a mimeographing shop to do the job. I told Dobie that ours would be three times bigger than last year's, that we would print three hundred copies and expected to break even, but that the print shop was asking for an advance. Before I could finish my explanation, he had his checkbook out and wrote me a personal check for fifty dollars. We put up booths out in front of the Union building and sold a good many, but by evening it was clear we weren't going to make it. Would Dobie autograph some copies so we could up the price to $1.50? He would and did: sixty copies. Next day we broke even. We paid him back. And he beamed.

My main memory is of his lectures. He'd say: "Today we'll talk about the mesquite tree." And we'd hear how you could stuff your hat with the leaves to keep cool, or chew them for a headache. Or rawhide: and we'd hear wondrous tales about its stretchability or its hardness when dry, or how Indians used it to bind and rack a spread-eagled victim, or how Charlie Goodnight threw a hide on the floor and told his guest, "Here, you take this. I'll rough it." Or we'd hear about bowie knives. Or prickly pear. Or herding songs. Or javelinas.

It wasn't just folklore either. His talk was a steady questioning of our insensitivity, and prodding us to open our eyes. It was above all a cultivation of our sense of vitality, but never a counsel of emotional abandon. He knew and respected the disciplines of good work: pointed them out in his stories, practiced them in how he told and wrote them, and demanded them of his students. His teaching was about the Southwest, but at heart it was liberal education of a very high order.

And it was not antiquarian. It pushed its way into the world we lived in. We were left with no illusions about who was for and who against the university. Or about the war and its issues, and his hunger to get in it. Or about his belated conversion to liberalism. Liberal education and the Southwestern past and the social, economic, political future all became one in this bountiful man, on whose tongue it achieved flavor and humor and sounded right.

He was accessible to us. His office was not only open to us, it was also cool, and the atmosphere could be inhaled. I once helped him hang an exhibit of Western prints in the main building. It took about an hour, and I improved the opportunity by getting him to talk most of the time. When we were through, he said: "Come on over and let's talk." So, over we went to B Hall, past that door-bone with its ominous inscription, and we talked. And I left with another inscribed volume. Several books he gave me at different times, usually inscribed by name. And I rather think mine was the typical experience of his interested students.

Maybe I could tell more, but let that represent what I could contribute: the reminiscence of a student during the prime years of that remarkable course on life and literature of the Southwest ("Not much literature," he said the first day, "but lots of life").

It was teaching about something, and done with high fidelity. It set strenuous academic standards. It was relevant to the times we were living through. It communicated the spirit of a wise and passionate human being. It was done with humor, not the least of the excellences. And at its center was a free, warm accessibility to students. Someone called him "the best professor that ever got on a horse." I don't know about the horse part, but I can vouch for the professor.

After finishing *The Longhorns,* Frank was torn several ways in regard to his next book. He wrote Ray Everitt, his editor at Little, Brown, that he would like to write next a long-projected book on the coyote, but he was also collecting material on "Bears and Bear Hunters" and he wanted soon or late to write a book on "Mustangs and Spanish Cow Horses," plus a work on the Old Trail Drivers. As he often said, he had "many more books" inside himself, including one on legendary tales of Texas. In the summer of 1940, he wrote Ray Everitt that "what keeps wanting to get out of me next is *Bears and Bear Hunters.*"

He began work on the archetypical hunter Ben Lilly in 1940, on trips to New Mexico and all the way up to Montana. In Roswell, New Mexico, he visited with the novelist Paul Horgan, whom he greatly admired. He worked his way on up to Denver, and after leaving that city, drove into a "leaf-storm," not a sandstorm, but a storm of millions of leaves blown by a strong east wind in the November weather. He longed, he wrote Bertha, to get out of the car and fly through space himself; above all else, he longed for Bertha's presence, to share the unusual and delectable experience with him. Later, from the Marcus Snyder Ranch, at Bighorn, Montana, he wrote her that in his research on Ben Lilly he had become as obsessed with the bear as Captain Ahab in *Moby Dick* had become with the whale. In modern jargon, Frank Dobie had a great capacity for empathy.

Snyder found him a fine interpreter, through whom Frank got some "wonderful bear stories" from the Crow Indians. He also got Cheyenne stories, and went on to the Blackfeet Reservation to collect still more. He worked two days in the "well-stored Montana Historical Library at Helena, where I learned a lot." On his way back, he drove out to Arizona "to see a bear man in Tucson and one in Phoenix" and then visited in El Paso with Tom and Sarah Lea. Bear material had not been his exclusive interest on the trip. Charlie Russell preempted some of his time. Frank went to Great Falls to see the great collection of Russell paintings belonging to Sid Willis of the famous Mint Saloon. He longed to buy three canvases of powerful appeal; he wired his bank in Austin for a loan so that he could buy them, and had them expressed from Great Falls. He wrote to Tom Lea that he himself couldn't afford to keep them, but "we'll get them in Texas and place them where eventually they will become public property." He had no doubt that Russell collectors Sid Richardson and Amon Carter of Fort Worth would want them. Richardson did in fact buy two.

After such labor in research, he who pretended to despise the primary virtue of the Ph.D. cult felt entitled to accept an invitation to a December deer hunt in La Salle County. "It is a waste of time to do anything else when I might be out in the pasture, down in the Brush Country, hunting deer. Before the week is over I am going to quit wasting my time." Thus he wrote Tom Lea, and left for the hunt the next day.

Once again the late winter desolated him with his annual bout of hay fever. The attack of December 1940–January 1941 was a monster, as he wrote Tom. It was the worst attack he had ever had, leaving him almost insane and utterly demoralized. He left Austin at the end of December, having delayed his departure because Bertha was suffering from her yearly battle with the flu. He went to Beeville, but was incapable of working. He moved on to the La Mota Ranch near Cotulla, owned by his friends Mr. and Mrs. Jim Bell, and adjoining Uncle Jim's old ranch. Seeking the solitude he needed for writing, he stayed at a little house two miles from the main ranch house, drawing his daily supply of water from the Nueces River, a hundred yards away. But he found himself still unable to write. Significantly, he wrote Tom: "If Bertha were well [he had talked with her by telephone from Cotulla], I might have some peace of mind."

There was another reason why he was distracted. He confessed to Tom that whenever he was in ranch country, he always wanted to ranch. "I am all ribbed up to borrow every dollar I can possibly raise and put the money into a bunch of cows on this ranch. I am seeing a loan company representative in San Antonio tomorrow, I can make a wad — for non-capitalistic people a wad — of money on the cows or loose [sic] everything I have. I feel like gambling." He did borrow the money, branding his new herd with the old D Dot: Ɒ.

He resumed teaching in February; he had an enrollment of 175 students in "Life and Literature of the Southwest." Between classes, which Bertha sometimes met for him, he worked very hard making "personal appearances" in Texas and Oklahoma for the promotion of *The Longhorns*. His good friend Holland McCombs, bureau chief of the Southwest office of Time Inc., managed a good story about the author and his book in *Time;* the book sold very well in the region, and quite respectably in the nation. Another bright note: Tom Lea got that spring a grant from the Rosenwald Foundation.

Bertha made a trip to the Mayo Clinic that autumn. She could not use her eyes for long without severe pain. The Austin doctors thought the cause lay "hidden in her system," and recommended the famous clinic as a last resource. The doctors there found, after tests, that there was nothing wrong with her eyes muscularly. They diagnosed the weakness as an aftermath of the severe attacks of influenza she had suffered in the preceding winter and spring. She felt so reassured on her return that Frank took off in November, only a fortnight before Pearl Harbor, for a hunting trip in the Davis Mountains of West Texas.

After Pearl Harbor, *Life* magazine commissioned Tom Lea to be a "war correspondent" for the publication, using painting instead of words in his reports. He was sent to the South Pacific. And after Pearl Harbor, the War Department commissioned Frank Dobie to make talks to the trainees at army camps in Texas. But Dobie was engaged in another war, a battle over academic freedom in the University of Texas. As the ringleader of the "liberals," Dobie was leading the fight against the demagogic governor W. Lee ("Pappy") O'Daniel, an overnight phenomenon in Texas politics and living proof of Barnum's famous dictum.

The so-called Rainey controversy at the university was already on the boil. In its first half-century, the university had grown steadily but unspectacularly, its air of pleasant tranquillity and competence stirred to storm by only two external events. One was the attempt, around 1917, by Governor Jim Ferguson to control the university as his own personal domain: a vain ambition that succeeded in unifying against him the faculty, the students and the regents. That time, the university escaped the danger of being a political football. The second was the discovery, on university-owned land in West Texas, of vast oil reserves. The oil boom, beginning in the twenties, had enormously enriched the university by the time Homer Rainey took over as president in 1939. Rainey inherited an institution conscious of its exciting future.

The university, however, had a constitutional weakness, in that its board of regents was appointed by the governor. O'Daniel had "inherited a decent set of regents, but when he got through with his two sets of appointees he had turned the board into a group whose only view of the university was negative." This quotation is from an essay by Joe B. Frantz, Walter Prescott Webb professor of history and former chairman of the History Department at the university. Writing in 1971, in the Austin *American*, Frantz provided an objective and temperate overview of the whole row, and I am much indebted to him in this account.

At President Rainey's first meeting with the new board of regents, he was handed a list of four professors who had to be fired. Rainey protested, pointing out that such "precipitate dismissal flew in the face of the tenure rules." He was told to get rid of the tenure rules.

Rainey's resistance startled the regents. He had all the credentials of that local ideal, "a good ol' boy." Born into poverty in Texas, he had pulled himself up by his bootstrings, had gone to a church college, was a four-letter man in sports, later played professional baseball for a while, became an ordained Baptist preacher and president of a Baptist college, and later had been head of the American Youth Council in Washington. But he was evangelical, and he thought many things in Texas needed change.

O'Daniel's appointed regents did not. They were (with a few exceptions) conservative men of wealth and power, haters of Roosevelt and the New Deal, fearful and resentful of intellectuals. They had decided, as Frantz puts it, "to suspend old rules, to make new rules of convenience, and in general to reorder life in the university so as to stifle outspoken liberalism and broad questioning." The university became the focal point of what was virtually a civil war in Texas.

In the thirties, Dobie had made sporadic forays against "the Establishment": as in his fulminations about centennial statuary, or his much-publicized day in jail for refusing to pay the one-dollar parking fines. He had changed his thinking about Roosevelt, probably influenced by his nonconformist friends Roy Bedichek, Walter Prescott Webb, Mody Boatright, Wilson Hudson, John Henry Faulk and others — all "liberals" (an awful word in Texas in those days). These friends, his closest companions, had helped to move his mind from an intense interest in the past on to a more profound concern about the injustices and cruelties of the present. "I don't live in the past of the open ranges — as I did before 1940," he was to write in 1948 to the editors of *Holiday*, then planning a three-issue survey of Texas.

A note he filed in one of his "Autobiographical" boxes reads: "About the time World War II arrived, I was, without being conscious of the fact, becoming my own contemporary. I simply could not see the Nazis bombing English civilization out of existence and go on sporting with Amaryllis in the shade. I simply could not watch the Fascist spirit asserting itself at home and go on tall-taling about Texas as if all were right with the world."

By the early forties, Dobie was widely regarded as a subversive, a traitor to Texas tradition and values. One of his Sunday columns, that of August 1, 1943, seems to have been a declaration of his independence from the past. It was also a siren alert of the alarming concentration of political power in the hands of the rich and their corporations. He wrote it as a warning that the regents were determined to dismiss Rainey, and that their manipulations were a threat to "all men whose outspoken political and economic beliefs are contrary to those that seem comfortable to reactionary millionaires and corporation lawyers." As he saw it, Texas history had reached a point where a fight had to be made to guarantee intellectual freedom and the life of the mind as inalienable human rights.

There is little doubt that the battle and its consequences set the intellectual life of the state back by about two decades, and it is quite reasonable to wonder whether it might not have had a different outcome had Dobie not been removed from the arena. He was due to leave for England in September 1943 to succeed the renowned Henry Steele Commager in the recently established professorship of American history at Cambridge University. "I think it a wonderful opportunity for him," Bertha had written his mother. "He no longer needs the prestige it will give, but the experience will be enlarging." He left Austin on his fifty-fifth birthday and, after various delays typical of wartime, arrived in England on October 5.

His experience there was one of the three or four most formative of his life.

5

A Certain Development

> There are no substitutes for nobility, beauty and wisdom. One of the chief impediments to amplitude and intellectual freedom is provincial inbreeding. . . . I'd like to make a book on Emancipators of the Human Mind — Emerson, Jefferson, Thoreau, Tom Paine, Voltaire, Arnold, Goethe. . . . When I reflect how few writings connected with the wide open spaces of the West and the Southwest are wide enough to enter into such a volume, I realize acutely how desirable is perspective to patriotism.
> — From a letter to Herbert West

His first lecture at Cambridge was scheduled for the middle of October. He lectured at Emmanuel College every Tuesday and Thursday at 5:15 P.M., on American history from 1774 to the present. Never in his life, he wrote Bertha, had he so dreaded making an appearance before a new class. But, "it did not take me long to lug in Sam Houston and then I felt more or less at ease." He was a success from the start, although he was boning up before each lesson, just barely staying ahead of his class assignments. And he had little time for preparation. "So many people ask me to tea and dinner — dinner mostly in the colleges — that I have to keep a calendar. I can never pay the calls back. And the groups that want me to talk are thicker than the invitations to tea."

Although he was prepared to accept the inconvenience of wartime restrictions, he was surprised at how much he missed meat at the otherwise ample meals. He was quite frankly unhappy at first, mainly because he missed the brimming Texas sunlight, but also because the damp and the chill so permeated his bones he felt he would never get warm. His thoughts turned homeward. He wrote Bertha to watch out for land deals; maybe she would find in his absence the ideal spot for them to build on. He loved their place on Waller Creek, so near the campus, but he also loved the Otherwhere, and he preferred an Otherwhere almost tropical in its heat to an Eden of wet and cold. In time, thanks to the good charcoal fires, his bones got warmed. In time, he was as happy in Cambridge as he had ever been anywhere, and a good deal happier than in most other places. But all that winter he felt poorly and was miserable from coughs and colds. "Only once a week or so do we get any fresh vegetables — a salad." He deplored the

British habit of boiling everything, "even fish," and adds in wonderment and dismay that they would even cook lettuce and watercress, the latter comment revealing likewise that he was no true gourmet.

London was a really powerful magnet for him. Many American acquaintances, involved in the war effort, passed through. He spent Christmas Day at Cambridge, but hurried on to London the day after, staying a week at Dartmouth House, the seat of the English-Speaking Union, "of which I am a member, with all rights and privileges." He had extremely enjoyable visits with the publisher Victor Weybright and fellow Texan Jim Dan Hill, who had earlier come to Cambridge for a visit, among others. Although the regular students at Cambridge left on December 16 for a six-week vacation, the RN and RAF students returned on January 4. Nonetheless, the Christmas interval gave him the feeling of "owning time instead of being owned by it," and he was delighted to be free of his engagement calendar. He grew homesick when an American woman he met at an embassy affair told him of her delight at finding in the English countryside a "barbed-wire fence." He was flooded with memories of home when she explained that the sight of the bob wire (as Texans call it) "allowed her to get a sense of space. It did not shut her in like the everlasting and continuous hedges that divide most of the land into plots." Dwelling on the fact that barbed wire lets you "see through," he added, "I wish I could analyze the effect that space has had on the American genius. However, I am much more interested in drawing several more breaths out of space than in analyzing it."

Letters from home, and especially from his mother, served as sharp contrast with his daily life. He heard that his new brother-in-law, T. Rucker Stanford, was buying heifers to breed to his Santa Gertrudis bulls; the news filled him with longing to have some cattle again of his own, and he wrote Bertha, "I guess if I were not tied down over here I'd have some more by now."

Bertha could not, under wartime restrictions in England, have considered going with him. But almost as soon as he left she came down with the flu, as she did almost annually. Before Frank's departure, she had been in good health all summer, and had made twenty-nine quarts of Frank's favorite summertime drink, his "parasite beverage," mustang grape juice. As she wrote to her mother-in-law, who as usual was spending the summer at her cottage near the Methodist Assembly Grounds at Kerrville, "by dint of swimming in Barton Springs and drinking quarts of mustang grape juice and eating cold watermelon, we survive" (the summer heat). But her autumn case of the flu was one of the worst in her life, second only to the attack she suffered in 1918-1919, the first time Frank had gone off to Europe, that time in the army, this time in some connection with the State Department and again during wartime. How psychologically conditioned was her vulnerability to the flu? She got it so often in her eighty-four years of living, and since she had been nearly given up as lost in a terrible sickness as a child, one must suppose that her physical strength, unlike her iron will, was extremely fragile; it was always threatened by her malady of anemia. And she well knew the pattern of Frank's "arrival and departure" style of existence, she was accustomed to the rhythm of his alternating strenuous action with solitude and repose, in which he gathered his inner forces. This basic duality she knew well; she was quite clairvoyant about her husband.

The bond between them, which stretched elastically because of Frank's alternating needs for society and solitude, was very strong indeed. To Frank, it seemed at times a yoke as well as a bond; he had to deal with alternations too, as Bertha swung from the need for intellectual lucidity and precision to one, equally compelling, for blurring sharp perceptions that collided with the conventions of the genteel tradition. Luckily, she realized this weakness in herself, though she defended it at times, if only to assert her own and equal right to be muleheaded or wrong.

But on the intellectual premises that meant the most to Frank, his dedication to enlightened use of freedom and to "progressive" thought, she was in entire agreement. Like him, she was a deist if not an agnostic. She quarreled with him over matters of taste — elegance of diction, for one thing — but their intellectual positions were largely identical. On recovering from her bout with the flu that spring of 1944, she took up the gauntlet in defense of beleagured President Homer Rainey of the University of Texas, as Frank did in articles and letters he sent back from abroad. In an action rather more characteristic of him than of her, she even fired off personal telegrams of "astonishment" to two of the most important newspapermen in Texas, both of whom she knew personally: the distinguished publisher of the Dallas *Morning News*, G. B. Dealey, and an old friend on the Houston *Post*, Lloyd Gregory. "The rank, malicious lies that are being told about Dr. Rainey amaze me," she informed them. She girded for the obviously forthcoming battle when the board of regents would drive Rainey out of office. Her health improved, and a real comfort came to her in September when her beloved nephew, Edgar Kincaid, "moved over after the opening of the fall term." Thereafter, this gifted, unusual young ornithologist (Frank wrote Bertha from England at the time that he thought Edgar had a touch of genius) was to be an integral part of the Dobie household on Waller Creek.

A movement back home of certain of his friends and admirers to "draft" Frank as a candidate for governor tempted him not at all. On first mentioning it, he told Bertha, "I'm not going to do it." For fear that his vanity, or his love of the unexpected, might carry him away, as it sometimes did, she wrote back strongly urging him to put a stop to the efforts at once. To make it stronger, she added that his mother was equally opposed to such a theatrical prospect. Mrs. Margaret Reading was identified in a San Antonio newspaper story about the draft as the spearhead of the movement, with headquarters in Austin. She told the reporter that cables urging Dobie to run were going to Cambridge at the rate of about ten a day, but so far no response from him at all. The newspaper article stated that "Dobie in his later years has turned to political pamphleteering," but gave no evidence of it. Actually, John Henry Faulk was master-minding the "draft Dobie" movement.

In the end, he too was sensible about it, and refused. No doubt he was tempted in a way. He had become a public figure in London, and he enjoyed the publicity and power of making radio broadcasts beamed at America. He went to hear Churchill speak at a meeting of Parliament; a good part of the meaning of his experience at the time presented itself in political terms. Though he deferred any active participation in politics, this first taste of the heady and tonic brew of political activity lingered in his mind.

The relentless pressure of social obligations, of making talks at American army installations, of receiving drop-in visits from young soldiers on leave in London, of being forever accessible, began to weigh on him that spring. In addition to teaching his scheduled classes, he undertook special writing assignments for army pamphlets, and faithfully delivered his Sunday columns, about which he felt a curious compulsion never to allow a single break. He cited to Bertha a favorite remark of Napoleon's: "Ask me for anything but time." He repeated that nobody could accuse him of "hoarding myself." He began one letter: "Dear Burbie: They are getting too many for me again — people." When not bone-weary, he enjoyed these encounters immensely and understood their impulsion. As he wrote Bertha, "Lots of these boys are lonesome and they want to see somebody from home — the last ten days they have made a stream." More practically, he wrote her of the dangers of postwar inflation, and as a hedge against it he told her to take the $4,000 worth of stock he owned in an Austin bank and buy land at Velasco with the money.

He was too busy to think very seriously about the "draft." He wanted to travel as much as possible, and made trips to Wales and to Scotland. Moreover, despite his yearning to get back to his native soil, he wanted even more to stay on longer in the excitement of wartime England, especially with the constant rumors circulating that the Allies would soon invade Normandy. Bertha was not surprised when he decided to remain beyond the Cambridge contract; his mother was, and wrote to wonder if he did intend to return to the university that autumn. When she learned that he planned to delay his return only until the first of September, she wrote him of her relief, and admonishing him as usual, pointedly observed that Bertha was a really wonderful wife to allow him to stay away from home so long. Mixing her genuine pride in his achievements with a constant concern for his departures from the conventional life she advocated and lived herself, she expressed her great pleasure in the fact that the Ministry of Information was organizing a farewell dinner in Frank's honor.

The year at Cambridge crystallized many points of view for Dobie, ideas that had invigorated and enlarged him in the past but that had never dominated his thought. As he once said, he realized — from the civilized perspective of Cambridge — that it was more important to his students in Texas to read about Socrates than about Sam Houston. He had always, however, known this in the back of his mind. Some things had to be overemphasized at certain moments just because they also had suffered from a false perspective, or even from total neglect. Wartime is a time of simplified choices, even in thought. Dobie's "divided self" adhered to a culture that stressed the universal, but it also remembered the immediacy of the local. By the end of his inspiriting stay abroad, he was yearning characteristically to get back to the Southwest in order to write a book on coyotes.

It was not the special, even local, nature of such a book that appealed to him most. His Cambridge stay matured his notions about his attachment to the metaphor of "the earth." The earth had a very long memory; and telling stories about this and the effect of earth's "remembering" on its human occupants and its animals was a way of expressing universal, not geographic, truth. He wrote to Bertha that in the many talks he made for the army at camps throughout England, he tried to talk sense "rather than to tell stories" — but he added, "I want to tell stories." He wanted to say to his youthful audience, "Let us sit upon the ground and tell sad stories of the death of kings," because, as he wrote Bertha, "there are only two parts of the earth that do not fade — the earth of nature and the earth of imagination. Waters on a stormy night will never become less fair; the horse of the Rider of Loma Escondida will not play out, even though he is not a Pegassus [sic]."

His respect for the imagination, as understood and celebrated by Blake and Coleridge, emphasized a growing distaste for its cousin, professional illusion. At Columbia as a graduate student, he claimed to have learned more, added more to himself, by going to the theater than by attending classroom lectures. But three decades later in London, he was surprised to discover how indifferent he had become to the stage. After seeing only two plays, he wrote Bertha: "I don't care whether I see any more or not. Many things are as fresh to me as they ever were, nature especially, but I have undoubtedly lost my zeal for plays."

Another "realization" he greatly valued from his stay in England concerned his long attachment to the writings of W. H. Hudson. At various stages in his life, Dobie professed his favorite writer to be Stevenson, then Conrad, then Hazlitt, and now Hudson. He wrote to Bertha at the end of his Cambridge lectureship that although he himself was not a naturalist, "Hudson comes nearer confirming in me the way I want to travel than any other writer I have ever found and I believe he teaches me more." He reported that he had now acquired all of Hudson's works and "they have cost me more money than I care to think about."

Also by the end of the term, he had decided to write a book on England; he was greatly pleased with an article on Cambridge he had written for the *Saturday Evening Post* on assignment. This decision meant, he told Bertha, that he would have to stay on for another month. The structure of the book was clear in his mind: the chronology would follow that of his Sunday articles: "letting the reader share in a certain development of the point of view."

That "certain development" was in part the vivid love Frank had developed for things English, a development of his youthtime enchantment with English poetry at Southwestern amplified by his intervening experience of life. A major privileged moment for him was his visit to Oxford — in July, after the Cambridge stint was finished — and his delight in the Shelley statue in University College. He went to see it twice, and wrote Bertha, "To me it is inexpressibly beautiful." After citing some lines from "Adonais" engraved on the monument, he says: "God knows that 'the world's slow stain' has marked me, but I thank Him for giving me capabilities that make the loveliness of Nature and of Poetry and of Art as lovely and as fresh to me as it ever was."

He spent all the time he could walking in the English countryside on its hills. The Oxford landscape seems to have bowled him over; he found it "easier to walk in the country in Oxford than in Cambridge," and adds of Oxford that he quite "fell in love" with the city.

He queried his old friend and editor, Ray Everitt, about the book project; Everitt sent a cable, "O.K. friend we'll publish." Frank thought he could finish the manuscript by the end of August, and filed an application for departure September 1, telling Bertha that if he had not completed the book by then he would finish it at home.

By August, he was longing for the Texas weather he had missed for a year. If he could just have "an hour of straight sunshine," he'd willingly accept the one-hundred-degree heat it would entail. He missed the sunlight most of all, and added that there was not enough money in the Bank of England to make him "spend another winter in these quarters."

His Texan bones needed drying out. His varicose veins were bothering him again, so much that he was denied the great pleasure he took in mere walking. He needed new shoes, and still wanted the kind he bought in Austin from "Doctor" Vosberg; he wrote Bertha to order him some at the shop there: "he knows my size and knows what I wear." This was an important detail. Frank had "pigeon feet," the toes turning sharply inward, and shoes were a problem. (Back home in Texas, however, he discovered he preferred British cobblers and for a time ordered shoes from England. He could never resist the charm of the Otherwhere.)

But hard as he worked, he discovered he could not finish the book as early as he thought. Mid-September found him still writing at Cambridge — and full of thoughts of home. He wrote Bertha that on his return he wanted at once to take her to New Mexico or Arizona "to breathe the mountain air." Early that summer of 1944, he had told her that many people felt the war would soon be over. Late that summer, since it wasn't over by a long shot, he was still finding it hard to get passage home. While waiting for word of sailing orders, he did several programs for the BBC, reviewed D. W. Brogan's *American People* for the Manchester *Guardian*, and attended dinners in London when he was summoned there to await sailing directions. He gave his portable typewriter to Brogan, whom he liked and admired.

He was finally able to leave in late October; on November 5 he wrote Bertha from Ray Everitt's home in Massachusetts. He had sailed on October 28, after midnight, on the *Queen Elizabeth*, and arrived at Boston on November 3, to go over the manuscript of the book on England with Everitt. The latter's large eight-acre property, thirty miles from Boston, seemed to Dobie an ideal place to work. "We've got to get a bigger house," he wrote Bertha. And he did enlarge their home on Waller Creek, mainly his study.

Once home, after a pollen-season vacation with Bertha in early 1945, Frank hurled himself at once into what he described to Tom Lea as "the university fight." What Dobie meant by this he explained in his letter: "It is nothing more than an attempt on the part of O'Daniel and Governor Stevenson appointees to the board of regents of the university to pitch out, batten down, wall out, starve, strangle and emasculate so that it can no longer breed [any] liberal thought, [any] play of mind on anything pertaining to economics in any way, and to do all this by any means."

He could not evade the limelight, even had he wanted to, which he surely did not. Through his books, his syndicated Sunday columns, his numerous public appearances, his teaching at the University of Texas, his radio programs, his now international eminence, he was for many "Mr. Texas." He had taught the citizenry more about its past, and the glories of that past, than any other man in the history of the state. Always a man with a mission (remember, he went into teaching because he thought that by teaching poetry to his students "they would fall in love more deliciously"), he now had, with the perspective gained in his European sojourn, to teach them the facts about their present.

He had been a public figure for a dozen or more years; he now cast himself in the role of a public conscience. Most contemporary Texans, but by no means all, would say, "Thank goodness." But in 1945, J. Frank Dobie, he who had been scored for worshipping the past, was now far out in the future, way ahead of his region. He was no longer Mr. Texas to many of his early admirers, no longer the darling of the "rugged individualists." Public stands he had taken on two burning problems new to Texas were the primary cause of this renunciation: Courageously in 1943, in his February 21 Sunday column, titled "Divided We Stand," he had defended the right of organized labor to strike, even in wartime, which automatically brought the charge that he had turned "red." And now, in 1945, again courageously — as one regent of the board of the university pointed out in defending him — he vigorously championed full voting rights for Negroes in Texas and their right to demand as good an education as the state provided whites. He received violent letters from former partisans (or so they called themselves) who could not stomach a speech at Fort Worth in which he said he would welcome qualified black students to the University of Texas. He was reviled in the state legislature; speaking engagements (on his experiences in England) were canceled; some letters told him he should have died right after the glory he gained from *Coronado's Children* and *Apache*

Gold and Yaqui Silver, a glory now betrayed since he had "become a public stench in patrician nostrils."

For him, the "university fight" had come to seem a battle against Fascist and Nazi theories of power and government. This was grossly oversimplified, perhaps, but it had a core of essential truth, in witness, the Texas Establishment's support soon after of Senator Joe McCarthy's ignoble bullyboy tactics, a national drama of which the local fight was an ugly foretaste.

He shared with Tom Lea a growing contempt for the "provincial outlook." He said, "I get belly tired of Texas bragging and nationalism fever. The truth is that I felt freer in England than I feel in this land of the free and home of the brave. What our people need is less satisfaction with themselves and more civilization that consists less of machinery. The time when I rated Custer's last stand painted on a wagon sheet as more important to the West than the *Blue Boy* is past. I still want to tell bear stories, but I think it is as important to know something about the Russian Bear as the California grizzly, and the Frogs of France are more important than the Frog of Calaveras County. This view has been growing on me for several years. The year in England made it inevitable. I may teach Life & Literature in the Southwest again — I don't know; if I do, I will teach it in a different way."

He was scheduled to resume teaching in the spring term in March, but he applied for a leave of absence, which was granted. In mid-June, as he wrote Tom Lea, he got a call from the War Department, inviting him to take a teaching post in the U.S. Army University being organized in England. He accepted, passed the physical examination, and agreed to a seven-month assignment. He explained to Tom Lea that no passport was available for Bertha during wartime, but he hoped she could come over next spring, "which is the right time to see England." His next letter to Lea was dated September 5, 1945, from Shrivenham, in Berkshire. He apologizes for not writing the long letter he intended to send before leaving but which he failed to write in the "busy-ness of departure." He confirms what he had stressed before leaving the States, that despite having lived so long imaginatively in the past he now finds in himself "a welcoming to change. . . . I cannot live without feeling, and most of my feeling is for the revolution I see coming."

He confesses that he is "scared" because "all those books about the past I stored my system with and was ready to pour out when the war came seem as remote to me now as the girls that I loved as a school boy and never told." He might warm the books over if he sequestered himself, but "they do not come and lure me in the night."

He found the Shrivenham experiment to be an army camp, not a university, but he greatly admired the young soldiers studying there. He discovered in himself a developing distaste for teaching; at least, as he wrote Tom Lea, he doubted he would ever go back to teaching again. As often as he could get away, he went up to London. But in that essential polarizing of opposite pulls in his personality, he meditated another escape: "I don't have to make a living. The only thing for me to do is get away from the political-economic battleground and live with the coyotes and bears."

He emphasizes, seeming to gainsay his correspondence of only six months earlier, that "the soil and the people of the soil are as dear to me as ever. . . . I think I'd like to be alone in the middle of London for a year and out of my inner consciousness write an autobiography — the first half of it a lullaby and a poem; the rest brimstone."

The work of the staff at Shrivenham was heavy. Dobie began the week at 9 A.M. on Monday, and worked every day of the week until 5 P.M. on Friday. He made himself readily available all the time to the students, whether enrolled in his classes or not. He taught courses in freshman composition, in the American essay, and in English poetry, with his usual great success. He was struck again, as he wrote Bertha, by the fact that English folk of the country were simple in the way of the Mexican *gente* of the country. As might have been expected, he was indignant at the amount of army red tape and "high-handedness" that prevailed at Shrivenham. He would travel on weekends and let off steam or forget his anger; he found Stratford a good cure.

He was always shrewd about money, and fancied himself a bit as a financial wizard had he really wanted to put his mind to it. Bertha wrote him of a check they had received from Rucker Stanford for their share of the farmland crops in the Rio Grande Valley, of $4,269.13. This seems indeed to have been for only one-third of their acreage under cultivation. Frank wrote back, "If you think General Electric a good purchase, buy 100 shares. Don't buy less." Bertha matched his financial acumen. When she died, ten years after his death, she was, by Texas standards, a rich woman.

He wrote her from Shrivenham that he was searching for the material and the theme of his next book. He would like to write another work on a civilized theme, like his *Texan in England*. He is wavering in regard to his long-projected book on the coyote. "Maybe," he tells her, "I can by imagination work back a gusto, but the coyote no longer cries to me in the night." As for his teaching career, he wrote Bertha on September 11, 1945, that he might not ever again teach at the university. "The prospect does not sadden me in the least. I am not resigning yet, however. I should force that board of regents to fire me and may do that when I get home." One must note, however, that all this was simply a preface to his insistence that all he wanted to do was to write his books. But he felt, as he said, an obligation to "help Rainey next summer" (Rainey, deposed, was going to run for the governorship of the state). He added, "Obligated not to Rainey but to society and to civilization. After that I am most emphatically through with causes."

Dobie's first wish on returning to England was to spend a week of vacation back at Cambridge, which he did in October, with great delight. He also went to Oxford in November to be "on a Brains Trust" program at Rhodes House with Gilbert Murray, Arthur Rowse and two other eminent professors. Meantime, he was invited to teach the following summer at the University of Minnesota. He wrote Bertha that he would accept "if I do not have to lecture too many hours and if the pay is good."

He took time out during this stay to write a long letter to a little Austin neighbor boy, Thomas, who regularly paid visits to Bertha "to cheer her up." And indeed she was quite cheered by the favorable prognosis on her eye trouble — the exercises she was scrupulously doing would correct the condition almost entirely. He still wanted a larger home, and wrote Bertha to go right ahead and buy one if she found what they were agreed on needing. Eating and drinking were on his mind when he wrote that he wanted to build a replica of the Stratford-on-Avon "William and Mary Bar" in their home, if ever they got to build one. The Shrivenham venture closed down in December, but he was scheduled to go on to another army university project in Germany, and would not be back in Austin until the spring of '46. He asked Bertha to hold a sum of $500 for a bronze he wanted to buy as a gift for Cambridge when he got back home: "I want to send something beautiful that represents the part of America that I represent — a Remington bronze or something like that."

He received his annual Christmas fruitcake that was Bertha's mother's specialty and wrote that he intended to save most of it to take with him to Paris, where he would spend the Christmas season. "From Paris, I will go to different camps in the Occupation zone. I don't intend to stay very long. . . . I would not feel easy, with this opportunity, unless I saw and heard with my own eyes and ears something of Germany." It was his last communication with "Dear Mother McKee"; she died two weeks after that Christmas Day.

Bertha was with her mother till the end came. She remembered, as she sat beside her mother's bed and heard the birds punctuating the silence of the quiet countryside, that Frank, as he once watched beside his mother's sickbed, had heard the jackdaws' incessant call, and had written a short poem about it.

Remembering led her to reflection and in this letter she recorded a deeply felt observation on their life together: "As I strained for my mother's breath to catch again, I found myself thinking of you at last without bitterness. You were not meant for marriage. Marriage, like a world organization, requires a certain surrender of sovereignty." They had been married thirty years.

Martha Dobie drove over from Beeville for the funeral, and some six weeks later, drove over again to take Bertha back to Beeville — to recuperate from an attack of the flu that had struck her after her mother's death. From Beeville, Bertha wrote Frank that he really liked Mrs. McKee for the same reason that she liked him: an eager attitude toward life. For once at least, her line of thought lacks the vigorous clarity typical of her, for she adds cryptically, "You stand without the gate because you do not care to lift the latch."

Frank did not get to stay long in Paris. New orders "billed him to Frankfurt," for which he left the day after Christmas. On

December 27, he reported to Intelligence and Education Division headquarters at Heehst, a suburb outside Frankfurt, having spent part of his last day in Paris writing and mailing back his Sunday column. His first lecture in Frankfurt was at a Red Cross Club that occupied what had been a big department store. "I think I ought to try to make men think, but they don't want to think." He suspected he would be sent on shortly to Vienna because, although there were many thousands of American soldiers in Frankfurt, a series of lectures on Germany that closed last week drew only "about 30 soldiers and 45 UNRRA people."

He had more success. On January 8 he was sent to Munich and made a talk that drew two hundred enlisted men; he was to operate out of Munich temporarily, making a talk a day. He wrote Bertha that he was appalled at the heavy drinking of the American soldiers and saddened by their lack of inner resources with which to counter the inevitable boredom afflicting armies of occupation.

On January 19, the army sent him on to Vienna, installing him in luxurious quarters at the Hotel Bristol; he made three talks in the city, then lectured at Salzburg and Linz. In Vienna, he went to the opera twice and heard one concert that gave him a Proust-like recall of his boyhood. The concert flooded him with memories of the ranch, of how he loved as a lad to hear an old vaquero named Rafael whistle melancholy Mexican songs — and especially the memory of one night when he got lost but found his way back when he heard Rafael. From Salzburg, he sent Bertha a "snow rose," one gathered "away up in the snow yesterday." It had been a magic day, one when he felt "free and happy up there, especially while I watched an eagle circle." He continued to have sharp recalls of home, as when the frequently served venison made him long to be "out on a ranch or in the Sierra Madre." He was ironic about his lectures, telling Bertha he saw one poster in an officers' Red Cross Club that advertised him as "World Famous After-Dinner Speaker . . . a Second Will Rogers." He commented: "The advertisers are afraid to announce me as a University Professor preaching 'The Necessity of Thinking'!"

Back in Munich two weeks later, he added a subtitle to his main talk, now announced as "The Necessity of Thinking, or, From Frontier Simplicity to Atomic Complexity." He noted to

Bertha, "I develop, unconsciously, the missionary spirit within myself every day." In fact, it had been present in him, in one form or another, since his childhood conditioning on the ranch, with his father's nightly readings aloud from the Bible and the strict Sunday observance of the Sabbath. He deplored the "hopelessness" of the Germans and the "purposelessness" of the Americans. "Yet the way to be hopeful is to be busy." He was in Nuremberg at the time of the war criminals' trial, and wrote his Sunday column about it. He went on to make five talks in Bremen, and thence to lecture in Copenhagen. To Bertha he wrote that when he got back to Frankfurt in April, he would ask for discharge in the hope of returning home around May 1.

He was eager to come home, as he wrote Bertha in an unusually gloomy letter from Denmark, dated April 1. "I feel I have done whatever bit of good I could do over here, and I'm through with seeing the country. I don't want to write a book about the scene. I have been utterly disillusioned by Russia — I think I have. I see no hope for a better world, except by long, long processes of communism into something else. I don't think anything can stop Russia if she is going to use just brute force. Conflict will bring more misery, and misery succumbs to communism. I'll just quit trying to save the world and write about my old friends the coyotes."

He had agreed to teach during the month of August 1946 at the University of Minnesota, and was already deploring the fact. "It may be the last time that I teach anywhere," he wrote to Tom Lea. After that, he was committed to helping out President Rainey's campaign for the governorship of Texas. And after that, he planned "to quit talking in public and do nothing but write."

He started on the coyote book that autumn, spending two weeks in Eagle Pass and its environs along the Rio Grande, "as fascinated as ever by the Brush Country and what it holds." Returning to Austin he was soon afflicted with his annual malady. He wrote Tom Lea a week before Christmas Day that "I am always in good health but would run across the world to get out of the cedars when they pollinate."

He noted that it had been five years since they had seen each other. He noted also that he hadn't been able to keep his resolve to quit talking in public. Just a few days earlier he had made a speech at a "mass meeting of several hundred university students and perhaps a thousand Negroes on the principle of equal educational opportunities for Negroes." He told Tom that "the injustice of it [barring Negroes from higher education] makes my blood boil sometimes."

He returned to work on the coyote book the first of the year, having to leave Austin "because of the damned cedar pollen," and going again to the cabin near Del Rio. A game warden lived across the road; Frank went into town every day to pick up his mail. Little, Brown was trying to persuade Lea to do the illustrations for the coyote volume, but Dobie advised him not to yield: "You have things inside yourself that have been ripening and that you want to get out." Lea was now writing as well as painting.

He interrupted his work in March to go to a UNESCO meeting in Philadelphia and on to a special Oxford-Cambridge dinner in Washington, to which Ray Everitt was also invited. He wrote the latter that he was "lugging along" his dress suit, "unworn for many years." At Cambridge during the war, he had been given the option of wearing or not wearing an academic gown at the nightly dinner at seven o'clock, the one meal of the day for which the dons assembled. Frank, of course, chose not to wear the gown. And his preference for evening clothes, in place of a dinner jacket or other formal wear, was always what became his trademark as well as Mark Twain's, a white linen suit. Somehow, Bertha almost never failed to find a red rose for the buttonhole, acceding in all matters large and small to Frank's wish to be "original and independent." Well, at least independent.

In May, his working retreat was another favorite, a cottage near Kerrville in the Hill Country about eighty miles west of Austin in the region most Texans love above all other native areas: an up-and-down region of long vistas and of brilliant but softened, even powdery, sunlight on most days, of limestone rocks and facings along clear-flowing and often beautiful streams. Its German-transplanted natives fill the air with baking aromas and, of course, the smell of free-flowing Texas beer — mostly from San Antonio, for a long time the only "hedonistic" center in the state, except maybe the harbor and port city of Galveston.

The news from Little, Brown that *The Longhorns* and *Apache*

Gold and Yaqui Silver were "going back into their original editions" made his "heart rejoice." And he was still hoping that Little, Brown would republish his *Tongues of the Monte* under their imprint, not merely because it was perhaps his favorite book among his writings, but, exception allowed for *A Texan in England*, it was "in some ways the most literary book I have written." He realizes that his "field" has been Western Americana, but also realizes that "I write more in the English tradition, which is the literary tradition, than I do in the American tradition. I know that."

In April of 1947, Dobie applied, through the Budget Council of the English Department, for a leave of absence for the fall term. As he was to write later, in a "public statement" on the row that followed: "I was aware of a rule passed some months back by the Board of Regents against extending leaves of absence except for special reasons. I gave as my reasons two: 1) I wanted to write. This is not an unusual circumstance with me. I have for more than a year been in the process of writing a book that combines natural history and folklore and that has entailed research in many fields. I am determined to finish this book and cannot concentrate on writing while teaching. 2) My main reason, however, is unusual. As I said in my letter requesting leave, along in December I always take hay fever from cedar pollen here in Austin. The hay fever season continues intensely into February. If I stay here I am simply devastated. All the membranes in my head become so raw and irritated that I cannot sleep or think or do any kind of work; then for weeks after the cedar pollen has ceased to fly from the trees, I still suffer. Severe hay fever, like habitual drunkenness, is funny only to people not connected with the curse."

The Budget Council recommended the leave Dobie had applied for, and passed the recommendation on through proper channels to the dean of arts and sciences, who likewise recommended it. Dobie continues his statement to say that "under date of June 26, the President of the University [Painter] transmitted to the Dean, to be transmitted to me through the Budget Council, a letter disapproving the application."

It will be remembered that President Homer Rainey had been fired from the university presidency in 1944. As Joe B. Frantz suggests, the regents and the men of wealth and power whose interests they represented had come to feel that Rainey and the faculty, which "sanctioned and even advocated change and tinkering, was subverting the Texas dream." Rainey was a competitive and combative sort, and for five years weathered the storm; but he may have had a martyr complex. At any rate, he had as much as asked to be fired when he called a public meeting to bring sixteen charges against the regents before the faculty and the students.

At the outset, all the major papers of the state, with one exception, had been Rainey partisans. And even in a center of oil wealth, the Wichita Falls *Daily Times* criticized the regents when finally Rainey was fired, saying, "This much seems clear, that the regents have not caught the vision which actuates Dr. Rainey." But when Rainey then carried his fight into a race for the governorship, his support rapidly fell away. He lost the gubernatorial election to ultra-conservative Beauford Jester.

Inevitably, the university had become a symbol of change. By 1950 it would be the second most richly endowed university in the world (second only to Harvard), with a remarkable library and facilities that attracted all sorts of "eggheads" and other "dangerous elements" to Austin. Yet the regents who governed it gave openhanded and notorious support to the political tactics now identified with McCarthyism.

Socially, Texas had evolved, almost too swiftly to be perceived, from an overwhelmingly rural and agrarian state with a corresponding ethos to an increasingly urbanized society, with half its population, which had also grown by leaps and bounds, living in its four biggest cities — Houston, Dallas, Fort Worth and San Antonio. These urban centers were likewise greatly changed by the removal to the state of heavy and light industry from the Atlantic seaboard, a change that made "labor" a power in a region where it had hardly existed as a political and economic entity before. Texas chauvinism, which Dobie had begun to deplore by 1940, had been not moderated but encouraged by the war decade. Texas was heady with power, and did not let the nation forget that Texas boys had practically won the war single-handed — with the help of that other determining factor, Texas high-octane gasoline and Texas oil. Texans like John Nance Garner, Sam Rayburn, Jesse Jones and the young Lyndon B. Johnson had gained great influence in Washington. The state had achieved a kind of surface identity, manifest in its braggadocio: it was, the natives liked to say, "a world in itself," an "empire."

The old problem of academic freedom, of the right to free inquiry, had arisen to plague the University of Texas campus at the worst possible moment. The faculty had been weakened by several resignations of outstanding members in the wake of Rainey's dismissal (particularly, Dobie felt, that of Henry Nash Smith, author of *Virgin Land: The American Dream in Myth and Symbol*, who went to Minnesota). When Dobie innocently asked for his leave of absence, his reasons were personal; but, in retrospect, it looks as though President Theophilus Shickel Painter may have found the request a golden opportunity to pacify his reactionary regents by swatting their gadfly and bête noire.

President Painter had a point. He laid stress on the fact that Dobie had been away from the university for four years. But as Dobie stated, two of those four years had been in the context of the "war effort": the year at Cambridge, "facilitated by and connected with" the State Department, and the following year with the Information and Education Division of the army "to teach in the GI university at Shrivenham and then to lecture to troops" in Germany and Austria. "In fact," Dobie says, "I was on leave most of 1943–1946 as a part of the war business." His absence for 1946–1947, the last of the four years cited by Painter, was "personal, for research and writing."

Dobie got the letter disapproving his request, through the intricate route of official channels, about the first of July, just as he was leaving on a lecture tour. He went to the chairman of the Budget Council, explained that he would be away about six weeks and repeated that he was not going to teach that fall.

He had not, in fact, taught in the autumn semester more than once in the past dozen or so years. His legendary course, "Life and Literature in the Southwest," probably the most popular course in the curriculum, was long established as a standard one-semester course, given in the spring semester.

For Dobie, his behavior in the matter was consistent with his past performance at the university, and was both logical and reasonable. On returning from his lecture tour about the middle of August, he went to pay a personal call on President Painter in the latter's office. In his "Statement," Dobie said that he found

President Painter "agreeable and courteous." "I told him I did not want to resign from the university and did not want to be fired, also that I was not going to teach this fall." He explained the convention of his springtime-only teaching over the past twelve years. Upon leaving the president, Dobie understood that his application for the leave of absence would be given further consideration.

But in September, the chairman of the Budget Council, Professor L. L. Click, told Dobie that the president and vice-president "had talked [his] case over and had decided not to extend the leave of absence." Again, Dobie told Click that he was not going to teach in the autumn semester. Click assembled the Budget Council for yet another meeting; again, the council recommended to President Painter an extension of Dobie's leave of absence. The next word for Dobie about the matter did not come through the official circuitry. On the morning of September 19, he read in his newspaper that President Painter had announced to the press that Dobie's application for leave of absence had been refused.

For the general public, Dobie was easily the best known, the most famous name, nationally and in the Southwest, connected with the university. As his closest friend, Roy Bedichek, said about him years later in summing up Dobie's character, his main flaw was overoptimism. Not vanity, or even pride, but a steady and constant cheerfulness seems to have misled him in this case. He was quite obviously caught by surprise at the outcome. Another good friend, Walter Prescott Webb, thought that Dobie had badly miscalculated the mood of the board of regents. Webb felt it was a mistake in judgment on both sides and worked to heal over the rupture. But this was not to be.

For Dobie, the line of decision seemed clear. The regents' adherence to their newly improvised rule of granting no leaves "except in special cases" proved to him that they esteemed "a technicality above a man" or else that they made the rule "to trap a man." If the first, he wrote in his public "Statement," they proved their smallness; if the second, their hypocrisy.

In two pages of notes on the Rainey controversy, filed away under the heading "Autobiography — University of Texas," Dobie wrote that when he first came to the university in 1914, "it had the simplicity of Southwestern." It changed character

He was, in fact, a Man for No Systems, an existentialist in embryo.

When Painter, the regents-appointed president who stayed on in office after promising the faculty he would serve only till the crisis had been adjudicated, finally resigned in the spring of 1952, Dobie wrote across a clipping from the student paper announcing the news, "A little man, a climber. He was forced to resign." On a clipping from the Austin *Statesman* he wrote of Painter, "His mission was to draw salary and act as waterboy for the regents."

In an article published in the Texas *Spectator*, October 13, 1947, Walter Prescott Webb recalled that in thirty years of service, Dobie had three times tried "separating himself" from the university, "but found so little satisfaction in having his body in one place and his heart in another that he always returned." The first was when he enlisted in World War I, submitting to a surgical operation to qualify for service. The second was his decision in 1920 to quit teaching in order to manage Uncle Jim Dobie's ranch, "but the bawling of white-faced calves could never quite drown out the call of freshmen and sophomores for an original teacher." The third was his exile to Oklahoma in 1923-1925, where he was instructing the Sooners when his first great contribution to the lore of Texas was published, *The Legends of Texas*. "By this time Dobie had matured his vision of a service which he could render to the culture of the state, and through the influence of a few farsighted men on the campus . . . he was brought back and given a freer hand than he had enjoyed previously."

From these three "arrivals and departures," so central in Dobie's equilibrizing his opposing impulses, Webb concludes: "Dobie is by nature a maverick, and has always been so. By maverick I mean that he wears no man's brand. He runs free and easy with whatever crowd takes his fancy, or if the crowd gets too big or in any way objectionable Dobie separates himself and 'runs in a herd by himself.' "

Webb asserts that it is this characteristic of Dobie's — his insistence on going his own way — that brought on the impasse with the regents. The regents, according to Webb, for a long time "took no notice of the bellowing and dust-throwing of their prize bull calf in the academic corral. They wanted him to be happy, when the discovery of oil on state lands allowed vast expansion. Dobie noted that this boon was accompanied by the increasing power in the life of the state of oilmen, whose business was naturally related to government in the matter of tax liability on great profits and government regulation of a natural federal resource.

In the politician W. Lee ("Pappy") O'Daniel, according to Dobie, the ruling class in Texas found their ideal weapon, statewide, for diminishing the effects of Roosevelt's New Deal reforms. Noted Dobie: "Pappy O'Daniel was somewhat like the Civil War — a rich man's war and a poor man's fight. He made himself the solace of the indigent and the ideal of the religiously ignorant; the rich made him a utensil, mainly to cut Roosevelt's throat. He began the process of stacking the board of regents of the university with the rich and the reactionary regardless of intellectual qualifications. The process has been continued by all subsequent governors. A regent who comprehended enlightened intellect or had even forgotten Emerson's 'The American Scholar' would now be as odd as a hen's tooth."

Dobie was exaggerating, and ignoring the minority element on the board, one of whom Dobie admired immensely and who has long been one of the most civilized minds and human beings in the nation, Major J. R. Parten. And with the advent of Harry Ransom as president-chancellor, the minority was not so small as in the Rainey days and their immediate aftermath. However unfair in that particular, Dobie was quite right, in a general sense, in writing that "ambitious smallness always distrusts largeness." Dobie concludes his notes about this in abbreviated form: "I don't know as they are any more distrustful of vitality than academicians themselves/Eng. Dept. professors never look for active intellects, only for scholarly records. The dullest of wits can add up footnotes as endlessly as an adding machine can add up figures . . . Dr. Callaway."

Frank did not merely feel that the majority of the regents had no idea of what a real university should be, but that they had no idea whatever of what the Southwest heritage really meant. What the Western inheritance meant for him was freedom from coercion. This freedom was the source of his later political liberalism — not adherence to Marxism or any "system," but a profound dedication to free expression, to the spirit of free inquiry.

and he was never known to be at peace with himself except when inveighing against something."

Webb thought that Dobie "walked with stubborn unconcern into a trap, that is, into a rule which on the whole was a good one. . . . Mr. Dobie should not have walked into it. The university is overrun with students and all good teachers are needed badly to handle them." So, to Webb's logical mind, Dobie's refusal to return to work from his leaves of absence forced the administration also into a trap. "Could it enforce a rule against every other faculty member and leave Mr. Dobie running free on the open range? There was only one answer to that question. The answer was no."

Now, said the reasonable Webb, "how can Mr. Dobie and the administration get out of the trap into which they fell together?" Webb argued that both sides could make concessions: "The administration can be generous and Mr. Dobie can be considerate." Dobie did not want to teach full time, so Webb contended that "in view of his larger contribution, he should not be required to teach full time." Let him teach his "famous course" on life and literature in the Southwest in the spring semester, for "there is no rule to prevent the employment of Mr. Dobie on terms agreed to by him and the administration." Webb stated unequivocally that Dobie's permanent separation from the university would be a loss to everybody, and that "Texas will lose most of all. . . . Surely a great university can be tolerant of personal idiosyncrasies of its great men." For Webb, only the reengagement of Dobie on such grounds could heal the wounds of a bitter conflict that might have been avoided. His sensible plea fell on deaf ears.

Francis Edward Abernethy later compared the impact of Dobie's teaching on Texans' consciousness to that of a vaquero riding into town: Dobie "looked up and down the lazy street and decided to whoop us into consciousness of what we had and what we have, and of the tremendous life and vitality of the things of which we are all a part." He was the only Texas writer generally and widely known to Texans. Some of the regents were taken by surprise at the public outcry after his dismissal, perhaps because they were more accustomed to dealing with the molders of public opinion than with spontaneous public opinion itself.

Despite many appeals, including an eloquent one from George

Sessions Perry, who wrote of his disbelief on hearing, after a long absence, that the university "has finally turned its back on great, lovable, intractable Frank Dobie, who for so long a time has been the state's and the university's ambassador to the world," the regents stood firm. Finally, a decade or so later, when Harry Huntt Ransom came to the presidency, he broached the prospect of return to Dobie at an informal encounter. Dobie declined to consider it, and asked his friend never, never to bring up the subject again.

Webb himself, one of the university's internationally recognized "glories," was prevented from getting the university's highest faculty accolade, the title of Distinguished Professor, for several more years by the opposition of a single powerful and hostile regent. Having lost Dobie and many other eminent faculty members, who resigned, the university entered on an officially announced "era of tranquillity." Luckily, a man of wisdom and integrity, James P. Hart of Austin, was appointed chancellor; his courage and moral strength started the university back on the upgrade, a comeback remarkably fulfilled under the administration of President, later Chancellor, Ransom. But the outcome of the Dobie firing was to affect the moral and cultural atmosphere of Texas for some time to come, in the direction of "toughness" and opportunism.

II

Whatever depression the University of Texas rupture caused Dobie, it did not survive his imperious urge to be on the move. He and Bertha promptly made what he described to Tom Lea as "one of the best trips ever," six weeks in the Rocky Mountains for research on the Ben Lilly book and also on a long essay about Charlie Russell, for which he interviewed around thirty people. This, he said, required him to "crisscross Montana." They could not stop at El Paso on their return to Texas because Frank had to meet an editor of *Holiday* in Austin to discuss a 15,000-word article on the state. Later he went to Chicago to conduct further research in the Ayer Collection and took time out to make talks in Tennessee and Mississippi. He could not turn down, he said, the "good money" offered him for talks. Following his dismissal from the university, his bruised ego needed solace, moreover, and the surefire magic he could often generate for a responsive audience must have been a comfort. He went on his annual hunt, this time to the Johnnie Barnes Ranch in San Saba County, and then on to the border to camp out near Eagle Pass "alone among the coyotes."

After Christmas, he went again to Fort Davis to work on the coyote manuscript, which he thought was the most original book he had done, indeed "the most original work in the realm of natural history that America has produced." Angus Cameron was now serving as his editor, a most able replacement for the late Ray Everitt. He and Frank conferred on the book that spring in Boston, Frank having gone to New York to talk with the editors at *Holiday* and to make a number of talks en route at various universities. In Boston, he got "fine word" about Tom Lea's novel *The Brave Bulls*, which Tom had submitted to Little, Brown.

By Frank's sixtieth birthday, September 26, 1948, the Ben Lilly manuscript was already in the Little, Brown office in Boston. "The next big job is the Mustangs." But, he told Tom, "I'd rather put it off and dawdle somewhere in a 'wise passiveness.' "

In October 1948, Ella Byler Dobie died at the age of eighty-seven. Frank wrote friends that his mother's death was "the most shaking" event in his life up to that time. He had gone to Beeville to pay her what they both knew would be a last visit before he and Bertha left on a trip to California. When the telegram came about her death, Frank called Bertha from the Huntington Library to be ready to leave "in twenty minutes." A fellow scholar at the Huntington, Wallace Stegner, volunteered to drive them to the airport.

Ella Byler Dobie, as her children have testified, was indeed a remarkable woman. Frank Dobie's tribute to her in *Some Part of Myself* may well be the most deeply felt pages he ever wrote. The flavor of her personality comes through sharply in her long correspondence with him, an exchange that lasted from his college days until her death. It was apparently not in the nature of Frank's father to be a patriarch; inevitably then, his strong-willed and capable wife became a matriarch. But she was not, as that word might imply, at all despotic. Her letters show her to have been eminently sensible and "human." Frank Dobie thought her life as a rancher's wife had been very limiting for her; he said she hungered for a fuller existence than range living could offer. But he did not think her unhappy. Most of her correspondence with him took place after her husband had leased the ranch because of his increasing illness and had moved the family "into town," in 1906.

Frank might very well have paid her the compliment she paid him in a letter of 1927: "Your utter reliability is a great comfort to me." Both were characterized by a profound sense of responsibility. To the end of her life, she was, unlike Frank, a true believer. In her late years, she grew hard of hearing, and invested $168 in a new kind of hearing aid, for her life had become miserable since she was unable to hear the sermons at the church services. She was not content just to hear the hymns, the music; her mind craved lessons. A typical sentence of her letter to Frank: "Our pastor has given us a fine series of sermons [at Easter Revival] on the last night's discourse of Jesus, basing his remarks on John's gospel 14–17 chapters inclusive." Frank faithfully wrote to his mother every Sunday during much of his life, but it was only in the early years of manhood that he spoke of going to church that morning. He wondered aloud, in letter after letter to Bertha, and to others, how his mother and the women of his tribe could "stand" all the various and frequent churchly "affairs" on their schedules. His mother, saddened by his falling away but trying not to make too much of it, occasionally rebuked him for his indifference to his early training. But this was perhaps "automatic maternity" as much as deep concern, just as she warned him, when he went to Cambridge, to keep his fingernails clean — "you tend to be careless about things like that." He was fifty-five years old when he got this reminder.

She had a deep feeling for a closely knit family, and after the children had grown up and moved away, was forever trying to arrange family reunions, a little tough since the Dobie clan were mighty travelers: Elrich spent years in Sumatra as an oil driller, Fannie went to Africa and to Siberia, Henry lived in California, and Lee was based in Chicago as an early pilot in commercial aviation. Only Martha stayed at home. She shared the usual fate of youngest daughters in those days — to be the family spinster destined to take care of her parents in their decline.

Frank sometimes rebelled against the notion of so much family unity, and could take a quite detached tone about his brothers, first for failing to make the grades in college he felt they should, and then for not being the "great" men he felt they could be. But just as often he was cheering them on enthusiastically, delighted to share in their successes. Elrich was the one in the family from whom the most was expected, more so than of firstborn Frank. Elrich was as much a "character" as Frank, and a good deal more of an active vagabond during parts of his life, the sort of man who could, whenever he wanted, charm the birds out of the trees. He inspired love in all his family — and to the end steadily surprised them.

The gentle and lovable sister Fannie, whom Frank adored, could, like the others, be independent. She volunteered as a nurse in World War I; all the Dobie children except Martha, who was too young, volunteered in World War I. Fannie later used her nursing knowledge to secure a long ocean cruise and a visit to Africa, taking care of a wealthy and aged invalid. When she decided in 1926 to leave Texas for good and live in New York, Mother Dobie was genuinely distressed. One purpose of Bertha's visit to Manhattan in the summer of 1927 was to try to bring Fannie back home. It was not like Bertha to adopt another woman's goals as her own, but she and her mother-in-law got along splendidly. Both women had "green thumbs," were born gardeners, both loved the outdoors. When Frank and Bertha bought their final residence, on Waller Creek, in the autumn of 1926, her advice to them was to be sure to plant pecan trees: the pecan was a tree both beautiful and practical. On her first visit, she said, she would bring Bertha two rosebushes for the new yard, "one dark rich red, very fragrant, the other a delicate, soft pink, very profuse bloomer." In writing Frank, she often alluded to Bertha as "that splendid wife of yours." She obviously loved and esteemed Bertha very highly, both as a wife to her son and as an individual.

Devotion to "gentility," or the particularly "ladylike," was more in Bertha's temperament than in Ella's. She valued, as her son did, independence and originality. Like so many intelligent and life-enhancing women, she had a very canny sense of business and commerce, and enjoyed using it. She was not frugal, what natives in Texas call "savings," so much as she was enterprising.

As early as 1928 she wanted to sell the remaining 3,919 acres of the family ranch, but changed her mind as the oil boom in Texas neared her land. A number of agents began consulting her about leasing the ranch for exploration, but at first their propositions were too vague to suit her. She was businesslike, perhaps to their surprise, but not to Frank's. She wrote him (he was working very hard then to finish *Coronado's Children*) that *if* she got the oil lease as she wanted it, she would be glad to lend him "one or two thousand dollars at 7% interest," for as many years as he liked, adding that she preferred the interest to be paid semiannually. When she got her first lease payment of $2,000 in December of 1928, she again offered to lend Frank "that thousand dollars." He quickly borrowed $800 from her; she loaned $1,000 to Lee, who had lost money in the 1929 stock market crash.

Frank remained pretty steadily in debt to her, but was careful to make his interest payments on time. Despite the Depression, he felt sure of his career. He was a very popular teacher, and he was a proven success as a writer. She probably valued more than did Frank his elevation to a full professorship in 1933. She continued to share her oil-lease money with her children. As Frank was leaving for Mexico in August 1934 from El Paso, she sent a wire telling him, "Closed oil lease $10 per acre one thousand is yours." She gave each of her five other children the same amount. In 1941, she gave each of the children several thousand dollars, and wrote Frank that she had enough money to live without anxiety or want. She worried about Frank's rebellious nature in 1942, and writes that she is concerned about his controversy with the regents of the university and hopes he is "at the age of discretion, . . . at least on this subject." Every autumn finds her prescribing cures for Frank's hay fever; at one time, she seriously proposed that he try wearing a gas mask. She advised him to find a "good osteopath" for his neuritis; steadily counseled Bertha about the virtues of taking plenty of rest.

Three years after Mrs. Dobie's death, the heirs to the estate decided to sell the old family ranch. It was a terrible decision for Frank Dobie to make, how wrenching he did not fully realize until the sale was an accomplished fact — as he wrote Fannie on March 15, 1951. The Houston buyers closed the deal at $140,000, agreeing to the customary provision that the Dobie heirs would retain one half of royalty interests in perpetuity. He wrote: "I feel that an end has come to something of a lifetime. I could not feel thus towards any other plot of ground on earth, not at all towards these lots on Waller Creek where I have spent so many years. Something irreplaceable has passed from me. Perhaps I should have kept my part of the ranch and not have sold it, but I did not feel that I could keep up with the Houston millionaires, who will no doubt spend a deal of money on improvements. I know and like a great many people who do not mean so much to me as the ranch. It has been next to Mama in something to go to."

His final word about his mother, from the essay in *Some Part of Myself:* "If everybody were as genuinely good as she was and had as much common sense as she had, the world would not need much managing."

Dobie had a fondness for going up to the cabin on Devil's River Lake, a project of the Central Power and Light Company, especially in the month of January. He went there again just after New Year's Day in 1950, enjoying as usual his mornings of writing and afternoons of respite, riding horseback when he could arrange it, fishing and hunting, chopping wood or performing other country-life tasks. At night, he edited his morning stints of composition and read for relaxation and in preparation for the next day's work. In this stay in 1950 at Devil's River, he boasted to Bertha that the draws in this countryside grew good chapote trees, so he had cut a number of straight but short pieces to make picture frames. He was always in search of unusual woods for his frames and took great pride in matching the wood to the work of art. He also took pride in using woods most "professional" framers would have scorned: mesquite, bois d'arc (for its orangy tint) ebony, cypress.

He was now at work on *The Mustangs*, which was based on his insight that "no man by taking thought can add to his stature, but by taking a horse he can." Starting centuries back with the mustangs' Arabian ancestors, he showed how horse ownership had made domination possible for a handful of conquistadores, how it had utterly changed the culture of the Plains Indians, not only materially but in "dilating" their "imagination," how it literally created a way of life for Mexican and Anglo cowmen. He wrote of the mustangs' own way of life, the social organization of the great wild herds. He wrote of mustangs in captivity, of legendary instances of the men who hunted, tamed, and used them, and of their ultimate near-extinction. Dobie's love of the mustangs' free spirit, and his admiration for the hardihood of the mustang men, enliven every detail of this rich and eloquent book, which never sags into nostalgia or sentimentality. He had aimed and succeeded in the mission defined by Emerson: to discover the physical facts about the truth and then to discover the spiritual fact beneath.

As Frank worked on his book, he was eagerly awaiting a visit at Devil's River from his editor, Angus Cameron, a man for whom he had the highest admiration and friendship. Cameron arrived about mid-January; the article he wrote about his visit for the special Dobie commemorative issue of the *Texas Observer* (1964) remains one of the best things ever written about Dobie. Bertha got word from Frank that they were getting along very well; for example, "[we] just had a hearty breakfast off fried bass and biscuits and honey," and had a dinner of "frijoles and cornbread." The bass they had for breakfast represented three out of a catch of fifteen the day before; the rest were in the refrigerator.

He sent Cameron the manuscript of *The Mustangs* the following year, in September 1951. Cameron judged it to be "the best book of your life." Both he and Bertha Dobie had arrived independently at an identical criticism: several stories told in the first person needed to be recast in the third person. Cameron was Tom Lea's editor as well as Frank's, and when that year he was forced out of Little, Brown by outside charges of "being a Communist," the two Texans were dismayed and puzzled. On the day after Frank's sixty-third birthday (September 26), an article about Cameron appeared in *Time*. That same day Frank wrote to Lea, "In today's *Time* we get a little more light on him and his resignation," but "a very murky light, however. . . . I can't believe that Angus is a Communist. If so, he joined a long time ago out of idealism, and not to overthrow the government or reap popular and monetary awards by his stand, like the blackguard Martin

Dies, the unpitying Westbrook Pegler, the hairy ape McCarthy and many another now taking 'the last refuge of the scoundrel.' "

The previous April Dobie himself had been listed as a sponsor of the Mid-Century Conference for Peace, allegedly a Communist-inspired group. Dobie defended himself, Wilson Hudson notes, by saying that "he believed in peace and did not have time to investigate the membership of organizations backing causes which he approved of." He had also, three or four years before, lent his name to the Progressive Party. As he told Lea in his September 26 letter: "One night three or four years ago somebody called me over the phone and asked me if I would be honorary chairman or something like that of [the] Henry Wallace Progressive Party. My belly was full of Truman and many other things at the time. I said yes. I never did a thing and soon found that I did not like the party. Meantime I was being branded as a Communist and the Philistinic Press was noticing me only to revile me. Two or three of my friends who knew the way I was feeling about Wallace and his party advised me to publicly resign from it. I hated to kick a down dog and I did not want to be bullied by a cowardly public and a few contemptible newspapers. I said nothing. When the time came to vote I voted as usual, though without pride or hope, the Democratic ticket."

Dobie enclosed a carbon for Lea of a letter he had sent on September 24 to Angus Cameron at his home address in South Lincoln, Massachusetts. Dobie said that on September 21, he had received a letter from Stanley Salmen, vice-president of Little, Brown, saying, "By now you will probably have heard that Angus has resigned from Little, Brown." To Cameron, Dobie wrote: "I had not heard and had not even suspected." Speaking of the magazine *Counterattack*'s attack on Little, Brown, Frank wrote: "I have never seen a copy of *Counterattack*." He repeated his faith in Cameron, his admiration for his editorial talents, and deplored the event both as a friend and as a grateful author.

When the family ranch was sold in 1951, Frank began looking for a country place. True, his new study, after the addition to the Austin house in 1950, was "fine," as he wrote Tom Lea, but when spring came he simply couldn't stay in it, although he could "force my body to sit in it." The group of oilmen who had bought the Dobie ranch as a hunting place had invited Frank "to visit, go back there or hunt there for the rest of his life," but he felt he needed land of his own. He and Bertha bought an old farm on the San Antonio road, not very far beyond the Austin city limits; he busied himself with adding a fireplace and assured Tom that their country place was now "charming." He very much wanted a fireplace mantel made of mesquite wood but not even on the old family ranch could he find a big enough trunk to yield the slab needed. As he told Tom, "Slabs of mesquite have to be mortised together to get the proper dimensions." He did eventually get his mantelpiece and had carved on it what he thought to be a sentence of his own invention: "We sat down with earth's greatest philosopher — the Fire." He discovered later that he was remembering and unconsciously appropriating a favorite line from R. B. Cunninghame Graham. The farm was named Fieldlarks.

A farm, however, could not satisfy his need for a ranchlike landscape, so a few weeks later he had further good news for Tom Lea. He had just bought a place about thirty-five miles from Austin, "in the Spicewood country, north of the Pedernales, in the hills." It had fine flowing springs, good grasslands and an excellent house. Its 746 acres "will run about forty cows." As an oasis of solitude for a writer who thought he required absolute privacy, it was ideal. He even confided that it was also a splendid place for the traditional Mexican habit of taking an afternoon siesta, a habit Dobie loved to practice.

The place was named Cherry Springs, for its wild cherry trees and its abundance of good water, and Frank became absorbed in making it productive. From the porch he could look out on an uncultivated, weedy field, full of wild flowers, and beyond that to a hill where some little bluestem grew. To this patch of good grass, and to the meadow, Frank added seedings of buffalo grass and sideoats grama. "In his eagerness," Bertha wrote later, "he would get down on his hands and knees and look for sproutings." He paid a visit to a botanist in Waco, R. C. Mauldin, who raised native grasses for seed, and as a result was able in later years to show his family and friends "what native grasses had done to restore old wornout land" at Cherry Springs: not just little bluestem, buffalo grass and sideoats grama, but hair grama and some tall Indian grass beside the sloughs, and needlegrass to walk through on the way to the maidenhair fern on the creek bank.

He wrote at the time: "No matter what improvements are put on ranch land, its essential worth consists of the grass it grows and nothing else. The combination of the practical and the beautiful in grass is singular. The sight of a turf, whether of shortgrass carpeting the earth or tall grass waving in the wind, restores my soul. A valley of green grass is beautiful in the way that mountains, sea and stars are beautiful."

Even Cherry Springs could not give him the privacy he wanted for writing, and near the end of his life he bought another "place" in the hills west of Austin which he named Paisano, after his personal symbol, the little earthbound Southwestern bird known as the roadrunner. (Dobie liked to remind artists, and others, that two of the roadrunner's toes on each foot point forward, into the future; and two to the rear, into the past.) In an article in the Austin *Statesman*, in July 1962, Frank wrote of his new acquisition: "The front gallery is provided with a couch, a cat, a bench, and a diversity of chairs; O. Henry's Sam Galloway would have delighted in it. Sam never stood when he could sit, and he never sat when he could lie down.

"There I would like to emulate Sam Galloway listening, if the wind isn't too high, to the water over the riffles in the creek, just down a slope, gazing at faraway hills, especially a patch of bluestem grass.

"It's a fine place from which to look at the clouds along from the south, pecans, elms, sycamores and other trees . . . a fine place in the evening to receive a visit from a hog-nosed skunk lingering there; one can nearly always delight in the gracefulness of a buzzard in the air. . . . In the summer, scissortails, vermilion flycatchers, chimney sweeps and other feeders upon airborne insects, add to the charm of life."

A post off the front gallery held an oldtime family dinner bell; there were sawhorses for his saddles, pegs for his sweat-stained hats, his leggings and cow skulls and ponchos, and plenty of bookshelves. He had an alcove made for his bed in the fireplace room, so he could watch the fire die as he went to sleep. Part of the six-room house had thick stone walls over a hundred years old. Thanks to the generosity of Frank's old hunting companion Ralph Johnston, Paisano, under the Frank Dobie Fellowship, now exists to give shelter and privacy to promising young writers.

At the time Frank was telling Tom Lea about the joys of his Cherry Springs "ranchito," Tom was deeply absorbed in a book about the King Ranch of Texas, probably the most famous ranch in the world. Dobie worried as Tom grew more and more engrossed in its history, more emotionally identified with its mystique of "empire," of power acquired through rugged individualism. He felt that Tom was giving too much of his life to the King Ranch (the book occupied Tom totally for almost five years). He began in his letters to make suggestions, in a friendly way. It seems likely that Dobie, reared on a small ranch not very far from the overpowering King enterprise, harbored a prejudice against the King Ranch, because he was a man whom only external events could compel to examine his own point of view. Not that he had a closed mind: witness his disavowal of his early "race" prejudice and of his adolescent worship of the Confederate leaders, his evolution in regard to the importance of "regionalism," and so on. But his attitude toward the King Ranch was also conditioned by his indignation at the misuse of power, as he saw it, when the Texas "big rich" sought political control over Texas life, as in the "university fight," and on a national scale, as in their generous support of Senator McCarthy. Slowly but surely a rift opened in the sterling and mutually enhancing friendship of these two superior men and superior artists.

Two months later he confided again that his "ranchito" was still taking too much of his time, but "I can't put it out of my mind." He cursed what he called "the way I disperse myself" — he was writing from Arizona, where he gave lectures at the university at Tempe. He would, of course, stop over in El Paso on his way home, all the more since he and Tom had to confer on Frank's introduction to an album of Tom Lea paintings which Frank Wardlaw, the dynamic head of the new University of Texas Press, planned to publish.

Of Tom's superb charcoal portrait of Dobie, Frank reported a comment of the Dobies' maid when she first saw the drawing: "He sure looks displeased about something." Frank's own reaction to the portrait was anything but displeased. His response was similar to that of Bertha's nephew, Edgar Kincaid: "Bertha wrote you, I believe, of Edgar's elation. He is reticent in adverse opinion but ebullient in enthusiasm and as choosey as any critic I know. You got *it*, and I'm contented to 'go down to posterity' in these lines. Getting something delivered right out of myself concerns me more, however, than the attention of posterity." He added about the portrait, "I see more and more beyond severity."

The portrait is indeed severe; the subject looks challenging, perhaps enraged inwardly, granitelike in features and utterly natural and unposed. One glance at it and one knows a great deal about what Frank Dobie was really like. Nearly all the photographs of Dobie show him with his infectious grin and his general good nature; Tom Lea's portrait goes deeper and shows the man who called himself a liberal because a liberal "is a man who doesn't like to be fooled." Lea's portrait, a profile, shows above all else a clear-sighted, luminous man whose great strength of face seems to come precisely from that concentrated energy of a fearless glance.

In the same letter, he reveals — he was then sixty-five years old — that he now tires easily and can no longer "recoup" on "one good drink, one good meal and a few hours of sleep." When working on his introduction to the Tom Lea album, Dobie wrote Lea that he was using much quotation from Tom's letters. "It has been a spiritual experience. The letters make an extremely lucid miniature of your development over sixteen years of time." This comment is worthy of notice: "Tom, if somebody artistically discreet in omission should some day want to publish our correspondence, it will be all right with my ghost. I think I should make provision that these letters and all the Tom Lea pictures I have should go to the special Southwestern Room in your El Paso Public Library. Let us talk about this a little the next time we talk."

On July 13, 1953, Dobie wrote Tom of his delight that Tom expected to finish the King Ranch book "by the end of the year" (actually, it was not finished until three years later). In a letter of August 4, 1955, he returned to the matter. He had received a "liberating" letter from Tom, and replied that for the "last several months I have at times come near brooding over my responsibility for your getting into the King Ranch book." For a year, he said, he had thought that Tom was "having to surrender too much of his own life to the book." But it does not seem that Tom Lea felt that way at all. He told this writer, after he had spent five years on the project, that he thought it was an "enlarging" experience for him.

In 1957, when the book was at last published, he wrote, "Tom, you said for me to tell you and I said I'd say." He proceeded to a long, long analysis, which he admitted was severe. If he were not so proud of Tom — "and didn't love you so much — and you know it — I never would have blurted out so much so savagely." By comparison, his front-page essay in the *New York Times Book Review* was cautious, but Tom and a number of his friends felt that it was a betrayal. That Dobie did not anticipate this reaction is evident from his letter, for he ends with the eager anticipation of being in El Paso shortly for the launching of the book on a special civic Tom Lea Day in El Paso.

Tom Lea Day was a fabulous "celebration," attended by a number of the outstanding figures of the Southwest in education, writing, painting, finance, government and ranching, an occasion fondly remembered by all who were present. Frank wrote Tom the day he got back to Austin that he had given Bertha a worthy account of "the wonderful celebration," and added, "You are very dear to me. Frank." Even then, he did not realize how deeply he had wounded his friend.

But he learned, and both kept silence with each other for six or seven months. After that time lapse, Frank sent a conciliatory letter on June 3, 1958, following a visit that day from Sarah Lea, who was in Austin. Dobie insisted that "I never did intend to question your integrity." A year later, he could write casually to his great friend, "Having a letter from you was like old times," but the rift was essentially irreparable. One wonders (I don't think Tom Lea ever wondered this) if the older man unconsciously felt some jealousy of his disciple's achievement, or at least of his success, for *The King Ranch* was, and has remained, a publishing event of considerable magnitude. If so, it is the only instance I know when Frank Dobie could have been motivated by jealousy, for he was the most generous and least jealous-hearted of men. Lea was stricken the most, for he felt challenged about his loyalty to truth, however much his talents were praised; Dobie was immeasurably saddened, as though he had lost a son, inexplicably driven away.

Many of his friends' most characteristic memories of Frank Dobie sprang from a sort of annual "ranch holiday" that Holland

and Marjorie McCombs organized for a number of years, beginning just after Frank's return from Cambridge, at their picturesque spread on the Pedernales River, about eighteen miles from Johnson City, and then, after they sold that property, at their "plantation"-style, Texas-Republic ranch-farm at Wheelock.

A man of great organizing talent and with a flair for style, Holland McCombs began inviting a small group of friends for the July Fourth weekend. Marjorie McCombs and the wives of the guests commandeered the ranch house; the men had quarters in a nearby grove of trees with folding cots under a circus tent that McCombs rented and installed for the occasion.

The only purpose of the gathering was to enjoy companionable good talk, something Frank Dobie loved. There were long verandahs to sit on, live oaks and cypresses to sit under, retreating hills and pillow-shaped clouds to look at, several deep pools in the Pedernales riverbed to swim in, catfish to fry, tomatoes in the garden to pluck vine-ripened and hot with the sun. There were horses for Frank Dobie to ride, bluffs over the river riddled with cliff-swallow nests for Frank to explain, wild flowers for Bertha Dobie to identify. As Bertha recalled, "Frank and I began anticipating the next Fourth on the way home from the last."

The attendance varied from year to year, but the "regulars" represented a wide span of interests. Among these, in addition to Frank and Bertha Dobie, were the architects O'Neil Ford and Arch Swank and their wives (Wanda Graham Ford was a virtuoso modern dancer; Patricia Peck Swank, an accomplished musician); Tom and Sarah Lea, Tom often busy drawing portraits of the guests in a huge "souvenir" book that Holland kept; Carl Hertzog and his wife Vivian, who watched with admiration as Carl tried to convert us all to Buddhistic explanations of reality and to Yoga practices; the painter and museum director Jerry Bywaters and his wife Mary, who carted down at immense trouble an old-fashioned foot-pumped organ as a contribution to the McCombses' early Texas living room and to the nightly singsongs that made Frank Dobie rage ("Why waste time like that?"); Bill Kittrell, once the most powerful voice in the Democratic Party in Texas when the party was "liberal" and regarded by Frank as the best raconteur in the Southwest; Green Peyton Wertenbaker and his wife Barclay, both bringing to the event as well as to the

San Antonio they loved a Virginia style and a talent for leisure; Eugene McDermott, the celebrated geophysicist and associate of Everette DeGolyer in the Geophysical Research Corporation (both men had a passion for books); Elizabeth Ann McMurray, who ran, among many other things in Dallas, the famous McMurray Personal Book Shop; and William Weber Johnson of Time Inc. (The last two eventually married and moved to California, where he could write his *Heroic Mexico*. There were others, among them the intermittent guest George Sessions Perry, but it was Frank Dobie who was the catalytic agent that united the diverse personalities. He did so simply by being himself.

Not everything at the ranch pleased him, and he could be wrathy on occasion. He felt that the night was made to sleep in. Inevitably, the urge to sing took over in the late evening after the conversation and the stories had run down. Frank kept a horse of Holland's ready for his midnight exit; claiming that the rest of us spoiled his sleep ("Damn a man that murthers sleep!" he would quote with no redeeming grin in his eyes), he would ride up to his own private "camp" to wait for dawnlight to wake him. He claimed to have to move more miles away every night as the singing grew more lusty. On at least one occasion, Frank hovered around the tent after sunup, hoping for some sign of life from the late sleepers. Thinking he saw host McCombs stir awake, Dobie went up beside the cot and said, "Come on, Holland, wake up, you're wasting the best hours of the day!" Holland groaned but he was aware enough to register one remark before falling back asleep. "Your eyes," Dobie said to him scathingly, "look like two holes in a blanket."

In the mornings, he was the first to the kitchen, naturally, for breakfast; only Bertha, of the women sleeping in the house, was up to keep him company. The Negro cook, proud of her skill, plied Frank with hotcakes and eggs and bacon. His appetite was Gargantuan or maybe not quite that big; at any rate, he knew what he was eating and he appreciated it and he liked to make a ritual of mealtime, a ritual of companionability and zest. But despite his hearty breakfast, and a couple of cups of coffee, he was ready to chastise the late sleepers for missing the morning hours (he himself would usually go off on a long horseback ride) and for ruining the night. By lunchtime, he had forgiven all, and habitually mixed on his plate an amazing sort of appetizer consisting of boiled pinto beans, chopped onions, and whole *jalapeños*, doused with guajilla honey ("Wa-hee honey," said Frank, "is the best honey in the world").

He enjoyed equally the riverbank meal, for which Marjorie McCombs's father, Sam Cavitt, would fry catfish and hush puppies, and the nearly formal indoor final dinner, with white tablecloth and candlelight, featuring most of the time venison ("the best cooked I ever ate — maybe," Bertha Dobie remembered). He delighted, though not equally, in riding Holland's one-eyed horse, old Gotch ("so mean he needs riding," Frank would explain as he galloped off), and Holland's magnificent, pure-blood Arabian, Zarif. When Frank rode the latter, a sort of grapevine summons spread around, for all were agreed that it was a beautiful sight to see such a perfect blending or melding of thoroughbred styles, horse and master. Holland McCombs loved to point out that Frank Dobie was one man who knew how to sit a horse with effortless control and mastery.

Frank was a joyous swimmer. The Pedernales at this point runs swiftly over falls, but the river is so wide between its hill-high banks that many still pools remain where the channel once ran and which it now, in its main course, skirts. He seemed to swim, however, primarily for the pleasure of sunning himself later. He liked to drink in the sun, while most of us were heading for the shade.

This was all part of Frank Dobie's zest for living, his hatred to see time merely "killed." In one way or another, as Bertha Dobie said, his mind was always at work. But this requires understanding. The contemplation, that sort of inner attention directed to the outer world and yielding an especially acute awareness characteristic of him, involved a determined attempt to savor life as it passed by, to linger in response. He was not a mental machine or a busy automaton. Many of Dobie's friends, I imagine, would classify him as one of the happiest men they ever knew — and precisely because he had the wisdom to savor life, not to exploit it.

It takes courage, of course, to be independent of collective pressures. No doubt, to be so would be folly if you did not have a sense of humor. The sardonic side that led Dobie to deflate the counterfeits and the stuffed shirts perhaps explained his fondness for the short-lived annual meetings of the "Texas Institute of the Unlettered." This was a project launched by Bill Kittrell and a few others in Dallas who decided around 1948 that the Texas Institute of Letters was too impressed with itself and its prize awards. On the morning after the institute's annual awards banquet, the Unlettered staged a stag breakfast, garnering Dobie and most of the institute's better-known members such as Tom Lea and Walter Prescott Webb, plus a lot of political bigwigs and such rich bookmen as DeGolyer and McDermott.

This waggish occasion prospered for several years. Kittrell was so depressed, however, the year Eisenhower carried Texas for the Republican Party that he couldn't rally two weeks later to organize the usual unlettered romp, and after this break it was never staged again.

Kittrell and company were not mocking Texas writing and they really had no specific targets except for the Poetry Society of Texas (not part of the Texas Institute of Letters), which claimed there were two thousand poets in Texas because the society had that many members with paid-up dues. The Unlettered fraternity simply took advantage of the presence in town of a good many true writers in order to blow off steam and to have at breakfast the culled genuine talent separated from the hitchhikers and the hangers-on and, above all, the "lady poets."

It was for Dobie another convivial group of Texas thinkers, one effort to defeat the loneliness of the writer in the state, one effort to declare the solidarity of the civilized. With equal gusto, Dobie would attend, say, the annual meeting of the Texas Folklore Society, genuinely glad to visit with everyone there, lingering and savoring. And with the same pleasure he would serve as featured speaker year after year at Dee Woods' Southwest Writers' Conference in Corpus Christi. Since he was always a valiant supporter of public libraries, as of any means to spread a love of literature, he could rarely decline a plea to come and give a talk. I have seen him push himself mercilessly on a tight schedule in Dallas in order to accept an invitation to address, for free of course, some new branch library and let the kids see that "not all authors are dead." What they saw, of course, was a "man thinking."

At the closing banquet of the thirty-ninth annual meeting of the Texas Folklore Society, held in the venerable old Austin hostelry, the Driskill, on April 23, 1955, Frank Dobie was honored. Four speakers made brief talks of tribute. Having recently visited Cambridge University, the former chancellor of the University of Texas, James P. Hart, reported that after a decade Dobie's memory was still green at Emmanuel College, not only with faculty members and from students' hearsay, but with townspeople. Hart added that Dobie had "really won the heart of Mr. Jack Barrett, the proprietor of Cambridge's leading pub, who recounted to me almost rapturously the boating trips that he and Frank Dobie had taken together on the waters of the Cam." Hart singled out as the central characteristic in both Dobie's self and work the quality of *sincerity*, the product of "a man who looks you straight in the eye, with love in his heart, but with the courage to tell you the truth as he sees it, whether you like it or not." Roy Bedichek stressed in his comment the same quality of being sincere, as revealed in "his well-known, because outspoken, abomination of pretense in life and art [which] is only the reverse side of his passion for sincerity in his own life, personal and public, and in his own art." Bedichek, the friend who knew Dobie best, reminded the audience that "many people forget [that] Dobie is first and last a teacher, and one who takes his teaching seriously." Walter Prescott Webb chose to spice the occasion with a humorous piece in which he pretended to describe Dobie in precisely the terms of what Dobie was not; for example, "a second characteristic is his unfailing spirit of obedience, his submissiveness to authority." All who were there agreed it was one of the best "celebrations" ever staged for the man who had become, in national as well as local eyes, the symbol of what was *good* in Texas. In 1955, very few outlanders thought there was anything good in a state so castigated for boastful, braggart worship of "bigness." The national megalomania found in Texas, and with good reason, a perfect scapegoat, a ready-made psychological "transfer." The justice in this nationwide targeting on a regional life-style that absolutely betrayed Socrates' dictum "The unexamined life is not worth living" did not escape Dobie, who had ten years earlier renounced his onetime support of "provincialism," above all of chauvinism and jingoism.

Bertha's father, very old and very feeble, moved in with the Dobies in 1955; his needs deprived Bertha of the chance to make trips with Frank. A lecture trip in April 1956 included Ohio and New York, where Frank also made some recordings for a commercial firm and took advantage of the chance to visit with old friends. He never enjoyed New York so much as he did on this visit. He found again his once-atrophied love of the theater, the one thing reminiscent of New York that had absorbed him in his stay at Columbia forty years earlier. He wrote to Tom Lea that he went to see Beckett's *Waiting for Godot*, which one might not have expected him to like. "I was enthralled, as I was also at Tennessee Williams' *Cat on a Hot Tin Roof*. There is nothing like theater and acting. . . . I'd rather see plays in New York and London than fly to the moon." He very much regretted that Bertha had to miss seeing the plays. He relished his visits with Arthur Thornhill, Sr., and Ned Bradford of Little, Brown, as he did with his ex-editor Angus Cameron and his onetime student and "disciple" John Henry Faulk, the noted former Texan and television actor who had the courage and the skill to defeat a fanatical effort at "black-listing" him and other allegedly "extreme leftist" network personnel at the height of the McCarthy era.

Back in Austin in early May, Dobie took care of Mr. McKee while Bertha went over to San Antonio for a week to rest at the Menger Hotel, a famous old hostelry. She was suffering another of her bouts with ill health, this time an ulcer on her vocal cords. For weeks that autumn of 1956 she was unable to speak, and had to write on handy pads what needed to be said. But by December, Frank reported to Tom Lea, she was "talking all right and chousing around in a normal way."

Dobie went to New York again in February 1957, to confer with the NBC network on one of their "Wide World" features, a special program on Texas. Dobie served as a narrator, with his usual success in public appearances. In New York he spent, as he said, "three wonderful hours with Ned Bradford," who made Frank promise to put aside all other projects in order to concentrate on writing his autobiography. Other, similar pressure came from Walter Prescott Webb and T. V. Smith, the latter recently returned to Austin after a combined academic and political career in Illinois. Frank returned their sentiments, grouping the three into what he called his "Autobiography Club," to spur each other on in similar undertakings. The spur, as it turned out, was not sufficient for Dobie. Or the activities that would have to be shunted aside were perhaps too attractive.

Dobie could no more forgo planning, and making, trips across the Sierra Madre or throughout the West or back East than he could forgo horseback riding and swimming. He could not give up the visits with friends who supplied him with one of his greatest pleasures, good talk.

Other pleasures he found hard to turn aside were his old habit of reading and the long contemplation of nature. His letters from Cherry Springs are rhapsodic about watching the dusk and "lingering with nature." As he often said, somewhat cryptically, "Nature puts something into man." He felt a great pity for urbanites in whom this simple delight and strength had atrophied. He was less "philosophic" about this saddening loss in human response than is the Texas writer whose work since Dobie's time most resembles Dobie's: John Graves (*Goodbye to a River* and *Hard Scrabble*). Graves says in his first and best book, "You either like this sort of thing or you don't," and cheerfully lets it go at that. Dobie, maybe because of his puritanical childhood background, found it hard not to evangelize.

III

Pneumonia and consequent damage to his heart in 1957 kept him in the hospital six weeks and left him forever bereft of the exuberant energy that had characterized him before. He was sixty-nine years old and still had a dozen books he wanted to write. Typical of his complaints of the unexpected aftermath of his illness is a letter to the artist Howard Cook of May 1, 1959: His doctors, and he himself, are paying much attention to diet — no salt, no soda, no animal fats; he reminds himself of a Brahma cow he had a few years back. "She'd been exceptionally thrifty but lost her energy. I saw her staying by herself and lying down at hours when healthy cattle graze; then one day I saw her licking dirt on the bank of a creek. She had access to salt, bone meal and also a mixture of minerals. She needed something that she wasn't getting and she didn't know what it was. I feel hungry for something to put juice into me lots of times. I don't know what it is. The earth won't tell me. I *do* know the chemical apparatus in my body doesn't translate raw stuff into energy as it once did. What the world needs is more doctors who know more chemistry."

Mixing technical details with everyday jargon in his report to a colleague, Frank's physician, Dr. Herrmann, ruled out the presence of "paroxysmal nocturnal dyspnea or pulmonary edema," but noted that Dobie had experienced "runs of fluttering heart action half a dozen times or so." Dobie said that when "he is under emotional stress," he has noticed a "darting pain under the right lower sternum," and "he has noticed that when he gets stirred up, it takes more out of him than it used to." The obvious remedy, not to get stirred up, was certain to deprive Dobie of one of his keenest pleasures.

For his colleague, Dr. Herrmann inventoried a number of minor details, such as a persisting early-morning cough, getting up during the night to pass urine, but found no gastrointestinal symptoms, no vertigo or syncope. Frank's major problem was tiring rapidly to the point of total exhaustion by nightfall. Even the severe hay fever and sinusitis which had plagued him all his life had tapered off in the past few years, one of the small profits of old age.

Two losses, however, canceled out those slight benefits: during his illness he lost his taste for coffee and his taste for alcohol. The latter was temporary. Dr. Herrmann, presumably banning tobacco, writes that Dobie had been a "pipe smoker constantly for 50 years, a half to one can of Prince Albert a day." By Dobie's account, which will come as a surprise to his friends, his customary daily intake of whiskey was "one or two jiggers."

Allowing subjectivity to enter his report, Herrmann remarked that the patient "has been waltzed up and down the Rosenberg Library steps by admiring devotees and fans here who learned of his presence in the city and he was proud and did not want them to know of his infirmities."

While in the hospital, which Dobie entered on September 23, 1957, he apparently was able to dictate to his secretary from time to time. On a loose page of the notes in his autobiographic dossier, he has two comments, marked "dictated," one of September 28 and the other October 1. The former, in toto: "He struts around crowing over being master of his own destiny; he can't even direct his own bowel movements." And the second: "*Voices*. The only people who ever accused Joan of Arc of listening to voices were worldly and ambitious; that included the bishops. Anybody who has ever spent a night under the stars or in an oxygen tent knows that there are beautiful voices waiting to be listened to."

Dobie convalesced at home in the ground-floor "sun-room," since he was forbidden to climb stairs. He had to choose between being imprisoned upstairs or down, so he chose down, explaining to Herbert West: "I chose the ground floor so I can get out on the good earth — I'm always having books brought down and sent up. It's a great nuisance not to be close to my tools." He found a greater nuisance in having to dictate, for even using the typewriter was thought to be too taxing on his strength.

Three months after the Galveston stay, Dobie still had not received a bill from Dr. Herrmann, so he wrote to say he had tried to pay the secretary when he said goodbye but had been thwarted, since she told him she did not keep the books and that Mrs. Herrmann handled the accounts. "I think you'd better advise Mrs. Herrmann," Dobie wrote, and then turned to a cheerful health bulletin, adding, "I'm doing my best not to eat any salt, soda, or fat, and haven't gained any pounds." He was five feet seven in height and weighed 167.

He had sent Dr. Herrmann some of his books, and announced a new one in his letter. "For the past six weeks or so I've been working along on a very scandalous subject. No respectable publisher would want to publish what I'm writing, but I get fun out of it. . . . Whenever it gets printed, sub rosa or otherwise, I shall send you a copy. It won't be too thick to read." He was alluding, of course, to his proposed counterpart to *1601*, Mark Twain's "scandalous" fantasy of vulgar behavior at Queen Elizabeth's court, unacknowledged by Twain during his lifetime, and to Balzac's *Droll Stories*. Dobie's project was no secret at all. He appealed to close friends for suggestions. "Two weeks ago I dictated in a few days eight or ten thousand words on a kind of narrative essay that's going to compete with Mark Twain's *1601*, though I don't imagine any publisher'll want to put his imprint on it." On November 7 his optimism had diminished a bit: "I'm still working, but slowly, on 'One Touch of Nature, Plus.' That's the provisional title of my narrative essays on several 'unparlory' words, with accompanying tales."

Comfortable again in his relationship with Tom Lea, Dobie confided to him in November 1958 about his project: "I've been composing something quite ribald. I guess I wanted change. I am in permanent rebellion against censors and censorship of the language, especially. . . . What work I do is hardly worth mentioning. If I average an hour a day of actual composing, I think I do pretty well." And, in fact, he never again — after the terrible sickness of September-October 1957 — recovered the energy he had always thought was his unfailing birthright and security. (He said to this writer a few years later, speaking of the crippling result of his sickness, "I never supposed that what happened would ever happen, that I simply wouldn't have the energy to finish a dozen different planned books.") He did in fact finish his collection of essays on old-timers, *Cow People*, for which he interrupted his book of ribaldry.

His most valued friend, Roy Bedichek, died in 1959, at the age of eighty-one. Two years before, Dobie gave him a copy of A. E. Taylor's *Socrates: The Man and His Thought*, and wrote on the flyleaf: "Dear Bedi, I give you this book because I should be as bereft if you went away as Crito and the others were when Socrates went. As one of them said of him, I can say of you, my friend, 'the wisest and justest and best man that I have ever known.' "

On his seventy-first birthday, September 26, 1959, Dobie gave an interview to Lorraine Barnes of the Austin *Statesman*, telling her he was planning three more books, one of which would be "utterly different" from any before. "If that book gets published I will no longer enjoy the society of the respectable." Miss Barnes reported that as he said this he sounded "not at all nervous." There can be no doubt that Bertha Dobie was. Like nearly all intelligent women of her time and position, she placed a high value on respectability — which caused lifelong, vivid talk between her and her husband. Frank could not deny that respectability was a central virtue in his beloved mother's canon; he transferred his rebellion against her in this matter to Bertha, which she probably well understood.

He dictated about ten thousand words of his "shocking book"

to his eminently respectable, highly sensitive, and indispensable secretary of many years, Willie Belle Coker, who later became director of the Dobie Room at the university. Mrs. Coker testifies that the unfinished book was vividly candid but not "obscene." Both the manuscript and the books Frank assembled for it disappeared soon after Frank's death. There is reason to believe the manuscript will soon surface, at least for the use of scholars.

Dobie's letters to Herbert West contain no further reference to "One Touch of Nature, Plus." With glee (one of his favorite words), he informed West that on April 1, 1959, he would take possession of his new country place, Paisano. In the same letter, he told his friend about an arrangement made in 1957 with the University of Texas to buy his books, while he would donate his manuscripts and papers and art objects to the university. "I spent three days this last week in the study spending the night up there — my first visit since September 22, 1957. I'm still not walking upstairs." Bertha's nephew Edgar carried him up and down the steps. The checklisting of his books required five months of "library presence in the house. . . . Frank Gilliam comes here about three or four times a week for maybe two hours and appraises books. . . . The university is paying for all this work." He told West to bill the university for the appraisal West did on Dobie's W. H. Hudson collection. Jeff Dykes, a good friend and noted dealer in rare Western books, was appraising the Western collection.

Bertha's father died on February 27, 1960 — at ninety-seven. Frank wrote West of Bertha's sadness but confessed that, as for himself, "my only feeling is of relief. He had been a rebuke to vitality in this house for an unconscionable time." Mr. McKee, like Frank's father in his later years, was a very tame old party, who roused Frank's compassion but not his interest. He sometimes referred to his father-in-law as "that poor old man, unable to die."

Bertha now had only one patient in the house, for Frank was still a sick man, and would never be really well again. Both Dobies were fortunate in the presence of Edgar Kincaid, the son of her sister Lucile, who had nursed her so loyally during her first, almost fatal bout of influenza. Mildly eccentric, he was an enormously gifted ornithologist, with the passion of a naturalist for detailed observation, a gift Frank respected and enjoyed, and the responsiveness of a good listener. When Frank was yarn-spinning or reminiscing, he never had a more admiring or appreciative audience than Edgar Kincaid; and the young man also shared his uncle's Jeffersonian liberalism. He admired Frank as much as he loved him, and for Bertha he had long been a surrogate son.

Her sister Lucile had died when Edgar was still a boy, and he had felt somewhat "orphaned" when his father remarried and established a large new family. Though he remained devoted to his father — a role that Frank never tried to usurp — the pleasant house on Waller Creek gradually became a real home to him. For Bertha, he felt a truly filial love and loyalty. With Frank so weak — Frank who had been, as her old friend Mary Thomas Simons remembered, so "protective" of her for fifty years — she must have taken great comfort from Edgar's presence and strength, and perhaps have drawn on them. Frail, sick or half sick most of her life, Bertha in old age was as always a valiant woman. Still very pretty, still, with her magnificent eyes and alert regard, a considerable presence, she had at last grown stout; it became her. She dressed beautifully and expensively, and carried herself with an air. Her once-and-for-all dedication to Frank, not an instinctive emotion but one achieved and scrupulously tempered in their long courtship, had given her — at great cost to herself — a raison d'être. "One half" of Frank, it will be recalled, she thought as fine as man could be. After his death in 1964, she seems to have transferred this dedication to Edgar Kincaid, and to have fought the persistent specter of ill health for ten more years in the hope of seeing his professional fulfillment. In 1976, after his monumental addition to *The Bird Life of Texas* was accepted for publication, Bertha entered the hospital for what she thought was a minor matter and died the first night there, quietly, in her sleep. Her death was said to have been painless, "natural," as Frank Dobie might have wished. Friends especially close to her say she had no inkling that death was near. Perhaps subconsciously she realized that she had no more books integral to her life to see completed. After Frank's death, she had edited, and had seen through to publication in book form, two collections of his short pieces, as well as his autobiographical fragment *Some Part of Myself*. With Edgar Kincaid's book, the circle of creativity in which she dealt was closed.

But this is to anticipate. In improving health, but in chastened hope and diminished energy, Frank lived on for seven years after his hospitalization. Loyal to his vocation, he tried constantly to gather and focus his forces, his powers of concentration.

Early in January 1961, Dobie sent a significant letter to West: "Some men of years and debility regret the loss of vigor. I regret that, too, but I have enough vigor to accomplish something if it were directed to a point. I've known for a good while that my energies are dispersed on book collecting and on being an institution and on other things — all to prevent me from being a writer. I'm going to spend some energy very soon in an effort to cut off from everything and write. I'd be pleased to see you, but you're apt not to find me here in March." To West, as to others, he steadily complained of the impossibility of finding in his social environment an understanding of a writer's need to concentrate in solitude, perhaps least of all in the academic context.

West did come down in March. Dobie wrote him they would go out to Paisano, but West would have to drive: Frank could not use his right arm — he had bursitis — and "worse, all my juice seems gone." Weary as he was, he remained more alive and real, more natural a man than most men ever become. I remember him as he was that autumn, when both of us were invited to Brackettville to watch John Wayne's filming of a longhorn sequence in the movie *The Alamo*. Dobie was enchanted with a gnarled and magnificent old mesquite growing just outside the building used as a commissary. After breakfast that morning, he communed awhile with the mesquite. A photographer importuned him to hurry; John Wayne was waiting out on location to have some still shots made of himself and Dobie inspecting the replica of the Alamo that had been built on Happy Shahan's ranch.

"Here's the thing to photograph," Dobie rebuked him. "Get some pictures of that old mesquite. It has survived wind and weather for, I guess, several hundred years. You never saw such a big trunk on a mesquite. Now there's something noble. And send me some of the pictures. I'll pay for them."

The mesquite was photographed and the drive out to location began, with scriptwriter James Edward Grant at the wheel. Dobie was identifying everything that grew along the road. Suddenly he told Grant to stop. Dobie got out of the car and beckoned us all to follow. I thought of the thousand extras waiting for our arrival before shooting began, and tried to recall the figure I had heard about the hourly cost of this movie, not remembering whether it was thirty dollars or three hundred or even three thousand.

"Look, Jimmy," Dobie called, his face as bright as any wildcatter just bringing in a strike, "here's a juajilla bush. This explains that honey you liked so much at breakfast. It's the best honey in the world and all because the bees suck these 'wahee' bushes . . ."

A dozen cars back of us, carrying actors and crew, stopped to see the phenomenon. We started again and at last came to a rise where we looked down on Hollywood's re-creation of Old San Antonio. Parking there, Jimmy Grant pridefully turned to Frank and began:

"How do you like that, Mr. Dobie? We got a Spanish architect who studied old documents and —"

Dobie had turned to lean over a bush beside the dirt road. He hadn't yet directed one glance to the counterfeit set.

"Look, Jimmy," he interrupted, "here's another juajilla bush."

John Wayne came over and Dobie was feted the rest of the day. The big scene to be filmed was the herding of longhorns into the Alamo by the Texans. Bill Daniel had assembled for Wayne, with much ingenuity, a magnificent herd of two hundred longhorns, powerful monsters unlike the captives you see in Brackenridge Park.

Dobie was elated. To stars and extras and onlookers he explained about the breed. Wayne put him in his own director's chair, marked "The Duke." Ken Curtis and Chill Wills were summoned to sing for Mr. Dobie some of the songs Dimitri Tiomkin had composed for the movie. Frank seemed to listen, but on that brilliant sunlit morning he kept his eye on the movements of the longhorns as they milled around under the control of Bill Daniel and some Mexican riders.

Like the mesquite and the juajilla, the longhorns were part of the real thing. The music wasn't. "No, Duke," Frank told Wayne, "what you need is some of the songs the Mexicans really sang. I think you ought to make 'La Paloma' your theme song."

We had been flown over by General Motors to take brief part in a TV "spectacular" the company was making about the production. Frank was to be in an outdoor shot, seated on an old wagon in front of the herd of longhorns, whose history he was to suggest in three or four minutes. Hopefully, the TV men handed him a "suggested" script. He glanced at it, then said, "Give me a piece of paper. I couldn't possibly say this stuff." He thought and wrote. "This is what I'll say," he said. And he did.

When we left a day or so later, I saw him look with long affection at that old mesquite. He did not find the flora and fauna more interesting than the Hollywood people, just more real. But with his immense gusto and zest for living, with his ever-present curiosity about the new, he thoroughly enjoyed the experience of this alien world.

On the way over, flying in a Piper Cub between San Antonio and Brackettville, Frank had interpreted to me all the patterns on the land below, reading the deer tracks on the ground as he might have read place names on a map. During the entire trip, he found nature more rewarding than movie stars or Hollywood moguls or the many involved mechanical gadgets used in the moviemaking. But when we came away, I was startled at how much *human* inventory Dobie had been taking. Frank hardly stopped talking on the flight back. He had described nature on the way over; coming home, he was offering capsule psychological portraits of the sharpest acumen, with clairvoyant glimpses into human nature. Some were barbed, some were bemused, some sardonic, and all of singular justice, I thought.

The picturesque Dobie had indeed been present all during the trip; he had delighted nearly everyone, and especially John Wayne, with his genuine and immediate charm; and the Duke had treated him regally as a "grand old man." Inside himself, Frank Dobie was steadily contemplating, almost effortlessly it would seem. Not judging, actually, just contemplating.

It was then, I believe, that I began to think of him as a complete man, a ripe man, maturing all the elements of his nature harmoniously. He found life something to absorb, not gluttonously or in quantity, but in savory understanding. He understood much more, I suspect, than he ever had time to corral in all his books.

In January 1962, when Frank Dobie was still under doctor's orders to take daily rests and avoid activity, he nonetheless headed up a group of Texas literati from the Texas Institute of Letters in an attack on reckless and bigoted censorship before the state legislature. The Dobie name brought overflow crowds to the hearing. Dobie told the legislative committee which was hearing testimony for and against the content of certain recommended textbooks that "All we're asking is to leave freedom free to combat error. . . . A censor is always a tool. Or, as Hitler called Mussolini, a utensil. Not one censor in history is respected by enlightened men of any nation. . . . Any person who imagines he has a corner on the definition or conception of Americanism and wants to suppress all conceptions to the contrary is a bigot and an enemy of the free world. . . . I'm for textbooks selected on the basis of strength, vividness, justness and the beautiful. The more censoring of textbooks, the weaker they become."

In March 1962, John Ciardi devoted two columns in the *Saturday Review* to his filming at the DeGolyer home in Dallas of a TV special on Frank Dobie. For Ciardi, a close friend of Robert Frost's and longtime associate of the poet at the Bread Loaf Writers' Conference, Frank Dobie offered a Southwestern version, and a very good one, of Robert Frost's major ideas about life and about art. Like Frost, who insisted that he was not a "regionalist" but a "realist," Ciardi found that Dobie located the essence of poetry, or poetic truth, in the realm of the imagination.

Dobie was in the hospital again that year, seriously injured in a two-car crash near his home the evening of November 3. When he was rushed to the hospital, on a weekend night, his doctor was out of town. Luckily, a team of physicians was hastily assembled; they performed an emergency tracheotomy which proved to be a life-saving operation, for he had neck injuries and was bleeding internally, which obstructed his windpipe. The head injuries themselves were mild, but the tracheotomy was imperative. He could not talk for many days. Bertha Dobie recalled that after a week of answering her questions with his eyes, he finally managed to lift a hand to caress her face. It was a gesture he had always used to reassure her that he could cope. After twelve days he talked his way out of the hospital, but couldn't convince his physicians to let him participate in his annual hunt at Ralph Johnston's ranch, with Johnston, Walker Stone and John Joseph Mathews. The doctors made an exception to the no-visitors rule to let his hunting companions stop by. They promised to bring him a winter supply of venison on their way back. Bertha told a reporter that he was able to walk about the lower floor but was not allowed to go outside. They had a morning nurse for him but no night nurse. "He feels lucky to be alive," she said, "and getting well."

Aged seventy-five in 1963, he could no longer take the extreme heat of Austin in the summer. He wanted to complete a book close to his heart, memories of personally known and admired "cow people," and he simply could not find the energy to work in the broiling Texas summertime. He decided to spend the month of September in San Francisco, where his longtime friend Henry Nash Smith was nearby (he was chairman of the English Department of the University of California at Berkeley). He stopped over in Dallas on the way, where a friend gave him a copy of *The Letters of Robert Frost to Louis Untermeyer*, a book which, he wrote Bertha, stirred him powerfully. "Frost's foolery, common sense, sometime aspersions on such people as Carl Sandburg, Stark Young, Edgar Lee Masters, wit, wisdom, humanity and undeviating adherence to his own path cause me to read slowly. I don't know why I continue to read newspapers for information when I could stick to Frost for life itself."

The noise of being in a downtown San Francisco hotel disturbed his writing; Henry Smith soon arranged for him to stay at the Faculty Club in Berkeley. From there he wrote to Bertha: "Frost said that what does not add to writing subtracts from it. The older I grow, the more I value economy. The art of omission applies to facts as much as it applies to style. Yet I like some narrative, etc., too much to delete." He wanted to finish his manuscript by October 1, and he was, despite his age and severe illnesses, still able to write six or seven hours a day. In general, he was gloomy, for not all days were good days, and even at the Faculty Club he did not find the silence and concentration he wanted. He wrote Bertha that he had lost all interest in the Dobie Collection at the university; "if I am to be remembered at all it will be through my writing; what goes to the library is of little more significance than a graveyard monument."

He was ready to return home by the end of September, and had regained his optimism. He realized, he wrote Bertha, that his manuscript on cow people had far more "autobiography" in it than he had anticipated. He enjoyed the writing of it. "Ploughing on in the field of writing, no matter how many stumps in the ground, gives me satisfaction. Without writing, life is not living to me."

He had never fully recovered his normal energy after the bout with pneumonia in 1957 that left his heart gravely weakened; after the collision of 1962 he was even more bereft of stamina, but was still able at crucial moments to summon a burst of energy, as when in April 1964 he and Bertha traveled to the White House at the insistent invitation of President Johnson, whom he had long known.

Dobie's main political comment while he was in Washington those four days concerned Senator Ralph Yarborough's campaign for reelection to the Senate (the Texas primary was held that spring), or rather the campaign of Senator Yarborough's rival. Dobie was caustic about the latter, and observed that the "primary was a test whether Texans could make an independent choice or whether conformity induced by the techniques of . . . controlled mass media would dominate." As one commentator remarked, "When he [Dobie] has something to say, and he generally does about everything under the sun, it can be as sharp as a rattlesnake's bite or as staggering as a .45 slug — and very often both at the same time."

That year Ronnie Dugger, the young and talented editor of Texas' only, or almost only, "liberal" paper at the time, the weekly *Texas Observer*, a paper that was a training ground for young writers, including Willie Morris and Larry King and William Brammer, devoted a special issue of the *Observer* to assess the achievement of J. Frank Dobie. Dugger had done the same for Roy Bedichek and Walter Prescott Webb, following their deaths. This time the honoree got to read the critical assessments of himself and did so with considerable interest. All three memorial issues were later gathered by Dugger into a volume titled *Three Men in Texas* and published by Frank Wardlaw at the University of Texas Press.

Also in 1964, Dobie was appointed consultant in American cultural history to the Library of Congress, for a three-year period, beginning January 1, although the duties of the post would not begin until August. Senator Ralph Yarborough had played a central role in securing the appointment, not simply as a member of the Congress but as an enlightened and civilized student of American culture himself. Also appointed were two outstanding scholars in American literature, Jay Broadus Hubbell of Duke University and Howard Mumford Jones of Harvard. Curiously enough, both men had spent crucial years of their teaching apprenticeship in Texas, Jones at the University of Texas, Hubbell at Southern Methodist University, where he and John H. McGinnis had transformed the *Texas Quarterly* (which had been founded in 1915 by Stark Young at the University of Texas) into the *Southwest Review*.

Dobie was summoned on September 14 to Washington, to receive the Presidential Medal of Freedom, but was too ill to go. He had been bedridden at home for a month. His friend and editor, Ned Bradford, stood in for him at the ceremonies, which Bertha attended. On her return, when she handed him the medal, he smiled with deep satisfaction.

But another token of concrete achievement gave him even greater satisfaction: on the morning of September 19 he had received the first copy of his latest book, *Cow People*, which Ned Bradford had thoughtfully hurried on to him. Frank died that afternoon, during his siesta.

Arranged by Bertha Dobie and Frank Wardlaw and Joe B. Frantz, the services were held on the University of Texas campus in the Will Hogg Auditorium. Friends and notables from all over the state, and outside, thronged the hall, one building on the campus Frank admired. Before Frank Wardlaw pronounced a moving eulogy, four cowboy-hatted officials of the Texas Trail Drivers Association, who had requested permission to do so, delivered the traditional ceremonial final salute the association offers in tribute to its outstanding leaders, a silent ritual impressively conceived. Burial was in the Texas State Memorial Cemetery, an honor the state usually reserves for officials of the government.

6

A Joy to Him and a Joy to Hear

> Vitality is the primary requisite of all prose writing. No matter whether a writer writes to instruct, to convince or to interest and amuse, without vitality his work will never be read. Hence tons of academic studies that had as well be burned up.
> — From *44 & 44*

Toward the end of his life, in his Sunday column of July 26, 1964, Frank Dobie wrote: "I have for years known that my writing considerably on Southwestern and Western subjects has in certain quarters lowered my reputation for literary achievement. That regard has never bothered me. I have written the best I could on what I wanted to write about. In my own judgment, I have in several books written with more power, precision of diction, vividness and continually cultivated use of the English language than quite a few of the literati have achieved." This sounds absurd, since by any standards he was one of "the literati" himself; but the fact is that Dobie was trapped by the image he had so carefully constructed, and sometimes he wanted out. Of the charming Western novelist Eugene Manlove Rhodes, Frank wrote angrily that "a newspaper article . . . characterizes him as 'a bold, gallant, card-playing, pool-playing, cowpunching natural son of the American West.' It is this Philistine conception of what constitutes natural sons that makes the civilized pursuit of art and ideas so difficult everywhere in America and especially in the Southwest. . . . Being a good hand on horseback did not make Gene Rhodes a good writer, though pride and vitality are common denominators of both." It is generally conceded that he who rides may also read, even write; but Frank could never count on it. Like a wealthy bride, he was insecure about "being loved for himself," and was persuaded that few people read him for anything other than content, for information, for picturesque detail. It was the price he paid for being "Mr. Texas."

Since he was preoccupied by the question, let's look at it: had he not been raised in — and inspired by — the Southwest, would he have achieved as much as he did, as a writer? That he was born to write, his early letters show to be indisputable. That he would have written very differently is probable. His style, like his persona, was deliberately chosen. In his courtship letters range words occur, but festooned with invisible quotation marks, in the way a Boston Brahmin writer will spice his language with Yankee phrases. Later on, they were incorporated into his vocabulary. I think he would have been a storyteller anywhere; never a critic, since he did not enjoy the play of abstractions, and probably not a novelist: he was not introspective enough. "Formal" history would not have suited him, for he could not write impersonally. The style he evolved suited the man he was; bravura passages are carefully qualified (one can almost hear Bertha in the background, reminding him that he loves to overdo it), dreamy evocations are almost sung in a delicious legato, and his narrative passages bear every mark of having been rehearsed aloud, by a man who loves yarning to an audience. Moreover, Frank — despite his rugged independence — needed badly to be liked; the prose of most such writers has an intimate, seductive quality. Hear him reminisce:

There were two or three Mexican bakeries across the railroad tracks, and every afternoon a man with a face radiating good nature walked up and down the streets carrying on his head a large flat basket covered with a white cloth and containing loaves of freshly baked, still warm lightbread and buns. He balanced the basket on a coiled-up red Mexican sash around his head, and while carrying it did not touch it with his hands. Walking slowly, he would sing in long-drawn-out and faraway-sounding syllables the words *pan cal-i-ente, pan dulce* (hot lightbread, sweet bread). The cry, running far up the musical scale, was a joy to him, and it was a joy to hear. It was an added joy to take a nickel from Grandma and run out to meet him. He would uncover the fragrant basket and hand me a loaf of lightbread with the invariable *pilón* (lagniappe) — a very soft warm bun, as light as milk foam, which I devoured at once. Then he would walk on, trailing aroma and melody.

What relish, and what care to make us hear the peddler's call; and what a knowing lilt to the last phrase! If you try reversing the words "aroma" and "melody" you lose the fine dactylic beat . . . and with it, the whole careful effect.

Frank often said that writing was hard for him: an unconvincing statement at first look. His gift as a sketcher, his knack for conveying a place or a mood in a couple of strokes — and his pleasure in doing so — are clear in his letters, for instance in the mirthful description of the family ranch that he wrote for Bertha in 1914 (see page 30). But he worked hard to control his overbrimming facility. That he did so is partly due to Bertha's assiduity as his "pruner," and partly to his own probity. "Tell the truth," he was taught; "account for yourself." In his first real writings, his love letters, one is aware of his earnest desire to define what he thought he thought and what he thought he felt . . . as though he owed such honesty to himself as much as to Bertha. For a very young writer, self-definition is a choice of affectations — trying one pose after another to see which one fits — and emotions are uttered as much to verify them as to express them. "How do I know what I feel till I hear what I say?" For a very young *American* writer, especially at that time and in that region, identity was established under the constant threat of being thought "different" or an idler or a sissy. He had learned self-reliance in his boyhood, and self-confidence came to him along with prominence among the students at Southwestern and popularity with girls; but Frank was wincingly vulnerable, and too trusting to have the defenses of irony. In Bertha's letters, we may read between the lines that — at least sometimes — she knew his youthful pretensions for what they were. But she never failed to take him seriously. Fully aware of his impulse to grandiloquence, she pruned, she restrained, she cautioned; and she was indeed a great complainer. But she never once struck at his self-esteem. It must surely be due, at least in part, to her tact that there is nothing anxious, self-doubting or divided underlying the occasional swank and rant of the mature man.

Later, Bertha encouraged him to write lean, spare prose, to lasso his rhetoric. Over and over, in print, he thanked her, as in the dedication to her of *The Voice of the Coyote:* "Through the years I have derived as much from her habit of clear thinking as from her particular criticisms. She is the most incisive and the most completely constructive critic I have ever known."

Much of his work, for instance the weekly columns he produced for over a quarter-century, must be regarded as in first draft; he had to release it unpolished in order to meet his deadlines. But the manuscript pages of the essays and books he labored over look like the galley-proof revisions of Balzac, who used to drive Parisian typesetters to despair. And, like Balzac, Dobie never regarded type as inviolable. To cite a well-known example, he rewrote four or five times his famous story "Sancho's Return," about a longhorn's attachment to its birthplace; each revision was made after the preceding version had got into print, even into bound volumes. The pains Dobie took to carve his sentences into perfection have rarely been noticed. Bill Bedell, reviewing *I'll Tell You a Tale* for the Houston *Post*, gave an example of how fruitful such an investigation can be. Bedell was the first among reviewers to compare what changes from original versions Dobie had made in helping Isabel Gaddis prepare this "Dobie reader." Then, Margaret Hartley gave an ampler treatment in the *Southwest Review*, benefiting from her long association with Dobie through the magazine he valued so highly.

Anyone who heard Dobie's magnificent speech to the Texas Institute of Letters at the Houston meeting of 1959 would have been alerted to his concern for form and structure. He spoke memorably of pace and tempo in writing, above all of the importance of cadence, of rhythm. He said that often while riding horseback as a young man he made up sentences to shout aloud and to match his mount's movement. But he said his feeling for rhythm in prose came first of all from his reading of the King James Version of the Bible. He worried a manuscript up to the last minute of a deadline. (I knew he had left a council meeting of the institute early that afternoon in order to keep on polishing the text of his speech. He had the manuscript at the meeting; I saw pages on which the typed script was barely visible under the inked corrections. But if anyone else dared make a change in one of his manuscripts, he could throw a fit. Having handled shorter Dobie articles for thirty-five years, first on the *Southwest Review* and then on the book page of the Dallas *News*, I can report that in the early days many a hot letter greeted editorial bungling. Still, to cross him occasionally was worth risking, just for the pleasure of seeing such fighting rapture. I have never known any other writer who took his craft more seriously.)

But his revisions were not radical: he tuned his instrument; he never smashed it in order to rebuild it. Never questioning himself in earnest, he knew what he wanted to say. An extrovert in writing as in life, his goal was to show, not to explain. "Explanations are tedious," he said often, echoing his beloved Hazlitt.

Few of his later writings were to retain the sober, serviceable transparency of his first book, *A Vaquero of the Brush Country*. It is an admirable journeyman-piece. If you want to know how a typical cowboy talked, how he pronounced his words and in what rhythm; if you want to know what he wore and ate and did; if you are curious about the techniques in the Brush Country, as distinguished from the open range, of branding, trail driving, and brush popping; if you seek the precise meaning of words like *chousing*, *hide crop*, or *die-ups*, you will find this book a manual. Not only is Dobie precise in detail, he has the historian's alertness to the influence of climate, commerce and technology on a culture. Writing *as* the vaquero John Young, using the first person, Dobie neither stoops to dialect quaintness nor superimposes his own eloquence. Well aware that John Young's "unfenced world" was gone, Dobie records but does not lament the change "from free disorder to mechanical order, from waste to economic efficiency."

He was reacting then against the sentimental mythifying of outsiders, who from Owen Wister (in 1902, with *The Virginian*) to Zane Grey had distorted the West Dobie knew. In almost all his books, he proclaims a special entitlement. In *Vaquero:* "I 'speak the same language' that John Young and the people he worked among speak." In *Tongues of the Monte:* "I tell these few things of my childhood as a kind of warrant for my right in years long afterwards to write a book about the Mexican people." In *The Mustangs:* "To that plot of earth in Live Oak County, Texas, known as the R. J. Dobie ranch, where I was born and reared and where I lived with horses, I dedicate this book . . ."

"As the frontiers advanced," he wrote in *Vaquero*, "the best mustangs were sought for with increasing eagerness and the proportion of inbred and poorly shaped mustangs increased. . . . At a distance, one of them with arched neck, distended nostrils, and flowing mane and tail looked graceful, even magnificent, but near at hand he was likely to appear gimlet hammed and narrow chested." In *The Mustangs*, published twenty-three years later, Dobie is transported beyond prose:

*Sentinels of alertness in eye and nostril,
Every toss of maned neck a Grecian grace,
Every high snort bugling out the pride of the free.*

*I see them vanishing, vanishing, vanished,
The seas of grass shriveled to pens of barbed-wire property,
The wind-racers and wind-drinkers bred into property also.*

*But winds still blow free and grass still greens,
And the core of that something which men live on believing
Is always freedom.*

*So sometimes yet, in the realities of silence and solitude,
For a few people unhampered a while by things,
The mustangs walk out with dawn, stand high, then
Sweep away, wild with sheer life, and free, free, free —
Free of all confines of time and flesh.*

The two passages mark the limits of his gamut; and in both, Dobie would have said, he was writing in a true way about mustangs. He was faithful as a reporter, rapturous as a celebrant.

And he could combine the two in prose, as in this passage preceding the "poem" above: "No one who perceives him as only a potential servant to man can apprehend the mustang. The true conceiver must be a lover of freedom — a person who yearns to extend freedom to all of life. Halted in animated expectancy or running in abandoned freedom, the mustang was the most beautiful, the most spirited and the most inspiring creature ever to print foot on the grasses of America. . . . Only the spirited are beautiful."

It is notable that the "freedom" theme, paramount in *The Mustangs* and in *The Ben Lilly Legend*, which just preceded it, is echoed in Dobie's own life (he was working on both books when the University of Texas refused to grant him a leave and he quit). One doesn't want to force a parallel too far, but something similar does crop up earlier, when he was out "prospecting," as he put it, for stories and legends and folklore of the Southwest.

He saw it as a quest; and it is around "quest" stories that he organized *Coronado's Children* and *Apache Gold and Yaqui Silver*. He went searching for the lost Tayopa mine in 1927 with C. B. Ruggles — mountainman, trapper, hunter, prospector, mustanger, amateur medicineman, who had spent six years, on and off, crisscrossing the Sierra Madre, looking for the ancient Jesuit treasure trove. His sympathy with Ruggles carries over to his heroes of legend, though they have to be measured against a canvas too vast to allow for psychological penetration.

"The New World," he wrote in *Coronado's Children*, "has been a world of men neither lured nor restrained by women. It has been a world of men exploring unknown continents, subduing wildernesses and savage tribes, felling forests, butchering buffaloes, trailing millions of longhorned cattle wilder than buffaloes, digging gold out of mountains, and pumping oil out of hot earth beneath the plains. It has been a world in which men expected, fought for, and took riches beyond computation."

The purposes of such men are rarely related to any idea or any institution "bigger than the individual himself," in the words of William James. And their children — Jim Bowie, for example — usually lacked Coronado's dedication, at least self-styled dedication, to crown and cross. Men like these lived *in* the moment and *for* a miragelike future. Historian, folklorist, man of letters, Dobie's larger perspective was long in his sense of the past, broad in his human sympathy, deep in his awareness of identity with the natural world. His books are not literature made out of other literature; there is something concrete, something firsthand, about them all. They are universal to the extent that his themes reflect the American mystique: the love of nature, the courage to endure, the celebration of life, even its tragedies, and the enlargement of individual freedom.

Certain abysses he skirted or ignored. Equally American, but in his day more characteristic of the literature of New England, the themes of moral responsibility, of guilt, of universal compassion, and of sin and redemption are rarely central in his work. As a dutiful son, solicitous husband, generous teacher, and upright citizen, Frank had a comfortable conscience, and one suspects that such issues never worried him. Terrestrial love, which certainly did, he dealt with rarely and queasily. In the first-person, nonfiction (but not "literal") *Tongues of the Monte*, he tells of two beautiful young women at the hacienda where he was a guest: one a servant girl, the other, the daughter of the house. Sensing that he had roused them both to unholy passion — the way he could tell was that they kept offering him flowers — he discreetly went off on a pack trip. On his return, he found that the señorita had poisoned the servant; and he himself was saved from death at the hands of the dead girl's sweetheart only by the loyalty of his mozo — and the wrenched arm of coincidence. The plot line is obvious, but Dobie manipulates the scene with dramatic skill, achieving plausibility and suspense, enough to make one regret again that he turned away, after this, from fiction. It always puzzled Frank that *Tongues* was not more popular with readers. He concluded that the title was to blame.

Frank was more at home with the attitude of the famous hunter Ben Lilly: nagged once by his wife beyond endurance, he obeyed her insistence that he get up from the table to kill a chicken hawk — since, as she said, he "liked to shoot so well." Ben took his gun; the hawk flew; Ben followed. He did not return until more than a year later. "That hawk kept flying," he remarked by way of explanation.

Wild old Ben Lilly, a self-taught naturalist, bounty hunter for the United States Forest Service, guide to President Theodore Roosevelt, was a man who never hunted on Sundays, read his Bible regularly, and lived for killing. Any hunting dog that proved lazy, he clubbed to death. "Now," Dobie wrote, "twenty-one years after my one encounter with Ben Lilly" (an encounter that lasted several days) "I still see his clear, serene eyes, as limpid as childhood's. The power of harmony had given them an open assurance, and in one way they seemed to lack nothing. Certainly they reflected nothing of design on other human beings. Yet in a strange way they seemed to shadow personal matters never to be revealed."

"When I am around babies," Lilly told him, "I always tote them out on my arm in the evening and let them look at the stars and feel the wind. They sleep better for that. They would sleep better still if they had their pallets on the ground. I always sleep better on the ground. Something agreeable to my system seeps into it from the ground."

Dobie was not, I think, so much fascinated by the old man's paradoxical character — "the lover of the wild [who] went on annihilating it" — as by the single-mindedness of his obsession with killing predators (bears and mountain lions) and the feral freedom in which he pursued it. Dobie's sense of duty never let him feel entirely free; and he always thought the grass would be greener somewhere else. His own quest was not for mountain lions or gold or land, but for a state of being, something less than "grace" and something more than contentment, in which he could feel in harmony with nature and with kindred minds — and with himself.

At Cambridge, as he relates in *A Texan in England*, his imagination, nourished so long on Shakespeare and the Romantic poets, responded simultaneously to the English landscape and to English civilization in an almost atavistic tropism. It was a needed respite for him, that sojourn in another homeland: an ancient, well-cultivated country whose culture has fused land and language, where an indigenous literature has expressed and set in proportion every human wish or impulse. In England educated men seem to have a word — a word in common — for just about everything.

In his introduction to *The Voice of the Coyote*, his next book, Dobie speaks of the necessity of sympathy, that "sympathy that comes from a civilized perspective," for understanding men and animals alike. "This sympathy," he writes, "is found in the two extremes of society — savages and people with cultivated minds and sensibilities." And he adds: "Among the wise this civilized sympathy infuses knowledge. It is a kind of cultivated gentleness. It is foreign to harsh and boisterous frontiers and comes after many of the wild creatures to whom it is directed have been destroyed."

It was this sympathy, awake in Dobie from the first but always growing, that has made his books so beloved. He creates a bond, a fellowship, between himself and the reader. His attention, his faithful effort to reach out to his subject, is so rapt as to compel one's own. Rereading his work all at once, one is struck by his reverence for concrete particulars, and then by the fact that he never rates things by ranking them on a scale, never reasons deductively, never creates hierarchies. When he said casually that things that interested him seemed to come together, he was, perhaps, hinting at the guiding principle of his life as an artist: *Love and attend to what exists. Bear witness. Trust the grand design* you cannot see; it is there, and what you do is part of it. If there is a heaven, which Frank courteously doubted, I like to think he may — when not in search of the outermost cloud — be consorting with Geoffrey Chaucer, the master storyteller of them all.

His arrivals and departures, so often repeated at the same points of interest, testified to the overpowering respect he had intellectually for opposites. He needed to balance strenuous physical activity with long periods of repose; he needed to go into the world and then retreat from it while he ruminated on his experiences. He needed to explore the globe and to be at the center of action (as when he volunteered in World War I as soon as the United States declared war on Germany), but he also needed long isolations, alone in a cabin while he shaped up his books. Self-sufficient and almost a hermit, he lived mostly on corn bread, which he baked; pinto beans he cooked and flavored with honey, onions and the very hot jalapeño chile peppers of the border; jello; and milk, preferably buttermilk when he could get it at some countryman's place. He longed to live in Santa Fe, when he first saw it, for "the rest of his life"; he felt the same way about the Basque country in France, about spots on the Mediterranean, about desert Mexico, about California, about rural England, about life on oceangoing liners, about the Dobie ranch, about Austin, Texas — to which he always yearned to return from his vagabonding yet purposeful wanderings.

He escaped labeling because he was an unfenced man who didn't like artificial or limiting boundaries. Most of his life he was called by colleagues a folklorist, although he steadily proclaimed publicly that he was an amateur in this field and that professional or scientific folklore interested him mildly; others labeled him a historian, although he insisted he was a chronicler of facts, and often used facts simply as a storyteller. He was an open mind, a man open, in Heidegger's sense, to experience. But tradition and the past also enthralled him, especially in the first half of his life. Tradition meant a respect for convention, but Dobie regarded conventions as he did the rituals and the ceremonies of civilization — all the subconsciously sanctioned and mostly unexamined encrusted habits we inherit or develop, that condition our notion of selfhood and that require steady scrutiny.

Dobie's respect for the natural was the reverse side of his distaste for the artificial and the overstructured, but his respect for reality and for the authentic forestalled his taking simplistic views. Much as the mustang meant to him as a metaphor of free and spirited living, he never meant to champion in man a mindless spontaneity. For all his love of simplicity, he was not himself a simple man. He was too many-sided, too contradictory, or too "ample" — to use one of his favorite words — to be a one-note or single-cause human being. But he was not at war with himself. He was, most of the time, at peace with himself, in a harmonizing of contradictory traits. Both his life and his books reveal a respect for the natural, for simplicity, allied with scorn for the simplistic. For this wholeness, we might call him: The Compleat Texan.

In going through his "Autobiographical" boxes after his death, Bertha Dobie discovered a handwritten epitaph for his gravestone, headed "Epitaph composed May 1962," two years before his death. On the manila folder she wrote: "(Not seen by B.M.D. until late August. The gravestone was already up.)" Her note is undated. The epitaph reads:

He loved life and put a few fragments of it into writing. Because of deference to the well-mannered he failed to expose most of what he knew, enjoyed and hated. He achieved a liberated mind. Realizing that all gods and bibles are man-made, he had contempt for all creeds, and admiration for nobilities and sensible skepticisms. His faith in the geological processes of the universe, including the speck called Earth, was, like literature, a solace to him.

To write one's own epitaph is to sum up, not only what one is, but, given human vanity, what one has hoped to be. Frank's was, ultimately, a liberated mind; but he was never a wholly liberated writer. It is sad to see a writer of his age still fretting over "the well-mannered," sadder still that he stayed so far within his actual limitations, failing, indeed, "to expose most of what he knew." Trapped within his loyalties and his public role, Dobie the writer became predictable. Dobie the man, I think, never stopped growing. Loving life as he truly did, he approached it, not as a ravisher, but as an ardent pupil. Let his last word be taken from another penciled note in his Autobiographical boxes: "The only reality I refuse to accept is life without magic."

A Bibliographical Note

THE PRIMARY COLLECTION of Dobie materials — manuscripts, correspondence, his great library of books on range life plus other collections in his personal library, his papers, his paintings and sculptures and art objects of the Old West — is housed in the Harry Huntt Ransom Humanities Research Center at the University of Texas in Austin, where the major part of the research on this book was done under ideal conditions of cooperation, competence and helpfulness.

Three other Dobie collections are important, though on a smaller scale: Texas A & M University at College Station acquired in 1971 the Dobie collection of Jeff Dykes, an alumnus and a renowned rare-book dealer. A great number of items bear Dobie's own notations. In 1966 A & M had acquired Dykes's own range-life collection of several thousand volumes, a collection he holds to be nearly the equal of the Dobie range-life library, which he had appraised when it was acquired by the University of Texas at Austin. Dykes was one of Dobie's friends.

Southwestern University at Georgetown, Texas, has in its Cody Memorial Library a remarkable collection of Dobie material made by Isabel Maltsberger Gaddis of Cotulla, Texas, who compiled, with Dobie, the anthology of Dobie narratives *I'll Tell You a Tale* (1960). She had known Frank from the time she was a girl. He visited her parents and went on deer hunts with members of her family; and she was one of the early students in his "Life and Literature of the Southwest" course.

Baylor University at Waco has recently been given the private collection of Dobieana belonging to Dr. Frank Connally, a noted Waco cardiologist and a former regent of the University of Texas.

Three bibliographies of Dobie's writings have been published:

Mary Louise McVicker's *J. Frank Dobie: A Bibliography* and Spruill Cook's *J. Frank Dobie: Bibliography*, both brought out in 1968 by the Museum of the Great Plains, Lawton, Oklahoma; and Jeff Dykes's *My Dobie Collection*, issued in 1971 by the Friends of the Texas A & M University Library, College Station. The latest entries in the McVicker and Spruill bibliographies are dated 1967; Dykes's bibliography lists over two hundred additional items, of varying importance, that he managed to find between 1967 and 1971. Nonetheless, the completeness and the carefulness of the McVicker bibliography, which was compiled with Dobie's cooperation, makes it supreme; and it is enhanced by a fine introduction by the late Harry Huntt Ransom, former chancellor of the University of Texas.

The McVicker bibliography is limited to writings by Dobie himself. The Cook volume includes a section on writings about him; and the Dykes volume lists ninety-seven items in the Dykes collection that are not mentioned in the Cook "selective" listing.

There have been surprisingly few works about Dobie, but several very good ones are available, although brief or only partly about him. This may be because Dobie's own books contain a good deal of autobiography, aside from his one autobiographical volume, *Some Part of Myself*, which deals only with his youth and early manhood, before he had become an established figure in literature and education.

The first resource for students of Dobie, outside his own books, is no doubt the Dobie memorial issue of the *Texas Observer*, July 24, 1964. This, and two other memorial issues — one on Roy Bedichek and the other on Walter Prescott Webb — were augmented and brought out together in book form by the University of Texas Press in 1967: *Three Men in Texas*, edited by Ronnie Dugger. They all consist of essays by the friends and associates of each member of the "Texas triumvirate," and are rich in personal insights and anecdotes. Henry Nash Smith's essay on Dobie is an important critical assessment.

Winston Bode's *Portrait of Pancho* (Austin: Pemberton Press, 1965) is a reworking of a television special prepared for an Austin station by Bode, with the close collaboration of Bertha Dobie and Harry Huntt Ransom; of its 164 pages, more than one hundred are photographs or other illustrative material. The captions Bode provided for this absorbing pictorial record concisely but vividly enhance the text, which includes as much biography as portrait. Francis Edward Abernethy's paperback book of fifty-two pages, *J. Frank Dobie*, was the first volume in the Southwest Writers Series, brought out by the Steck-Vaughan Company of Austin, and got the series off to a brilliant start. Abernethy, a leading figure in the Texas Folklore Society, blends biographical information with lively and penetrating commentary on Dobie's books. It is the best critical survey of Dobie thus far published.

Lawrence Clark Powell, one of Dobie's most valued friends, has written some of his best essays on Dobie, notably in *Books in My Baggage* (Cleveland: World, 1960), in which the essay "Mr. Southwest" justifies the bestowal of that title on Dobie; the essay was reprinted from Powell's *Books: West Southwest* (Los Angeles: Ward Ritchie Press, 1957). Many references to Dobie are made in other books by Powell, especially in *Southwestern Book Trails* (Albuquerque, N.M.: Horn and Wallace, 1963), and another long essay on Dobie's work is in Powell's *Southwest Classics* (Los Angeles: Ward Ritchie Press, 1974).

A brief but penetrating piece on Dobie, especially on his political activities, is to be found in Ralph W. Yarborough's *Frank Dobie: Man and Friend* (Washington, D.C.: Potomac Corral of the Westerners, 1967). Yarborough was one of Dobie's valued friends, much admired; Jeff Dykes supplied an introduction to this privately printed brochure.

William A. Owens's *Three Friends: Bedichek, Dobie, Webb* (Garden City, N.Y.: Doubleday, 1969) is a compilation of letters that make a revealing portrait of each man.

Larry McMurtry, clearly the most thoughtful spokesman for the new generation of Texas writers since the fifties and certainly one of the most important Texas writers of this century, has written the most-discussed and the most negative assessment of Dobie's achievement — indeed, of Webb's and Bedichek's also — in his essay "Southwestern Literature?" which appears in *In a Narrow Grave: Essays on Texas* (Austin: Encino Press, 1968). McMurtry's book is indispensable to anyone who wishes to gain an objective view or who welcomes a challenge to his own predilections. (I must admit that although I value McMurtry's insights, and enjoy the play of his unique sensibility and his intellection, I believe his judgments on Webb and Dobie to be wrong.)

Ronnie Dugger's *Our Invaded Universities* (New York: Norton, 1974) includes an incisive, penetrating sketch of Dobie and numerous references to him.

Two recent reference books contain brief articles, mostly biographical, on Dobie: volume III of *The Handbook of Texas: A Supplement* (Austin: Texas State Historical Association, 1976); and *The Reader's Encyclopedia of the American West* (New York: Crowell, 1977). The Dobie articles were written by Winston Bode and Joe B. Frantz respectively.

Two unpublished theses consulted in the preparation of this book deserve grateful mention. Professor Henry Louis Alsmeyer, Jr., allowed me the use of his "J. Frank Dobie's Attitude Towards Physical Nature" (doctoral dissertation, Texas A & M University, 1973); and William Delaney allowed me to consult, with profit, his brilliant term paper written for a graduate seminar in American studies at Johns Hopkins University in 1974. An undergraduate honors paper by Paul Stone, written when he was a student at Harvard in 1974, deserves mention for its sharp insights.

In view of the compendious nature of the McVicker, Cook and Dykes bibliographies, it seems pertinent to list here only the books of which Frank Dobie was the author:

A Vaquero of the Brush Country. Dallas: Southwest Press, 1929.
Coronado's Children. Dallas: Southwest Press, 1930. New York: Literary Guild of America, 1931.
On the Open Range. Dallas: Southwest Press, 1931.
Tongues of the Monte. Garden City, N.Y.: Doubleday, Doran, 1935. Reprinted as *The Mexico I Like.* Southern Methodist University Press, 1942.
Tales of the Mustang. Dallas: Book Club of Texas, 1936.
The Flavor of Texas. Dallas: Dealey and Lowe, 1936.
Apache Gold and Yaqui Silver. Boston: Little, Brown, 1939.
John C. Duval: First Texas Man of Letters. Dallas: Southwest Review, 1939.
The Longhorns. Boston: Little, Brown, 1941.
Guide to Life and Literature of the Southwest. Dallas: Southern Methodist University Press, 1943. Revised and enlarged edition, 1952.

A BIBLIOGRAPHICAL NOTE   255

A Texan in England. Boston: Little, Brown, 1944.
The Voice of the Coyote. Boston: Little, Brown, 1949.
The Ben Lilly Legend. Boston: Little, Brown, 1950.
The Mustangs. Boston: Little, Brown, 1952.
Tales of Old-Time Texas. Boston: Little, Brown, 1955.
Up the Trail from Texas. New York: Random House, 1955.
I'll Tell You a Tale. Boston: Little, Brown, 1960.
Cow People. Boston: Little, Brown, 1964.
Rattlesnakes. Edited by Bertha McKee Dobie. Boston: Little, Brown, 1965.
Bob More: Man and Birdman. Austin: Encino Press, 1965.
Carl Sandburg & St. Peter at the Gate. Austin: Encino Press, 1966.
Some Part of Myself. Edited by Bertha McKee Dobie. Boston: Little, Brown, 1967.
Out of the Old Rock. Boston: Little, Brown, 1972.
44 Range Country Books Topped Out by J. Frank Dobie in 1941 & 44 More Range Country Books Topped Out by Jeff Dykes in 1971. Austin: Encino Press, 1972.
Prefaces. Boston: Little, Brown, 1975.

Frank Dobie's gift for friendship won him close association with a number of noted rare-book dealers — among them the delightful Charles W. Everitt of New York — both in the United States and in England. Some of these bookmen have issued catalogues of Dobie's writings. Jeff Dykes's *My Dobie Collection* lists twenty-five such, of which the most readily available and more important are probably these: *The West and J. Frank Dobie*, catalogue 99, J. E. Reynolds, Van Nuys, Calif., 1967 (Reynolds had memorable visits with Dobie and summarizes them in this publication); *Texas and the West*, catalogue 24, Price Daniel, Jr., Waco, Texas, 1963 (son of a former governor of Texas, Daniel moved on from bookselling to the law and then became a lieutenant governor of Texas); *A Catalogue of the Writings of J. Frank Dobie (1888–1964)*, catalogue 5, John E. Jenkins Company, Austin, Texas, 1965 (Jenkins is a bookseller-publisher whose writing and book career Dobie encouraged from the start).

Acknowledgments

SOME OBSERVERS WHO WATCH such things claim that J. Frank Dobie had more friends, more genuine friends, than any Texan of this century. It depends on how you define friendship, but there is enough truth in the claim to make it impossible to list here all the former students of his at the University of Texas, all the book-folk, regional and national, all his colleagues in education and journalism and writing, all his faithful readers, who have volunteered information for this biography, either upon request or by simple interest in Dobie himself. Many of them are mentioned directly in the text or otherwise acknowledged. It seemed needless to repeat here, for example, appreciation for comments or statements from such very close friends as Walter Prescott Webb, Henry Nash Smith, Wilson Hudson, Frank Wardlaw, Tom Lea, Holland McCombs, Joe B. Frantz, and John Henry Faulk. Still, some specific expressions of gratitude for help must be separately stated.

First of all, to Bertha McKee Dobie, who survived her husband by ten years, and who was dedicated to helping achieve a biography that, she hoped, would be objective and concise — an adjective she prescribed for Frank Dobie during all his writing life. When I was beginning the years of commuting between Dallas and Austin, she told me: "Set up a schedule for when you want to see me, and I'll hold it as sacred." So far as I know, she withheld no letter, no document, no information of importance, known to her. She directed me to a number of important sources of information I might otherwise have missed. She did not merely profess the ideal of objectivity but practiced it. Her nephew, Edgar Kincaid, the noted ornithologist, was of indispensable help. Dobie's surviving closest of kin, his sisters Fannie Dobie Stanford of Lyford, Texas, and Martha Dobie of Kerrville, were equally cooperative and helpful.

Fannie Dobie's husband, T. Rucker Stanford, and his brother John, both classmates of Frank and Bertha Dobie's at Southwestern, gave freely of their college-day memories.

Among those to whom Bertha Dobie directed me, none was more helpful, or more delightful, than Mrs. Lowe Simons of Austin, a vigorous, vital college classmate and lifetime friend of the Dobies', now in her late eighties and as "alive" as any of the UT undergraduates who pass her house on the way to and from school and who stop for inspiring visits.

This biography owes a debt beyond calculation to that admirable civilizing institution in the Southwest, the internationally renowned Harry Huntt Ransom Humanities Research Center of the University of Texas, now generally regarded as one of the great libraries of the world. Chancellor Ransom, its first director and "father," chose a remarkable staff. The second and present director, Warren Roberts, the D. H. Lawrence scholar, maintains a competent and courteous service that has delighted scholars from all over the world. Of the HRC staff, I must single out for special thanks David Farmer, William R. Holman, John R. Payne, Sally Leach, Lois B. Garcia, Warner Barnes, and Sheila Ohlendorf.

One other deserves special mention: Willie Belle Coker, in charge of the J. Frank Dobie Memorial Room from its inception until her recent retirement, and longtime expert secretary for Frank Dobie. Anyone who wishes to know anything about Dobie's writing and career is sent first of all to the incomparable Mrs. Coker.

Others close to Dobie's work and career who allowed me the use of papers and letters — and their own recollections — and who should be specially mentioned are Allen Maxwell; Margaret Hartley; William D. Wittliff; John Jenkins, Jr.; Winston Bode; Ralph Yarborough; A. C. Greene; Billy Porterfield; Victor White; Eldon Branda; Elizabeth Ann and William Weber Johnson; J. F. Bliss Albright; William H. Gilliland; Florence Rosengren; Carl Hertzog; Clara Lewis; Frank Tolbert; William B. Ruggles; John Graves; Martin Shockley; Hudson Long; Stanley Marcus; Jack Reynolds; and Mildred Gervasi.

For information on Frank Dobie's stay as visiting professor at Cambridge, I am indebted to Professors J. H. Plumb and C. P. Snow, and to the American professor who followed Dobie there, the Keats scholar Aileen Ward. For the use of a very rare privately printed pamphlet that attacked Frank Dobie at the time of the Rainey–UT controversy, I wish to thank Lee Milazzo of Dallas; and for two articles on the frontier tradition and its culture by Larry Goodwyn, I owe thanks to Ervin Eatenson of the Dallas Public Library.

For those who helped but shall be nameless here, such as many of Dobie's former students, I should like to recall a "Note from the Teacher" that Frank Dobie used to append to the mimeographed copies of his final examinations: "As Carl Sandburg always says, 'We're both young yet; we'll meet again.' When we do, forgive my poor memory and know that I shall be glad. Yours for Longhorn culture, J. Frank Dobie."

Index

Abernethy, Francis Edward, 203
Adams, Andy, 120, 143
Adams, Henry, 128
Aguayo, marqués de, 140
Atkinson, C. J., 67
Austen, Jane, 63
Austin, Mary, 116, 121, 161

Babb, Stanley, 123
Baker, Herschel, 120
Balzac, Honoré de, 225, 242
Barker, Eugene C., 115, 118, 123, 130
Barnes, Lorraine, 226
Barnum, Phineas T., 174
Barrett, Jack, 221
Barth, Karl, 170
Battle, W. J., 118
Beckett, Samuel, 222
Bedell, Bill, 242
Bedichek, Roy, 37, 176, 200, 221, 226, 234
Bell, Jim, 17
Bell, Mrs. Jim, 173
Bell, Raymond, 136
Benedict, Harry Yandell, 115
Beretta, Alice, 22
Bernhardt, Sarah, 85
Blair, Walter, 89
Blake, William, 186
Blakely, Bassett, 53
Block, Maurine, 169
Boatright, Mody, 37, 176
Boatwright, Eli, 116
Bonnet, Ellis, 137
Boswell, James, 58
Bowie, Jim, 157, 245
Bradford, Ned, 222, 235
Brammer, William, 234
Brewster, Oscar, 116
Bridge, Joe, 148
Brogan, Denis W., 188
Browning, Elizabeth Barrett, 64
Browning, Robert, 48, 49, 53
Bulwer-Lytton, E. G. L., 13
Bunyan, Paul, 128
Burns, Robert, 16
Byler, Fannie (aunt), 20
Byler, Frank (uncle), 7-8
Bynner, Witter, 121, 161
Byron, Lord, 16

Bywaters, Jerry, 217
Bywaters, Mary (Mrs. Jerry), 217

Callaway, Morgan, 31-32, 50, 51, 60, 76, 79, 103, 106, 147, 154, 201
Cameron, Angus, 205, 210, 211, 222
Cameron, Ewing, 157-158
Campbell, Killis, 64, 118
Carlyle, Jane Welsh, 64
Carlyle, Thomas, 53, 64, 86
Carter, Amon, 165, 173
Castañeda, Carlos E., 123
Cather, Willa, 161
Cavitt, Samuel, 219
Chaucer, Geoffrey, 248
Churchill, Winston, 184
Ciardi, John, 232
Click, L. L., 129, 200
Cloud, Joe, 116
Cobb, Ty, 78
Coker, Willie Belle, 227
Coleridge, S. T., 16, 111, 144, 186
Commager, Henry Steele, 176
Conrad, Joseph, 50, 108, 186
Cook, Howard, 223
Coppini, Pompeo, 156, 158-159
Coronado, Francisco Vásquez de, 245
Cortez, Santos, 101, 142
Crockett, Davy, 170
Crowell, Grace Noll, 123
Crozier, Harry Benge, 32
Cunninghame Graham, R. B., 212
Curtis, Ken, 230

Daniel, William ("Bill"), 230
Davis, Richard Harding, 33, 34
Day, Donald, 143
Dealey, George Bannerman, 118, 121, 184
DeGolyer, Everette, 218, 220, 232
del Bosque, Genardo, 30, 54, 56
Deschner, John, 169-172
Díaz, Porfirio, 161
Dickens, Charles, 13
Dickson, Raymond, 133, 148, 149
Dies, Martin, 210-211
Dimmitt, Mrs., 36, 58
Dobie, Ella Byler (mother), 3-22 passim, 69-72, 79, 87, 93, 105, 110-111, 182-183, 205-209

INDEX

Dobie, Elrich (brother), 5, 6, 19, 30, 56, 142, 206, 207
Dobie, Fannie. *See* Stanford, Fannie Dobie
Dobie, Frank (uncle), 54
Dobie, Henry (brother), 206
Dobie, Jim (uncle), 14–15, 51–54, 63, 67, 79, 93, 97, 99–102, 108, 110, 133, 141, 147, 165, 173, 202
Dobie, Lee (brother), 42, 57, 76, 206, 208
Dobie, Martha (sister), 71, 136, 193, 206–207
Dobie, R. J. (father), 7–15 *passim*, 20, 55–56, 69–70, 116, 133, 205
Dodd, Mrs., 72
Dos Passos, John, 115
Dreiser, Theodore, 118
Dubose, Ed (uncle), 33–34
Dubose, Friendly ("Grandpa"), 13–14, 17, 116
Dubose, Judge (uncle), 33
Dubose, Martha F. ("Grandma"), 12, 13
Duffus, R. L., 129
Dugger, Ronnie, 234
Dykes, Jeff, 227

East, Tom T., 159
Eckhardt, Wolf, 165
Eisenhower, Dwight D., 220
Eliot, T. S., 3
Emerson, Ralph Waldo, 53, 201, 210
Everitt, Ray, 172, 187, 188, 196, 205

Faulk, John Henry, 176, 184, 222
Ferguson, James E., 63–64, 174
Fisher, Theodore, 142
Fleury, Cardinal, 59
Forbes-Robertson, Johnston, 28
Ford, Lynn, 165
Ford, O'Neil, 165, 217
Ford, Wanda Graham (Mrs. O'Neil), 217
Frantz, Joe B., 175, 197–198, 235
Frost, Robert, 232, 233

Gaddis, Isabel, 242
Garner, John Nance, 198
Gilliam, Franklin, 227
Goldman, Emma, 28
Goodnight, Charlie, 171
Goodwyn, Frank, 170
Grant, James Edward, 229–230
Graves, John, 223
Gray, Mrs., 66

Greer, Hilton Ross, 121, 123
Gregory, Lloyd, 184
Grey, Zane, 120, 243
Griffith, R. W., 115, 118
Guajardo, Alberto, 133, 142

Hadley, Ed, 107, 109, 110
Haley, J. Evetts, 156
Hardy, Thomas, 46
Hart, James P., 204, 221
Hartley, Margaret, 242
Hawkins, Lyndsay D., 35
Hazlitt, William, 88, 164, 186, 243
Heidegger, Martin, 248
Hendaye, Frances, 90
Henry, O. (pseud. of W. S. Porter), 116, 213
Herrmann, G. R., 224, 225
Herrmann, Mrs. G. R., 225
Hertzog, Carl, 160, 217
Hertzog, Vivian (Mrs. Carl), 217
Hill, Jim Dan, 182
Hogg, Mike, 149
Hogg, Thomas E., 149
Hogg, Will C., 149
Horgan, Paul, 121, 172
Horn, P. W., 112, 113, 115
Hough, Emerson, 119, 120
Houston, Sam, 162, 181, 186
Howells, William Dean, 52
Hubbell, Jay Broadus, 235
Hudson, W. H., 111, 134, 144, 145, 186–187, 227
Hudson, Wilson, 176, 211
Huerta, Victoriano, 135
Hughes, Hatcher, 28, 121
Hugo, Victor, 44, 53
Huizinga, Johan, 78
Huxley, Aldous, 161
Hyer, Robert Stewart, 15–16, 17, 18–19, 22, 117

Jackson, Una, 22–23
James, Marquis, 162
James, William, 245
Jester, Beauford, 198
Johnson, Lyndon B., 198, 234
Johnson, Samuel, 58
Johnson, William Weber, 218
Johnston, Ralph, 107, 213, 232
Jones, Howard Mumford, 118, 119, 235
Jones, Jesse, 198

Katwijk, Paul van, 170
Keats, John, 16
Keithly, Lee, 147
Kemp, Lou, 156

INDEX

Kincaid, Edgar B., Jr. (Bertha's nephew), 184, 214, 227–228
Kincaid, Edgar B., Sr. (Bertha's brother-in-law), 84, 85, 86, 92, 93
Kincaid, Lucile McKee (Bertha's sister, Mrs. Edgar B., Sr.), 23, 68, 92, 93, 99, 227, 228
King, Larry, 234
Kipling, Rudyard, 160
Kittredge, George Lyman, 103
Kittrell, William H., 217, 220
Knapp, Bradford, 109, 114
Knight, Thomas, 129

La Farge, Oliver, 162
Lamy, Joseph, 161
Law, Robert Adger, 66, 106, 115, 118, 119
Lawrence, D. H., 161
Lea, Sarah (Mrs. Tom, Jr.), 172, 216, 217
Lea, Tom, Jr., 135, 159–168 *passim*, 172–174, 188, 190–191, 195–196, 204–205, 210–217 *passim*, 220, 222, 226
Lea, Tom, Sr., 135, 159, 164
Lee, Robert E., 17
Lewes, George Henry, 53
Lewis, Sinclair, 118
Lieb, Victor, 163
Lilly, Ben, 172, 204, 205, 246–247
Lomax, John A., 102, 103–104, 109
Longfellow, Henry W., 13
Lowes, John Livingston, 144

McCampbell, Joe, 116
McCarthy, Joseph, 190, 198, 211, 214, 222
McCombs, Holland, 174, 216–217, 218, 219
McCombs, Marjorie (Mrs. Holland), 216–217, 219
McDermott, Eugene, 218, 220
McGinnis, John H., 79, 107, 116–119, 120–121, 122, 123–124, 129, 235
McGinnis, Mrs. John H., 117
McGinnis, Karl, 122
McKee, Emily (Bertha's sister), 23
McKee, Lucile. *See* Kincaid, Lucile McKee
McKee, Ray Park (Bertha's mother), 71–72, 193
McKee, Richard Alexander (Bertha's father), 221–222, 227
McMurray, Elizabeth Ann, 218
Maguire, Jack, 170
Marin, John, 161

Marlowe, Julia, 28
Martin, Frank O., 129, 130–132
Masters, Edgar Lee, 233
Mathews, John Joseph, 107, 232
Matthews, Brander, 28
Mauldin, R. C., 212
Maule, Harry, 141, 143
Mead, Ben, 126, 127
Maxwell, Jesse, 155–156
Mencken, H. L., 119, 161
Meredith, George, 46, 91
Mérimée, Prosper, 43
Mirabeau, comte de, 59
Montaigne, Michel de, 88–89
Moore, S. H., 22
Morris, Willie, 234
Mouzon, Bishop, 37
Murray, Gilbert, 192

Napoleon Bonaparte, 185
Newberry, Lem, 134
Niebuhr, H. Richard, 170

O'Daniel, W. Lee ("Pappy"), 174, 175, 189, 201
O'Keeffe, Georgia, 22, 161

Painter, Theophilus Shickel, 197, 199–200, 202
Palmer, Alice Freeman, 58
Palmer, George Herbert, 58
Parten, J. R., 201
Parton, James, 15
Pater, Walter, 43
Pavlova, Anna, 28
Payne, Leonidas Warren, Jr., 112–113, 114–115, 118
Pearl, Ray, 111, 114
Pegler, Westbrook, 211
Pegues, Albert Shipp, 16–17, 24, 31, 42
Pegues, Mrs. Albert Shipp, 42
Perry, George Sessions, 203–204, 218
Poe, Edgar Allan, 20–21, 64, 118
Pope, Alexander, 115, 118
Porter, Jane, 6
Porter, Katherine Anne, 162
Proctor, A. Phimister, 159

Rabelais, François, 58
Rainey, Homer, 174–175, 176, 183–184, 192, 195, 197–198, 199, 200
Ransom, Harry Huntt, 113, 168, 201, 204
Rayburn, Sam, 198
Reading, Margaret, 184
Reagan, John, 32
Remington, Frederic, 159–160
Reynolds, Sir Joshua, 58

INDEX

Rhodes, Eugene Manlove, 239
Richardson, Sid, 164, 165, 173
Rodríguez, Rafael, 116
Roe, E. P., 13
Rogers, Captain (Texas Ranger), 14
Rogers, John William, 126, 130–132
Rogers, Will, 142, 163, 194
Roosevelt, Franklin D., 175, 176, 201
Roosevelt, Theodore, 134, 246
Rossetti, Dante Gabriel, 43
Rowse, Arthur, 192
Royster, James Finch, 46
Ruggles, C. B., 141, 143, 245
Rusk, Thomas J., 157
Ruskin, John, 52
Russell, Charles M., 159, 160, 164, 172–173, 204

Sabin, Edwin L., 129
Salmen, Stanley, 211
Sandburg, Carl, 125, 146, 233
Sanders, Shipp, 85
Savonarola, Girolamo, 59
Schoenbohm, J. G., 33–34
Scott, Sir Walter, 6, 13
Shahan, James T. ("Happy"), 229
Shakespeare, William, 44, 53, 58, 117, 118, 119
Shaw, George Bernard, 59
Shelley, Percy Bysshe, 16, 44, 64–65, 187
Sherman, William Tecumseh, 13
Shettles, E. L., 130
Simms, Ella, 10
Simons, Lowe, 17, 22–23, 32, 39, 40
Simons, Mary Thomas (Mrs. Lowe), 22–23, 36, 228
Simpson, Claude, 120
Simpson, J. Fisher, 18
Siringo, Charlie, 120
Sloan, John, 161
Smith, Erwin, 166
Smith, Henry Nash, 88–89, 120, 129, 139, 140, 199, 233
Smith, T. V., 222
Snyder, Marcus, 172
Socrates, 185, 221
Stanford, Fannie Dobie (sister, Mrs. T. Rucker), 5, 10, 12, 20, 33, 67, 76, 87, 206–207, 209
Stanford, T. Rucker (brother-in-law), 16–17, 18, 110, 182, 191
Stegner, Wallace, 205
Stevenson, Coke, 189
Stevenson, Robert Louis, 44, 53, 101, 186
Stoker, George P., 140
Stone, Walker, 107, 110, 232

Sullivan, Maud, 108
Sun Yat-sen, 161
Sutliffe, Milo, 130
Swank, Arch, 217
Swank, Patricia Peck (Mrs. Arch), 217

Taylor, A. E., 226
Taylor, E. H., 107, 109–110, 122
Tennyson, Alfred, Lord, 6
Thackeray, William Makepeace, 100
Thomas, Mary. *See* Simons, Mary Thomas
Thompson, Stith, 36–37, 102, 116
Thoreau, Henry, 154
Thornhill, Arthur, Sr., 222
Thorp, R. D., 154, 155, 156
Tiomkin, Dimitri, 230
Truman, Harry S., 211
Turner, P. L., 123–128, 129–132, 143
Twain, Mark, 13, 52, 88–89, 109, 117, 142, 163, 170, 196, 225
Tyler, R. G., 106

Van de Velde, Paul, 139
Van Doren, Carl, 130, 132, 161
Veramendi, Ursula de, 157
Verdeau, Julien, 116
Vestal, Stanley, 121, 162
Villa, Pancho, 33
Vosberg, "Doctor," 188

Wallace, Henry, 211
Wardlaw, Frank, 214, 234, 235
Wayne, John, 229, 230, 231
Webb, Walter Prescott, 118, 119, 121, 163, 175, 176, 200–204, 220–222, 234
Wertenbaker, Barclay (Mrs. Green P.), 217–218
Wertenbaker, Green Peyton, 217–218
West, Herbert, 225, 227, 229
Weybright, Victor, 182
Wilhelm, Kaiser, 71, 82
Williams, Tennessee, 222
Willis, Sid, 172
Wills, Chill, 230
Wilson, Woodrow, 59
Wister, Owen, 120, 243
Witt, Edgar, 153
Woods, Dee, 220
Woodward, W. E., 126
Wordsworth, William, 7, 16, 17, 53, 147
Wrather, William D., 129

Yarborough, Ralph, 234–235
Young, John Duncan, 122, 125, 243
Young, Stark, 233, 235